INUYASHA

VOL. 7
Action Edition

Story and Art by
RUMIKO TAKAHASHI

English Adaptation by Gerard Jones

Translation/Mari Morimoto
Touch-Up Art & Lettering/Wayne Truman
Cover Design/Yuki Ameda
Graphics & Design/Yuki Ameda
Editor (1st Edition)/Julie Davis
Editor (Action Edition)/Julie Davis

Managing Editor/Annette Roman
Director of Production/Noboru Watanabe
VP of Publishing/Alvin Lu
Sr. Director of Acquisitions/Rika Inouye
VP of Sales & Marketing/Liza Coppola
Publisher/Hyoe Narita

INUYASHA is rated "T+" for Older Teens. It may contain violence, language, alcohol or tobacco use, or suggestive situations.

Printed in Canada.

Published by VIZ Media, LLC
P.O. Box 77010
San Francisco, CA 94107

1st Edition published 2000

Action Edition
10 9 8 7 6 5 4 3
First printing, December 2003
Second printing, October 2004
Third printing, May 2005

VIZ media

store.viz.com

INUYASHA

VOL. 7   Action Edition

STORY AND ART BY
RUMIKO TAKAHASHI

CONTENTS

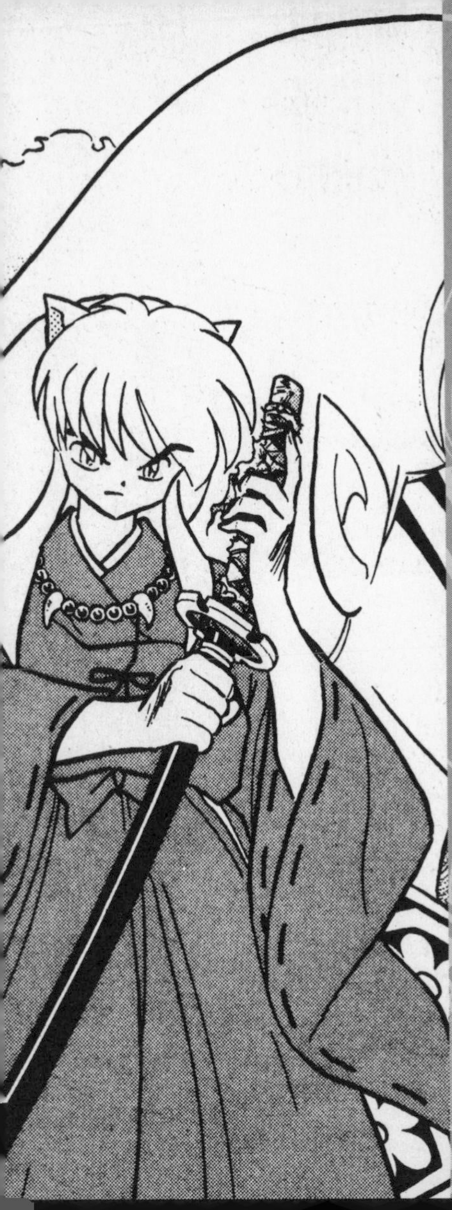

Long ago, in the "Warring States" era of Japan's Muromachi period (Sengoku-jidai, approximately 1467-1568 CE), a legendary doglike half-demon called "Inu-Yasha" attempted to steal the Shikon Jewel, or "Jewel of Four Souls," from a village, but was stopped by the enchanted arrow of the village priestess, Kikyo. Inu-Yasha fell into a deep sleep, pinned to a tree by Kikyo's arrow, while the mortally wounded Kikyo took the Shikon Jewel with her into the fires of her funeral pyre. Years passed.

Fast forward to the present day. Kagome, a Japanese high school girl, is pulled into a well one day by a mysterious centipede monster, and finds herself transported into the past, only to come face to face with the trapped Inu-Yasha. She frees him, and Inu-Yasha easily defeats the centipede monster.

The residents of the village, now fifty years older, readily accept Kagome as the reincarnation of their deceased priestess Kikyo, a claim supported by the fact that the Shikon Jewel emerges from a cut on Kagome's body. Unfortunately, the jewel's rediscovery means that the village is soon under attack by a variety of demons in search of this treasure. Then, the jewel is accidentally shattered into many shards, each of which may have the fearsome power of the entire jewel.

Although Inu-Yasha says he hates Kagome because of her resemblance to Kikyo, the woman who "killed" him, he is forced to team up with her when Kaede, the village leader, binds him to Kagome with a powerful spell. Now the two grudging companions must fight to reclaim and reassemble the shattered shards of the Shikon Jewel before they fall into the wrong hands.

INU-YASHA
A half-human, half-demon hybrid, Inu-Yasha assists Kagome in her search for the shards of the Jewel. The charmed necklace he wears allows Kagome to restrain him with a single word.

KAGOME
A modern-day Japanese schoolgirl, Kagome is also the reincarnation of Kikyo, the priestess who imprisoned Inu-Yasha for fifty years with her enchanted arrow. Kagome has the power to see the Shikon Jewel shards wherever they may be hidden.

KAEDE
The little sister of the deceased priestess Kikyo, now an old woman and head of their village. It's her spell that binds Inu-Yasha to Kagome by means of a string of prayer beads and Kagome's spoken word—"Sit!"

MIROKU
An easygoing Buddhist priest with questionable morals, Miroku is the carrier of a curse passed down from his grandfather. He is searching for the demon Naraku, who first inflicted the curse.

KIKYO
A powerful priestess who died protecting the Shikon Jewel, and has been resurrected by magic. She and Inu-Yasha once shared a special bond.

MYOGA
A flea demon and Inu-Yasha's servant. His bloodsucking seems to have the ability to weaken certain spells.

SESSHO-MARU
Inu-Yasha's half-brother by the same demon father, Sessho-Maru is a pure-blood demon who covets the sword left to Inu-Yasha by their father. The last time the two brothers clashed, Sessho-Maru lost an arm.

SHIPPO
An orphaned young fox-demon who enjoys goading Inu-Yasha and playing tricks with his shape-changing abilities.

SCROLL ONE

A MATTER OF ARMS

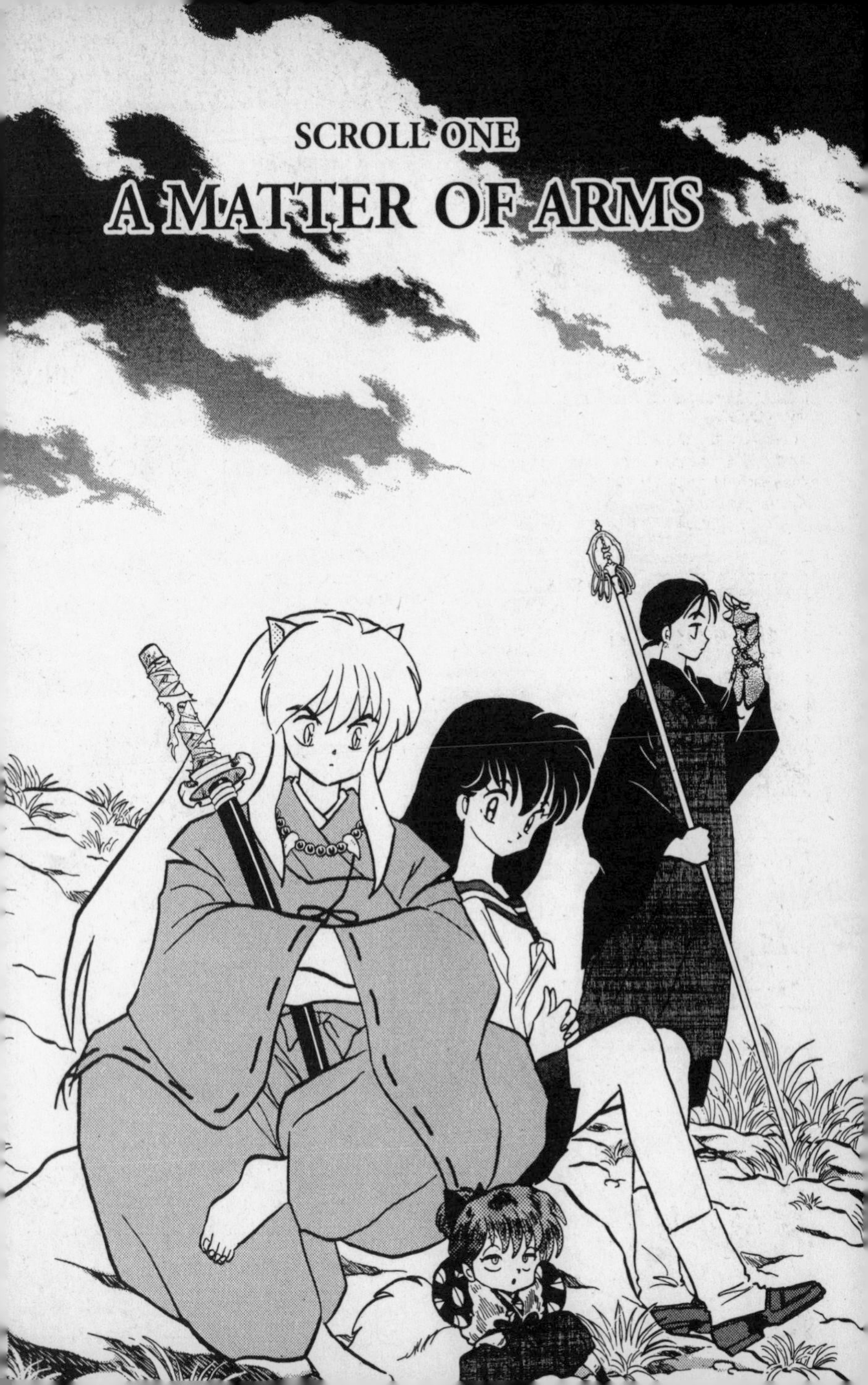

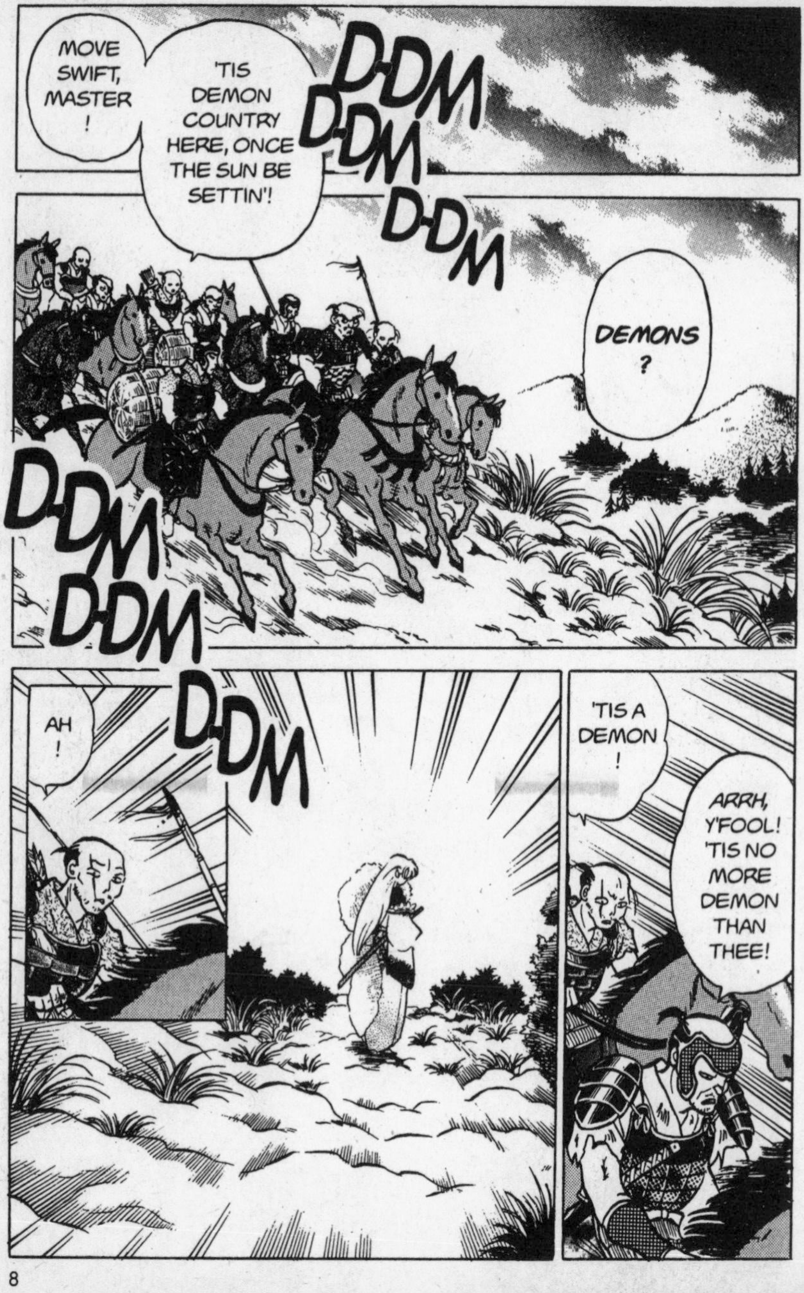
MOVE SWIFT, MASTER!
'TIS DEMON COUNTRY HERE, ONCE THE SUN BE SETTIN'!
D-DM D-DM D-DM
DEMONS?
D-DM D-DM D-DM
AH!
'TIS A DEMON!
ARRH, Y'FOOL! 'TIS NO MORE DEMON THAN THEE!

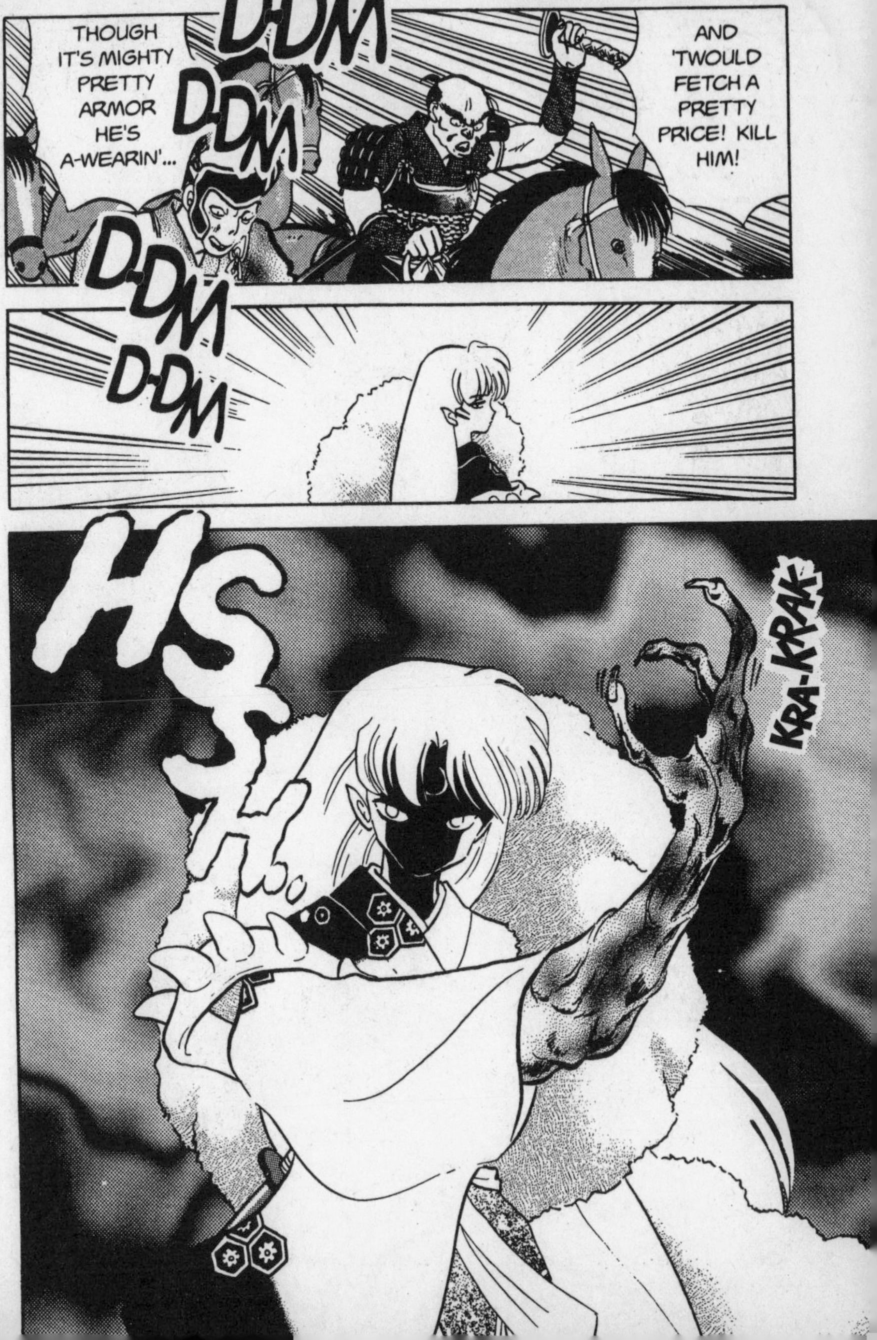
THOUGH IT'S MIGHTY PRETTY ARMOR HE'S A-WEARIN'...
D-DM
D-DM
AND 'TWOULD FETCH A PRETTY PRICE! KILL HIM!
D-DM
D-DM
HSSH...
KRA-KRAK

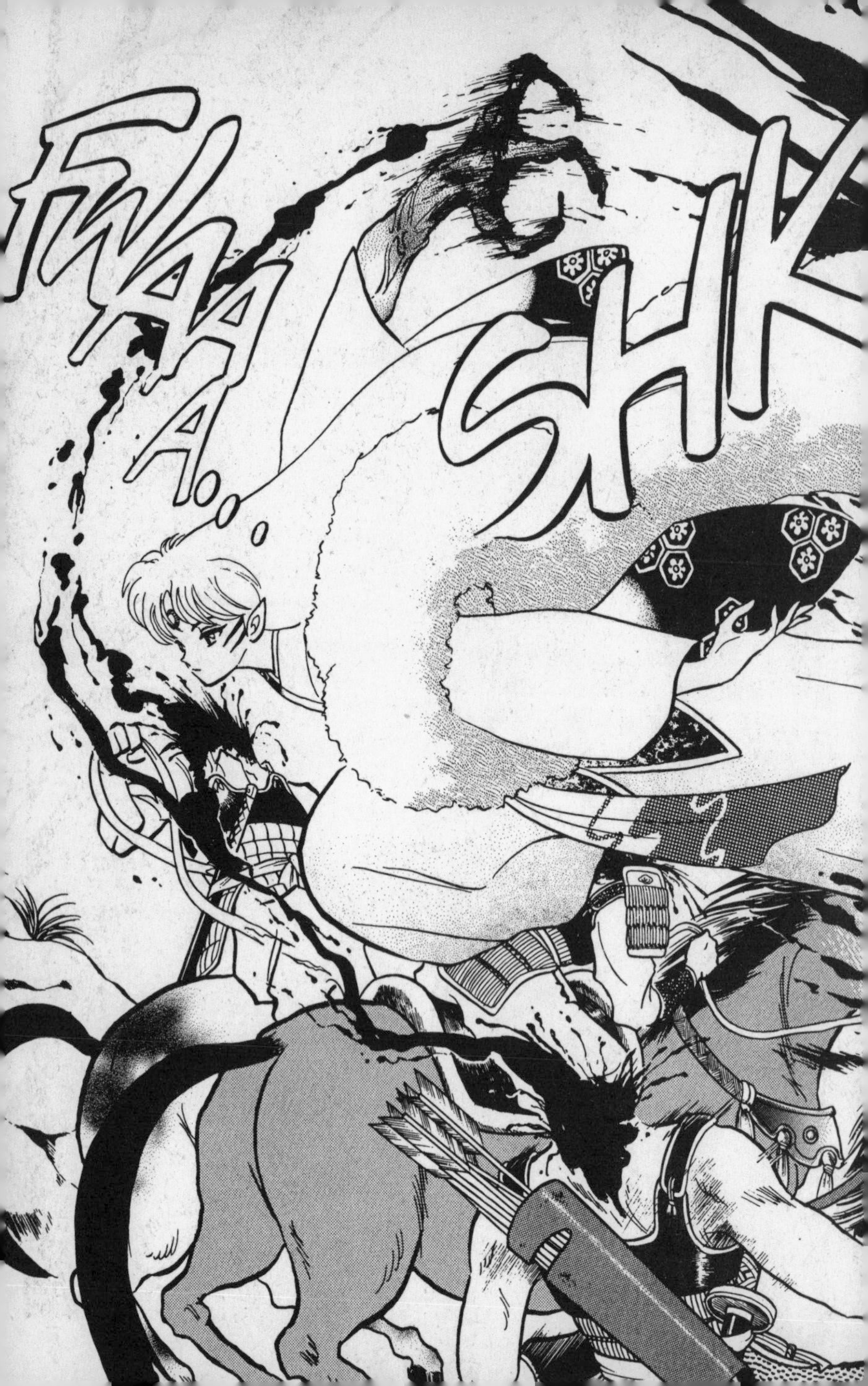
FWAAA...
SHK

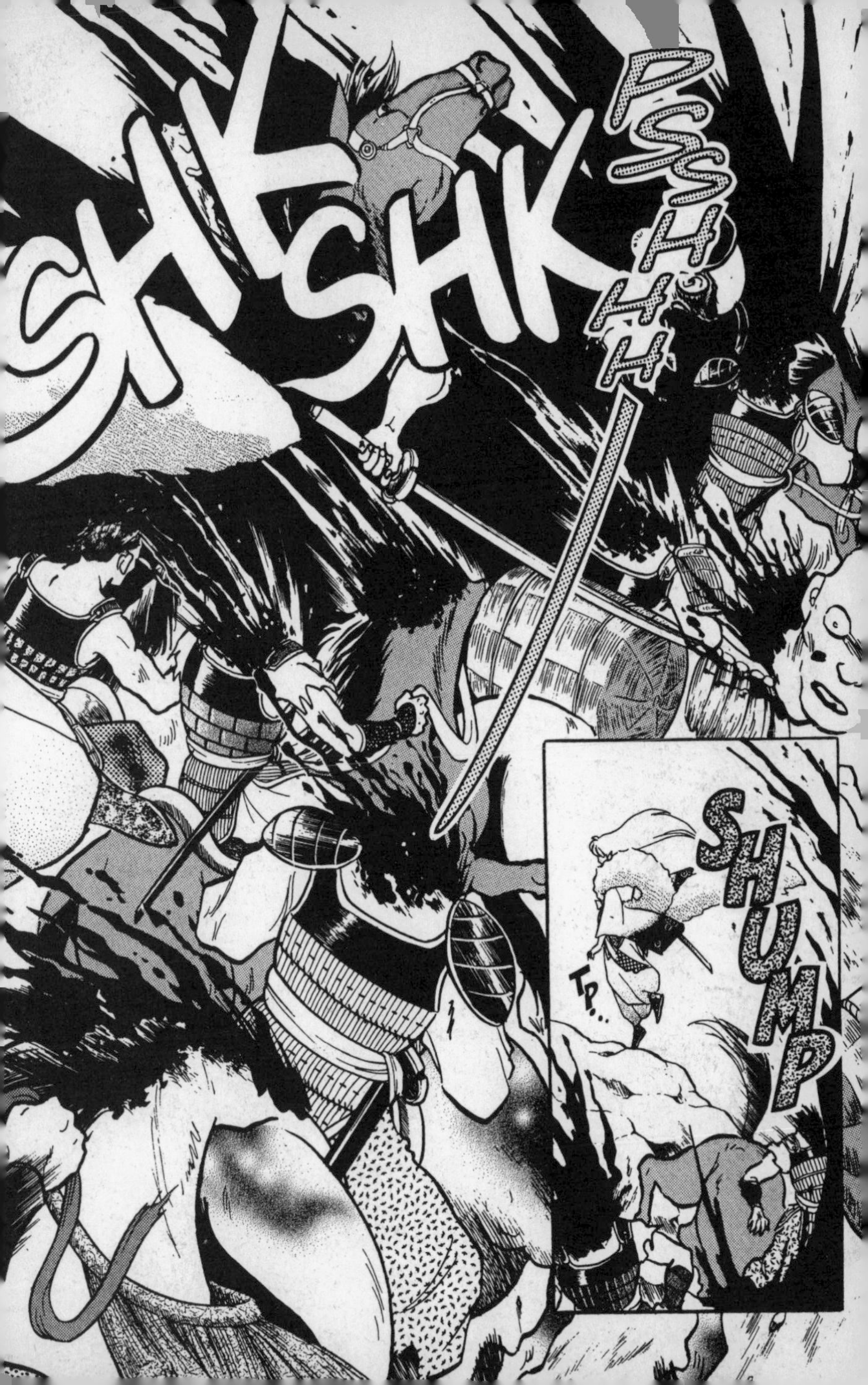
SHK SHK
PSSHHH
SHUMP
TP...

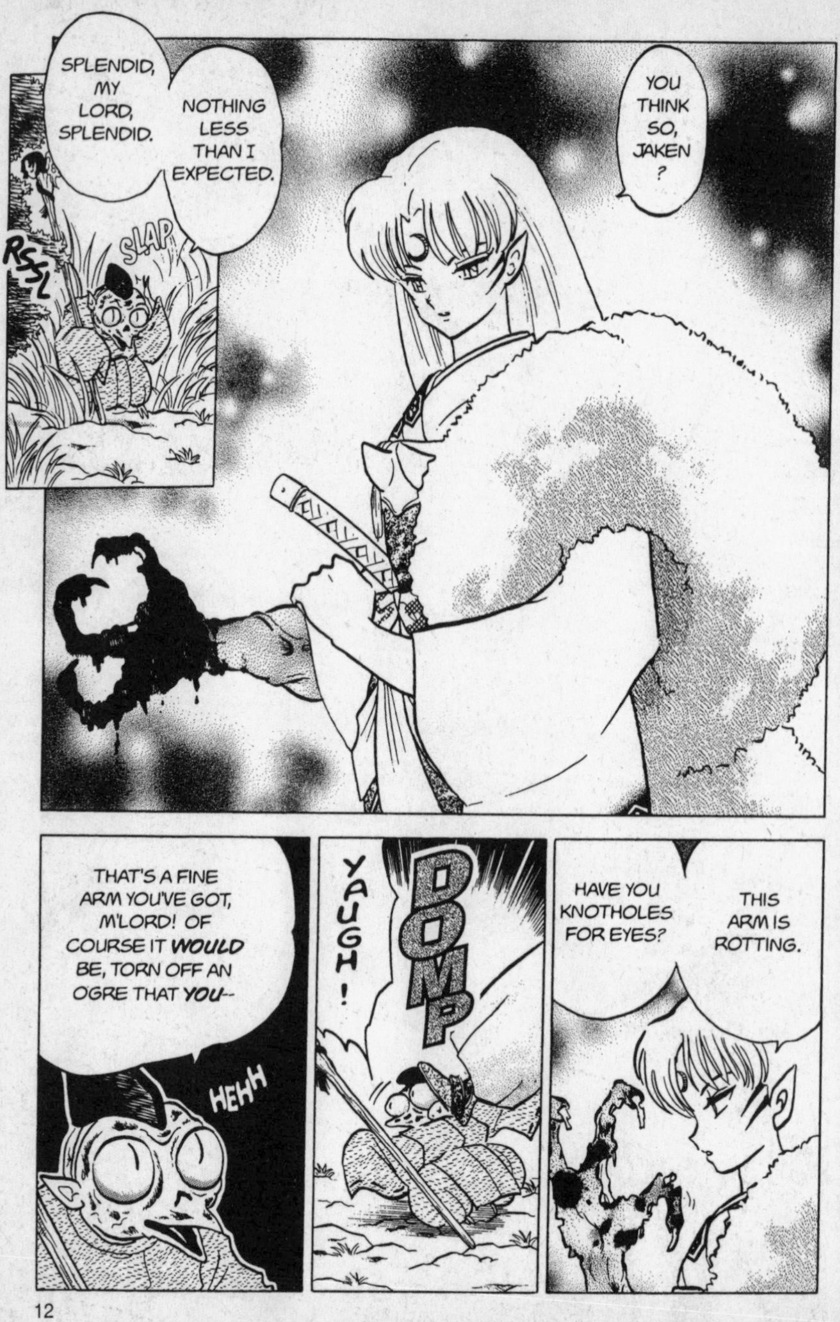
SPLENDID, MY LORD, SPLENDID.
NOTHING LESS THAN I EXPECTED.
RSSL
SLAP
YOU THINK SO, JAKEN?
THAT'S A FINE ARM YOU'VE GOT, M'LORD! OF COURSE IT WOULD BE, TORN OFF AN OGRE THAT YOU--
HEHH
YAUGH!
DOMP
HAVE YOU KNOTHOLES FOR EYES?
THIS ARM IS ROTTING.

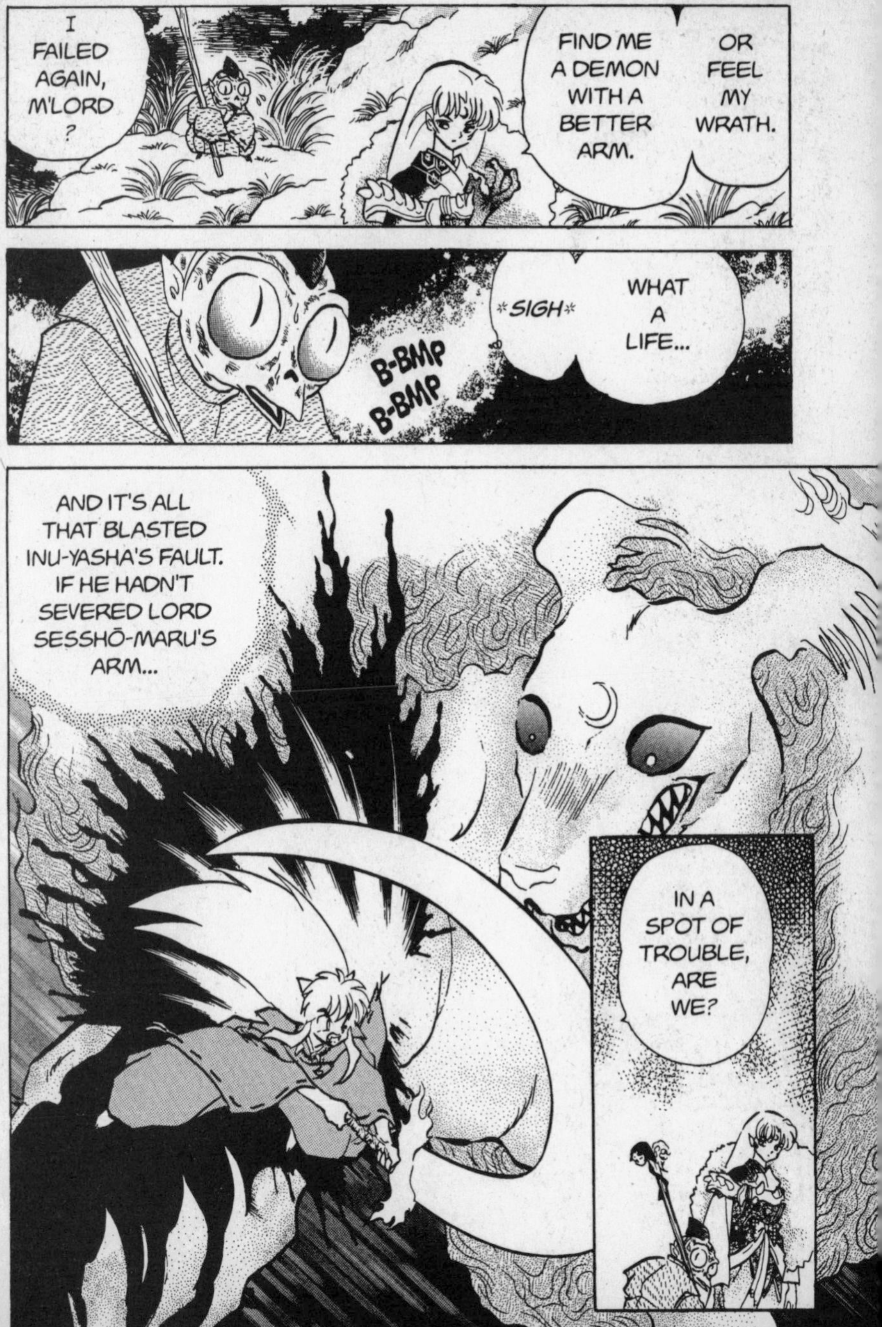
I FAILED AGAIN, M'LORD ?
FIND ME A DEMON WITH A BETTER ARM.
OR FEEL MY WRATH.
B-BMP B-BMP
SIGH
WHAT A LIFE...
AND IT'S ALL THAT BLASTED INU-YASHA'S FAULT. IF HE HADN'T SEVERED LORD SESSHŌ-MARU'S ARM...
IN A SPOT OF TROUBLE, ARE WE?

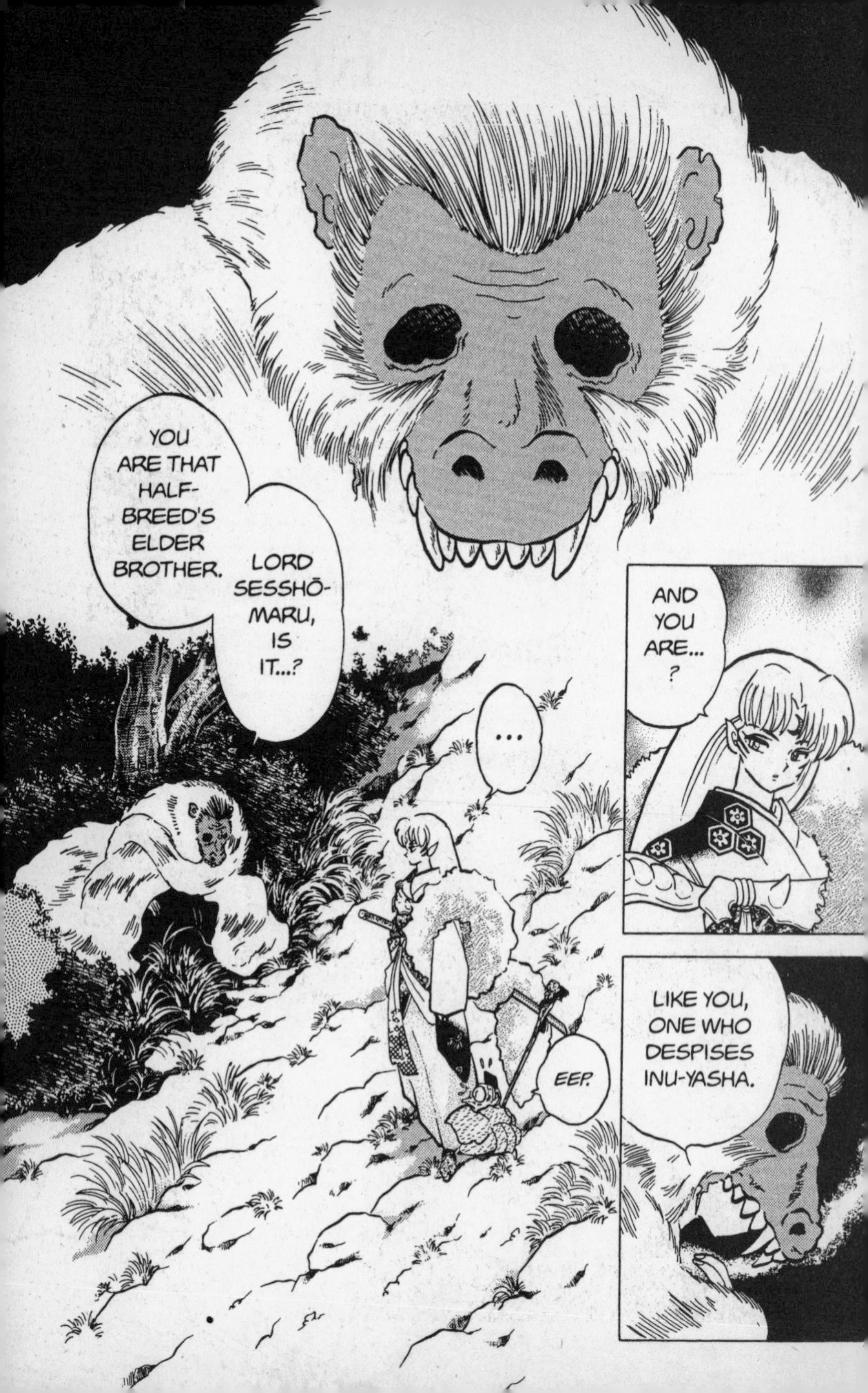
YOU ARE THAT HALF-BREED'S ELDER BROTHER.
LORD SESSHŌMARU, IS IT...?
...
EEP.
AND YOU ARE...?
LIKE YOU, ONE WHO DESPISES INU-YASHA.

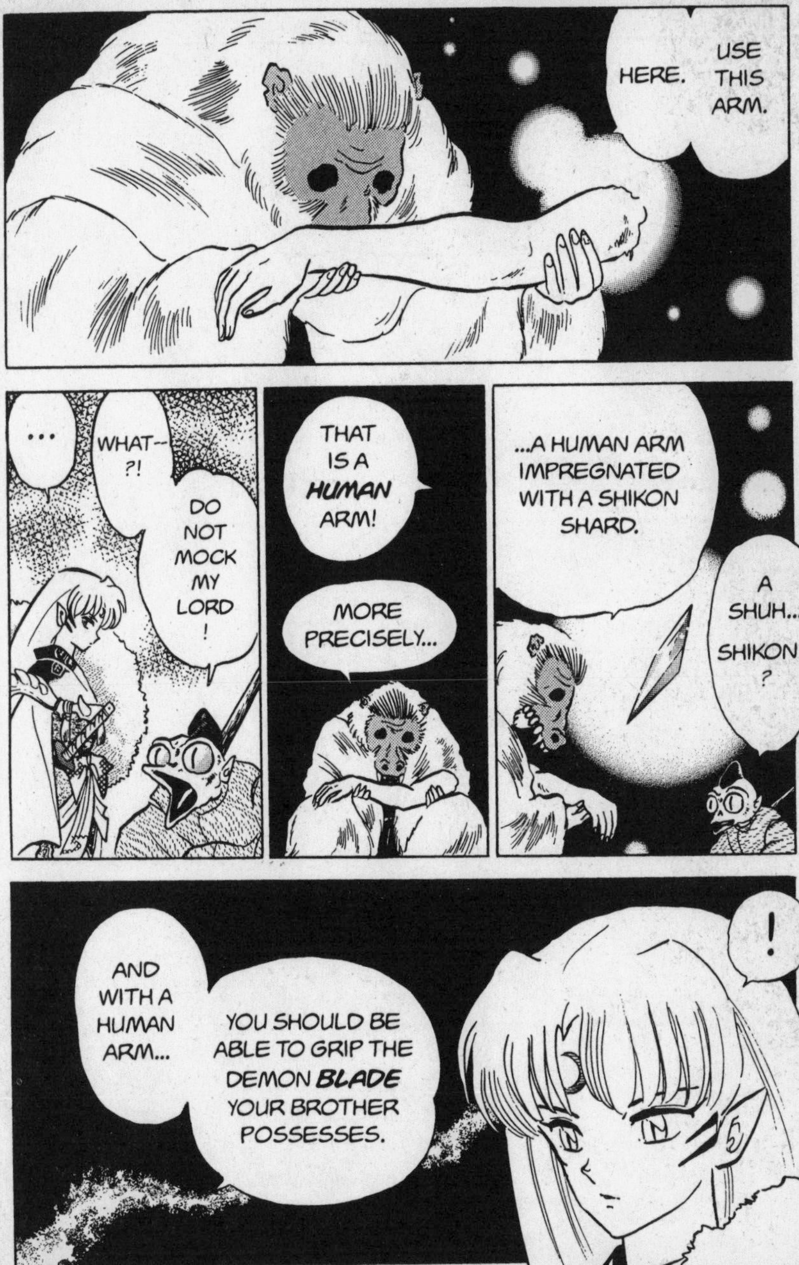
HERE.
USE THIS ARM.
...
WHAT--?!
DO NOT MOCK MY LORD!
THAT IS A HUMAN ARM!
MORE PRECISELY...
...A HUMAN ARM IMPREGNATED WITH A SHIKON SHARD.
A SHUH... SHIKON...?
AND WITH A HUMAN ARM...
YOU SHOULD BE ABLE TO GRIP THE DEMON BLADE YOUR BROTHER POSSESSES.
!

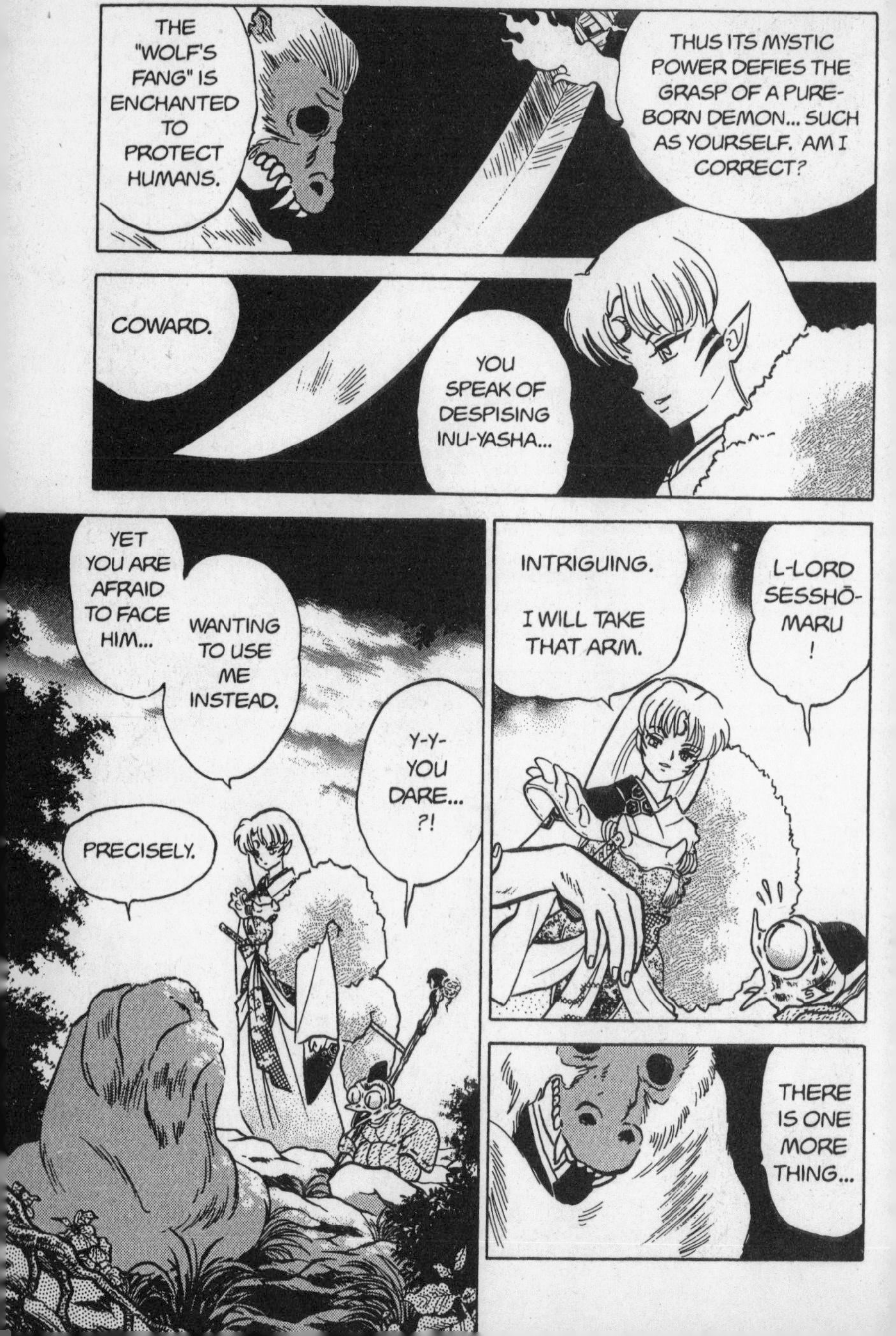
THE "WOLF'S FANG" IS ENCHANTED TO PROTECT HUMANS.
THUS ITS MYSTIC POWER DEFIES THE GRASP OF A PURE-BORN DEMON... SUCH AS YOURSELF. AM I CORRECT?
COWARD.
YOU SPEAK OF DESPISING INU-YASHA...
YET YOU ARE AFRAID TO FACE HIM...
WANTING TO USE ME INSTEAD.
Y-Y-YOU DARE...?!
PRECISELY.
INTRIGUING.
I WILL TAKE THAT ARM.
L-LORD SESSHŌ-MARU!
THERE IS ONE MORE THING...

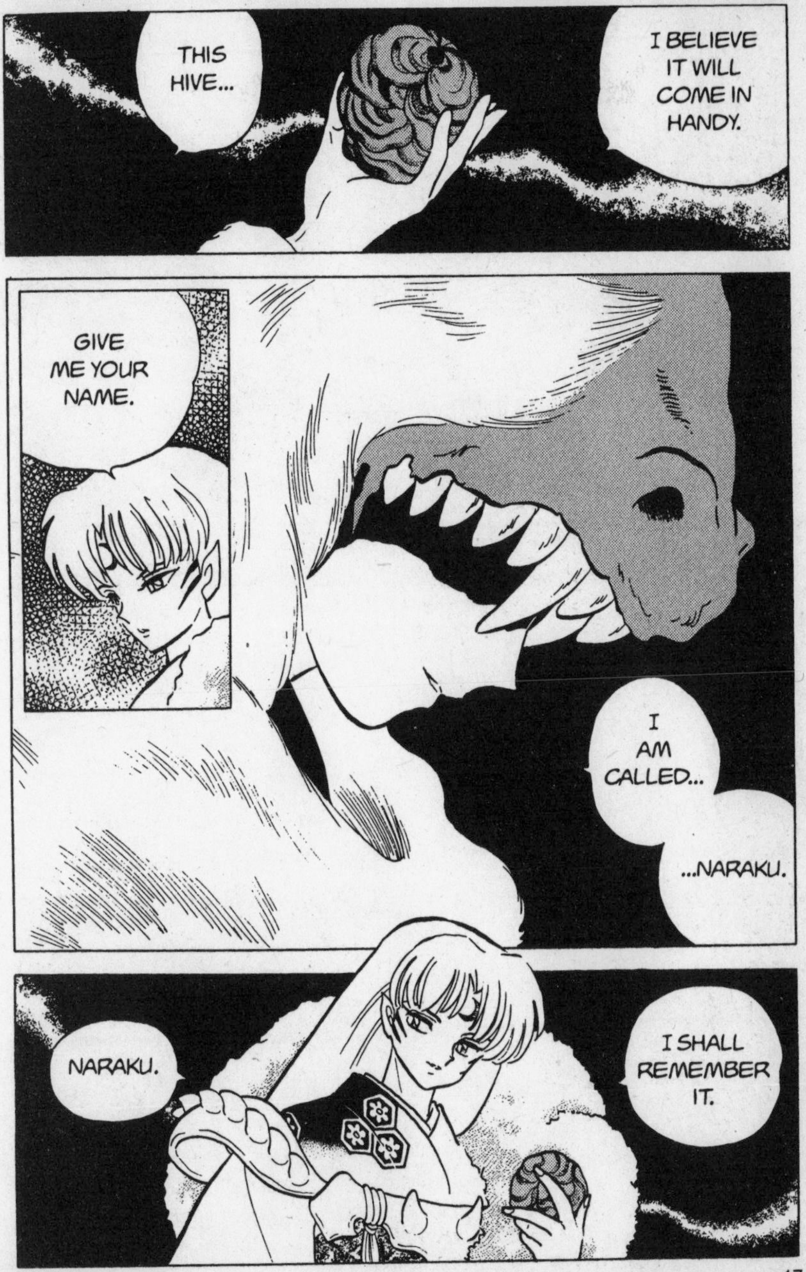
THIS HIVE...
I BELIEVE IT WILL COME IN HANDY.
GIVE ME YOUR NAME.
I AM CALLED...
...NARAKU.
NARAKU.
I SHALL REMEMBER IT.

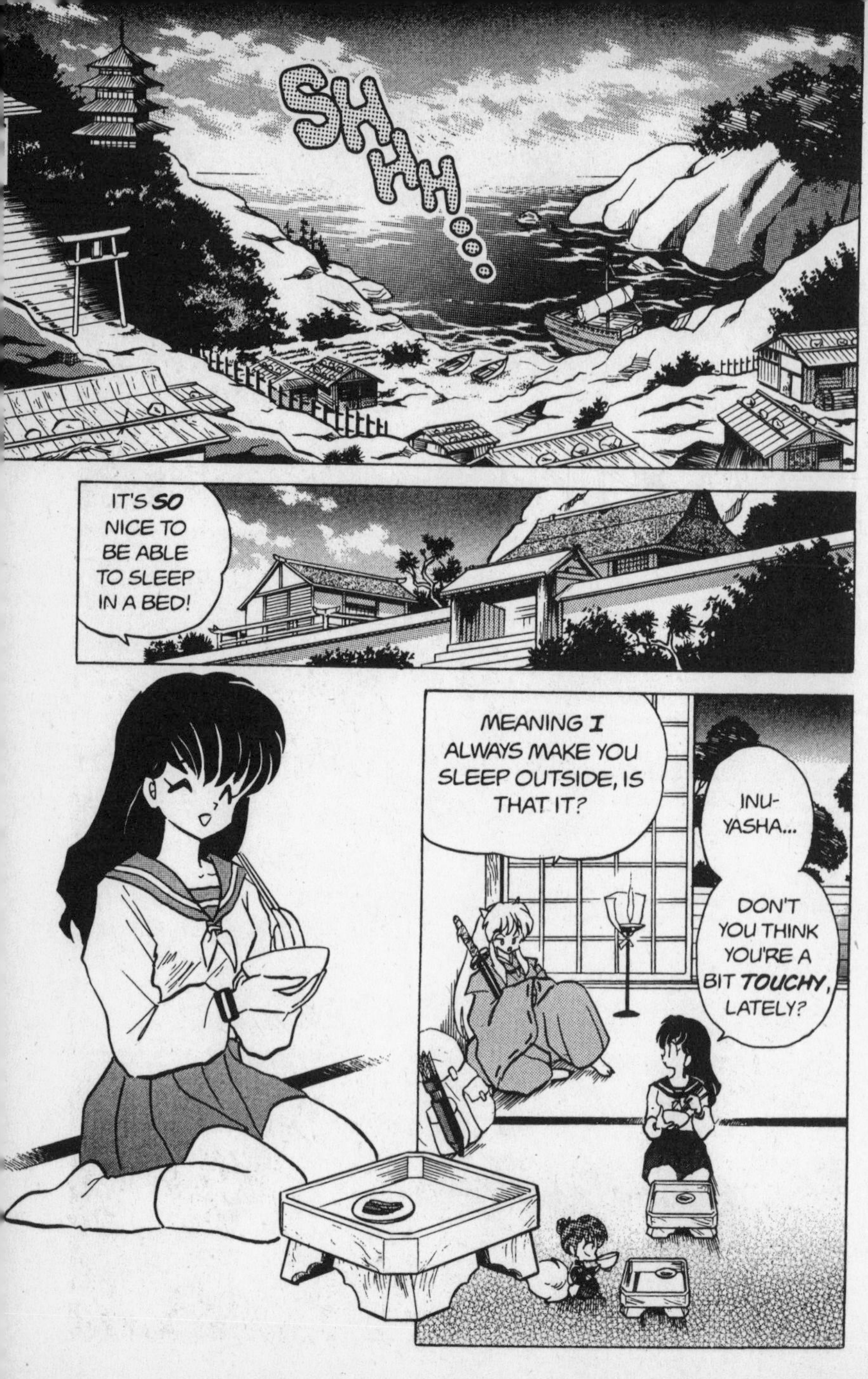
SHHH...
IT'S SO NICE TO BE ABLE TO SLEEP IN A BED!
MEANING I ALWAYS MAKE YOU SLEEP OUTSIDE, IS THAT IT?
INU-YASHA...
DON'T YOU THINK YOU'RE A BIT TOUCHY, LATELY?

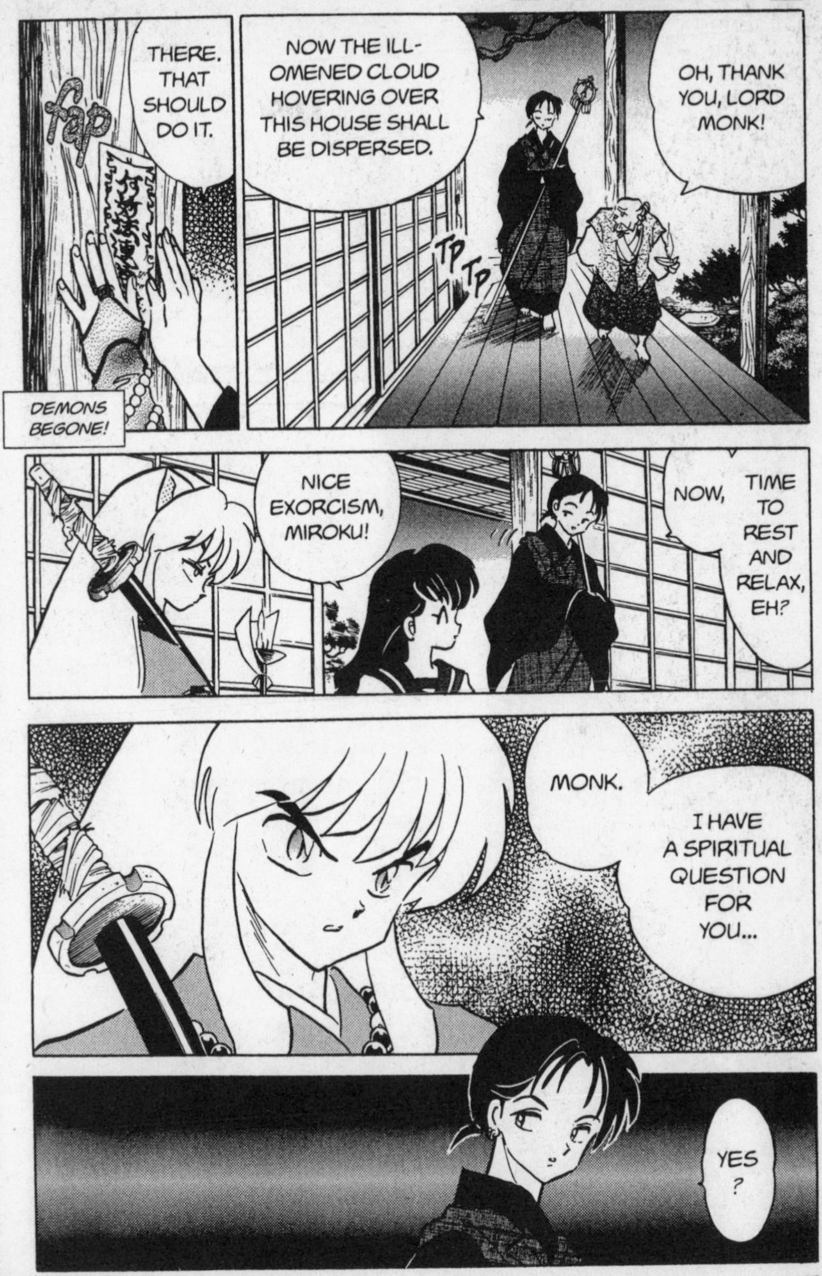
fap
THERE. THAT SHOULD DO IT.
DEMONS BEGONE!
NOW THE ILL-OMENED CLOUD HOVERING OVER THIS HOUSE SHALL BE DISPERSED.
TP TP
OH, THANK YOU, LORD MONK!
NICE EXORCISM, MIROKU!
NOW, TIME TO REST AND RELAX, EH?
MONK.
I HAVE A SPIRITUAL QUESTION FOR YOU...
YES ?

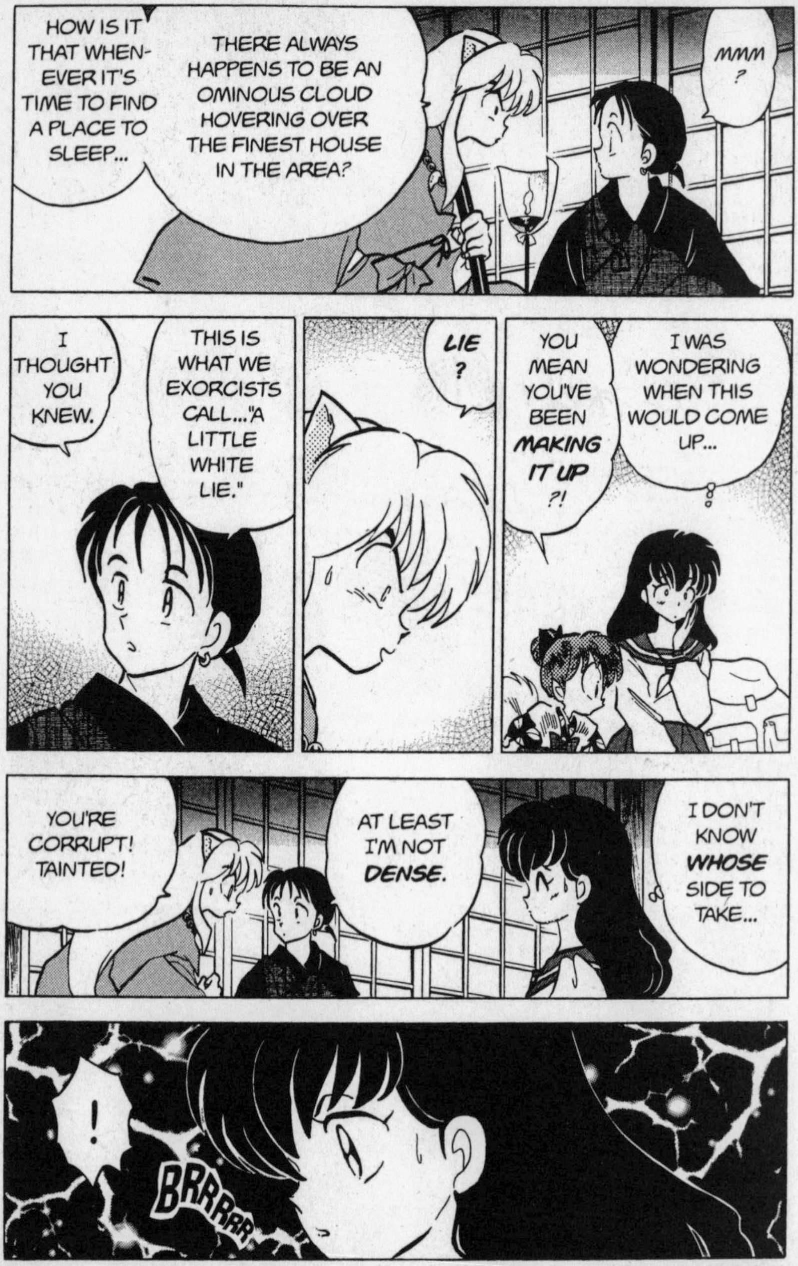
HOW IS IT THAT WHENEVER IT'S TIME TO FIND A PLACE TO SLEEP...
THERE ALWAYS HAPPENS TO BE AN OMINOUS CLOUD HOVERING OVER THE FINEST HOUSE IN THE AREA?
MMM?
I THOUGHT YOU KNEW.
THIS IS WHAT WE EXORCISTS CALL..."A LITTLE WHITE LIE."
LIE?
YOU MEAN YOU'VE BEEN MAKING IT UP?!
I WAS WONDERING WHEN THIS WOULD COME UP...
YOU'RE CORRUPT! TAINTED!
AT LEAST I'M NOT DENSE.
I DON'T KNOW WHOSE SIDE TO TAKE...
!
BRRRRRR

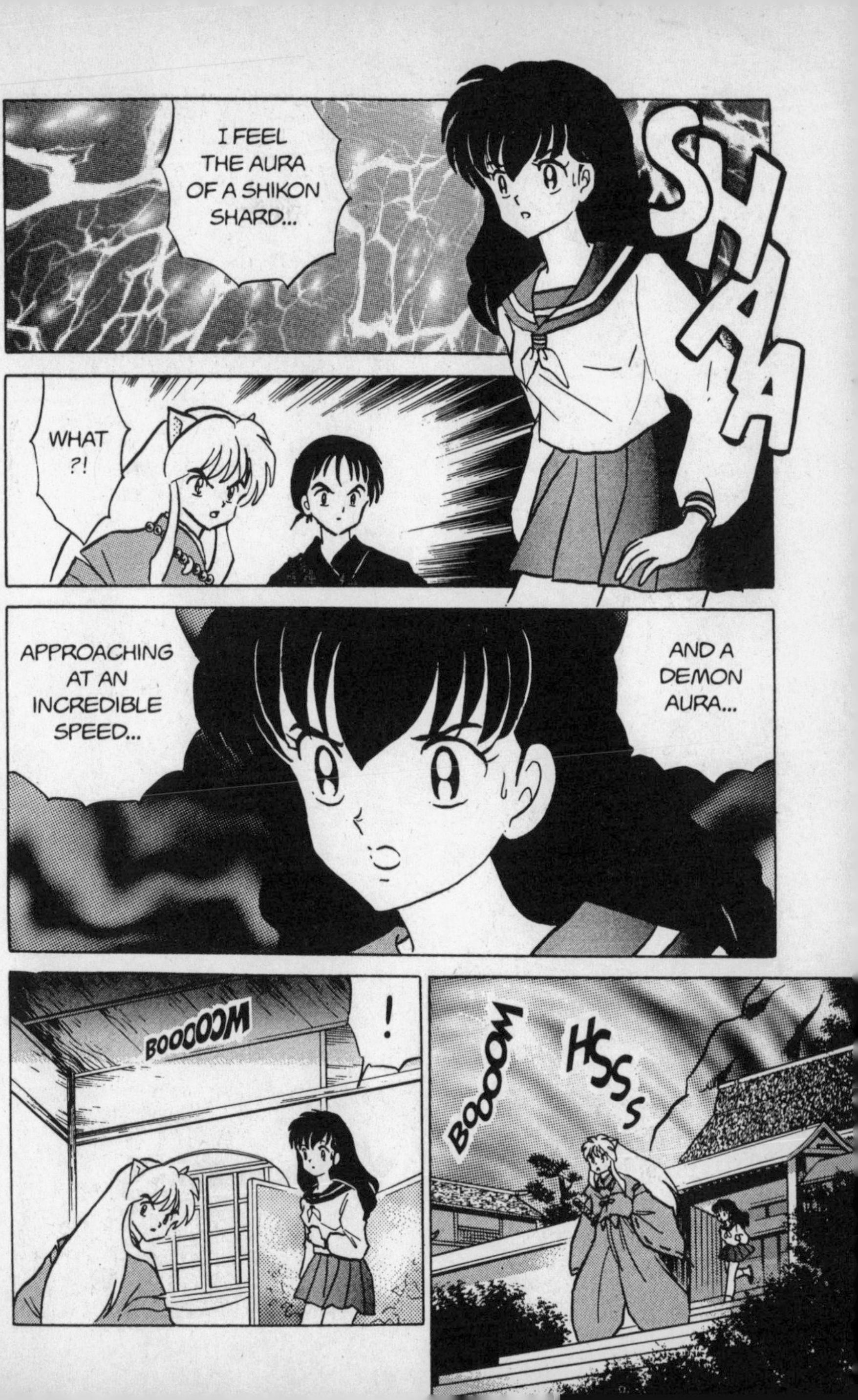
I FEEL THE AURA OF A SHIKON SHARD...
SHAA
WHAT ?!
APPROACHING AT AN INCREDIBLE SPEED...
AND A DEMON AURA...
BOOOOOM
!
BOOOOOM
HSSSS

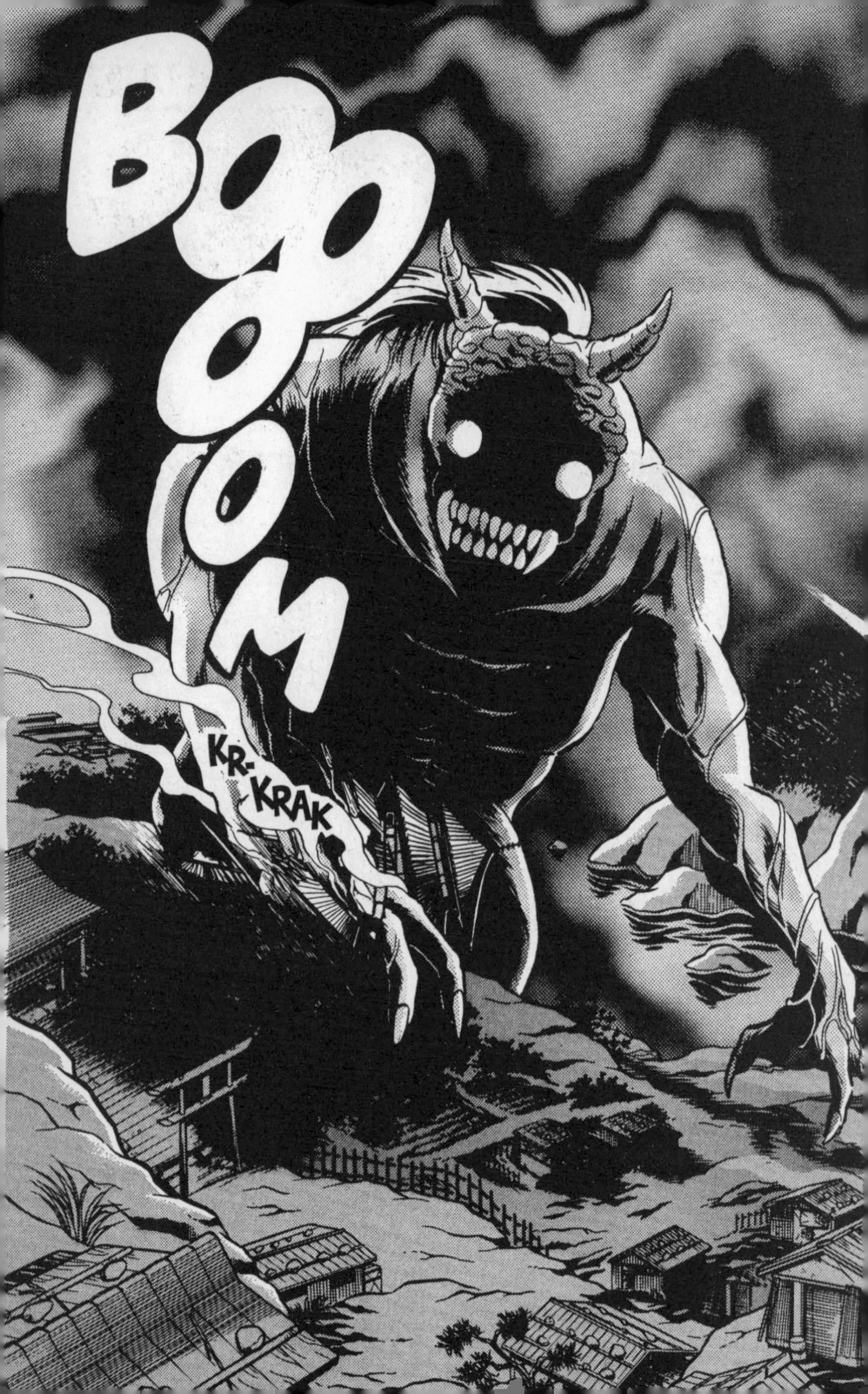
BOOOOOM
KR-KRAK

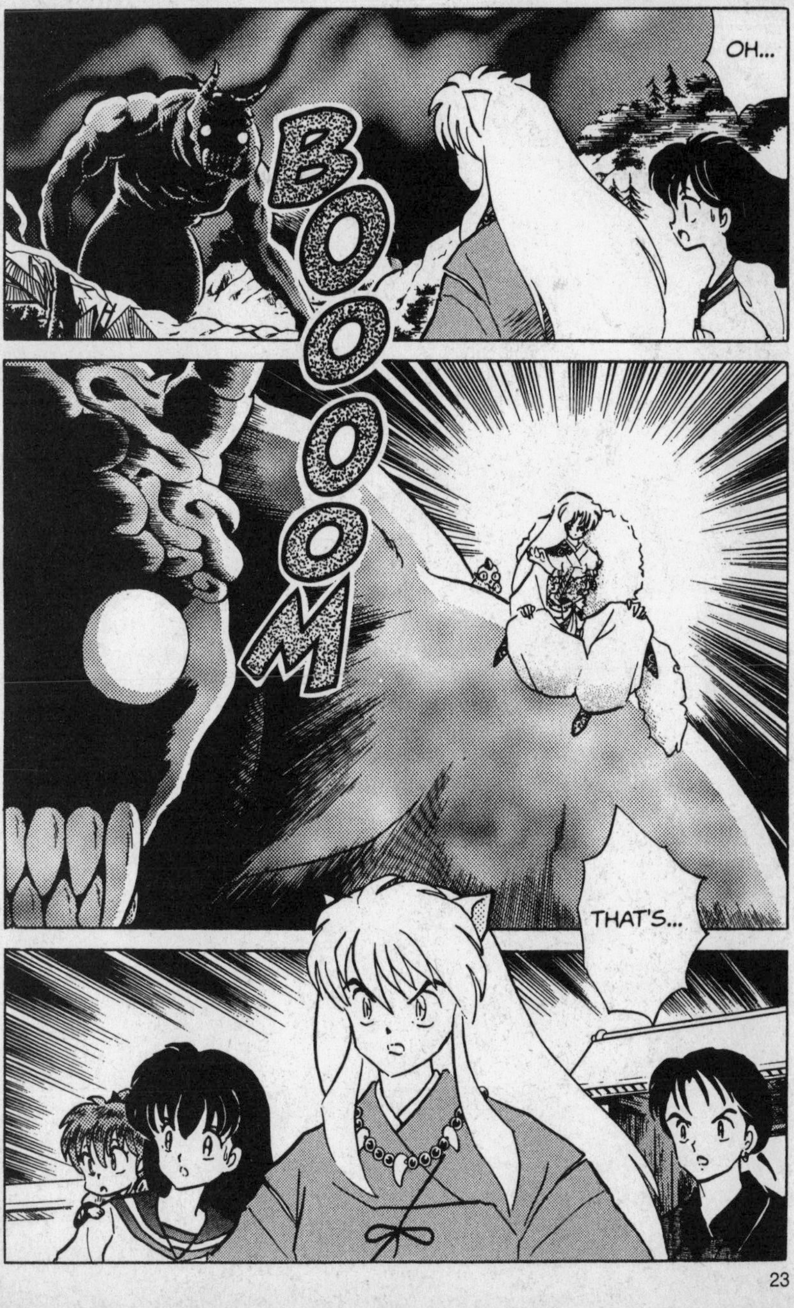
BOOOOOM
OH...
THAT'S...

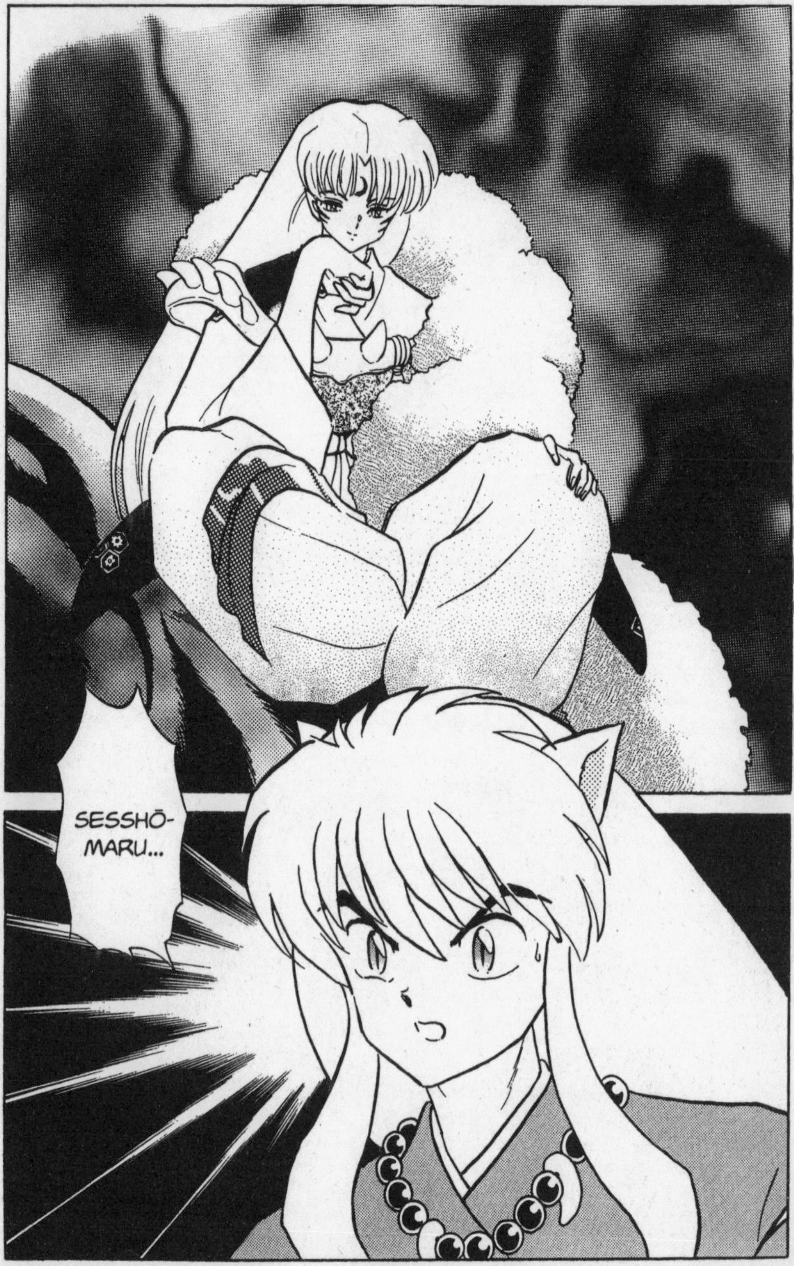
SESSHŌ-
MARU...

SCROLL TWO

THE POWER OF THE WOLF'S FANG

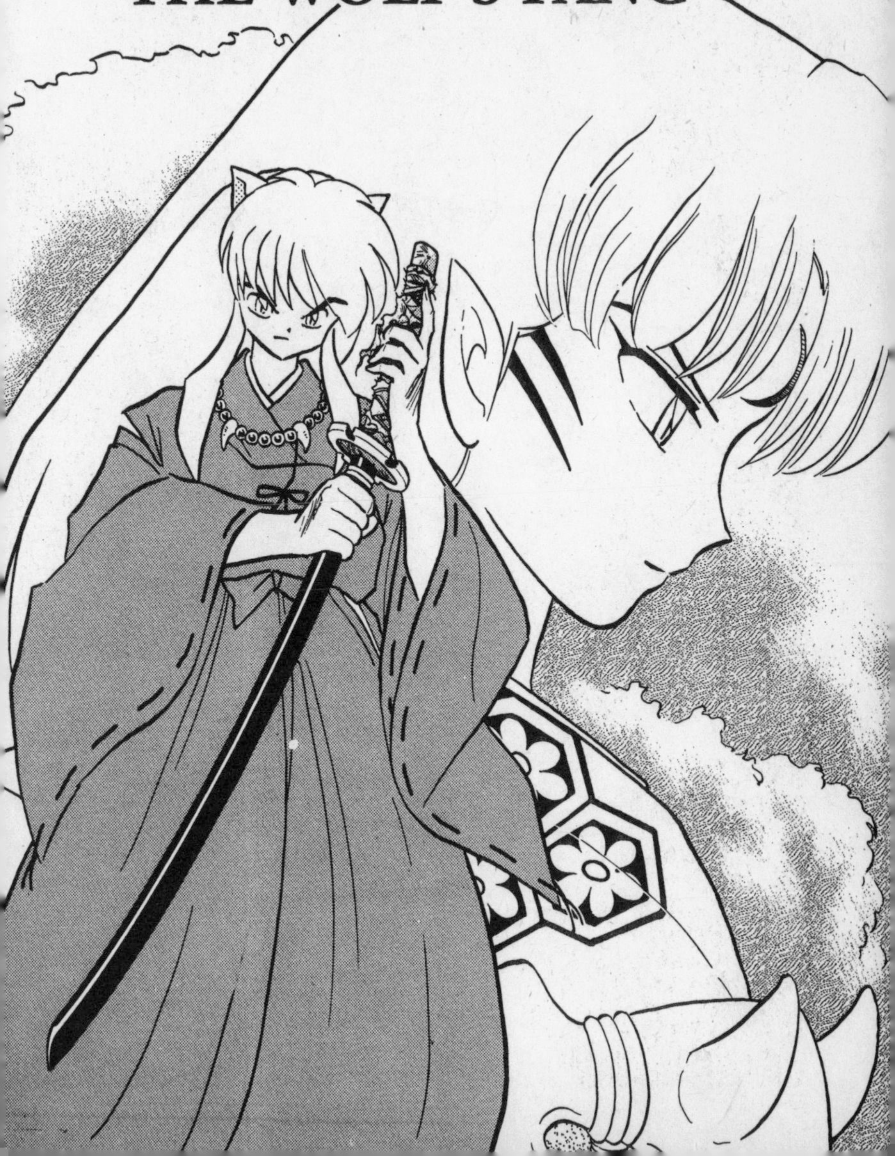

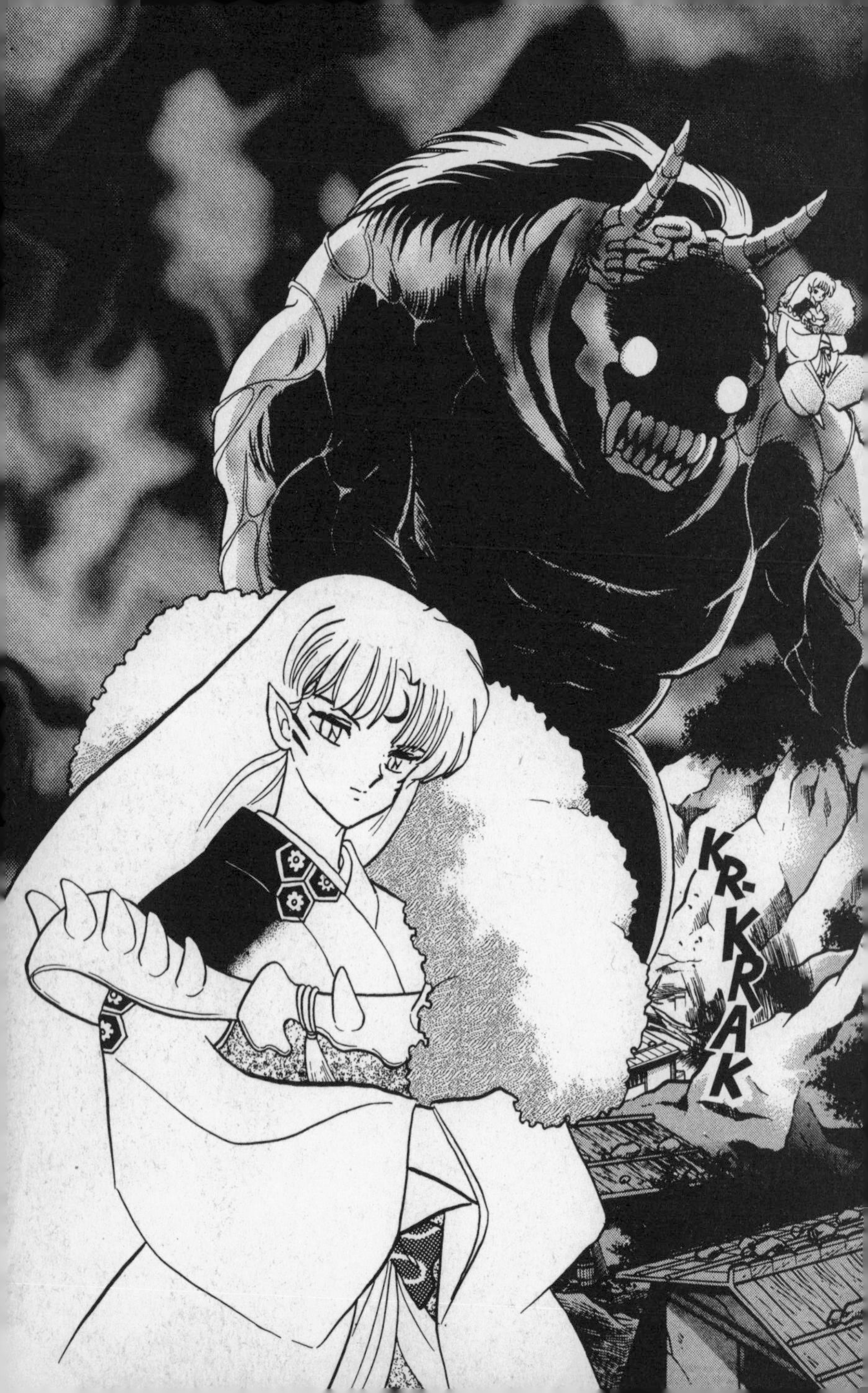
KR-KRAK

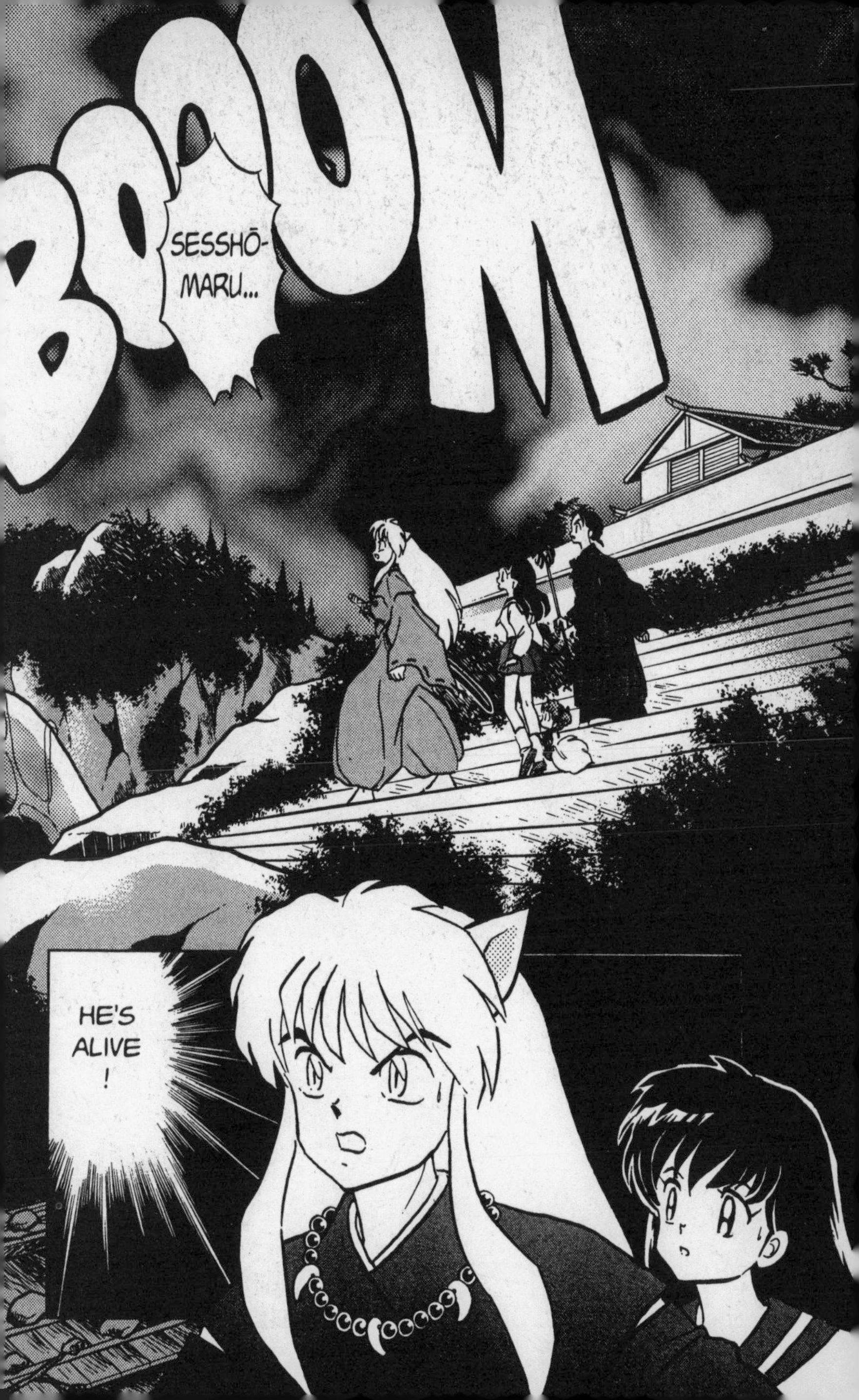
BOOOOM
SESSHŌ-MARU...
HE'S ALIVE!

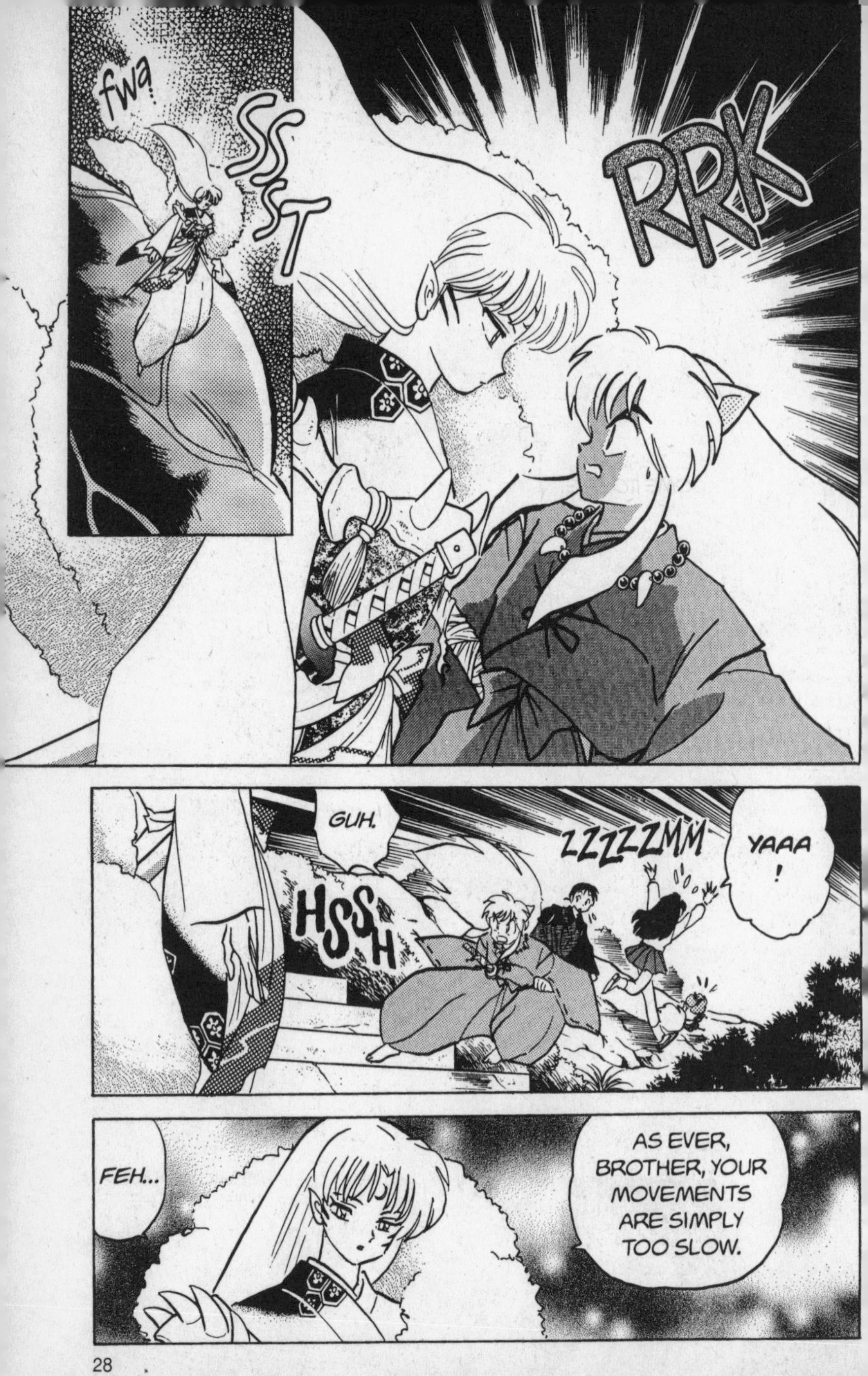
fwa
SSST
RRK
GUH.
HSSH
ZZZZZMM
YAAA!
FEH...
AS EVER, BROTHER, YOUR MOVEMENTS ARE SIMPLY TOO SLOW.

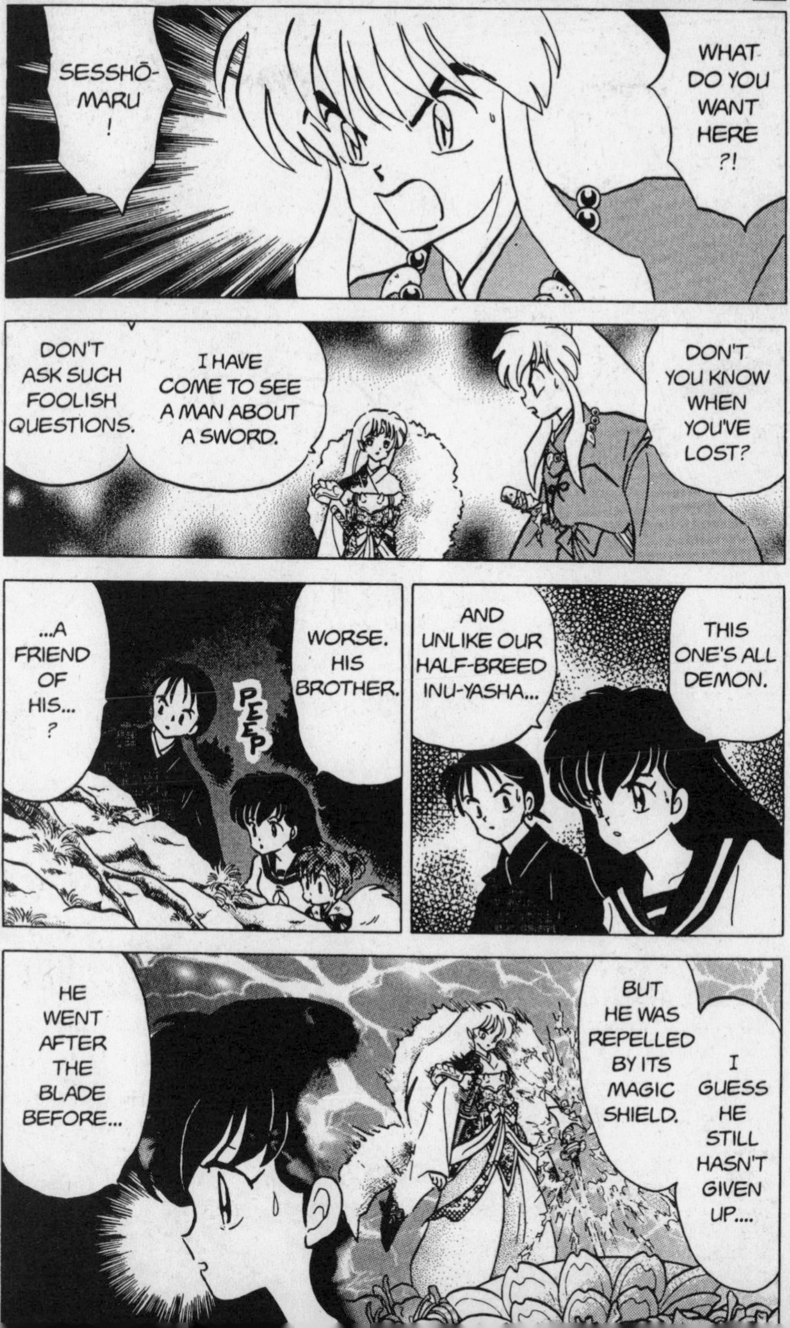
SESSHŌ-MARU!
WHAT DO YOU WANT HERE?!
DON'T ASK SUCH FOOLISH QUESTIONS.
I HAVE COME TO SEE A MAN ABOUT A SWORD.
DON'T YOU KNOW WHEN YOU'VE LOST?
...A FRIEND OF HIS...?
PEEP
WORSE. HIS BROTHER.
AND UNLIKE OUR HALF-BREED INU-YASHA...
THIS ONE'S ALL DEMON.
HE WENT AFTER THE BLADE BEFORE...
BUT HE WAS REPELLED BY ITS MAGIC SHIELD.
I GUESS HE STILL HASN'T GIVEN UP....

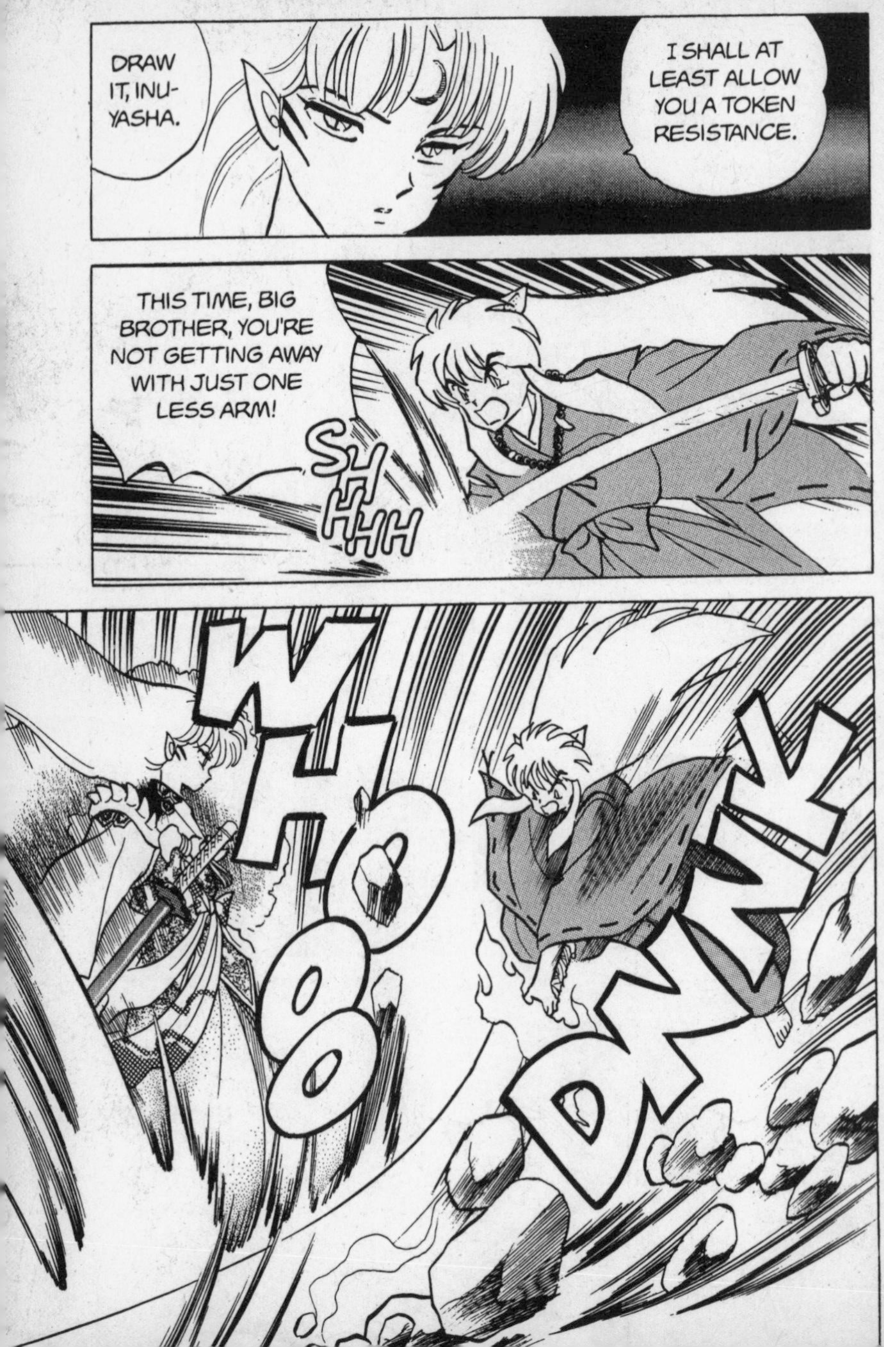
DRAW IT, INU-YASHA.
I SHALL AT LEAST ALLOW YOU A TOKEN RESISTANCE.
THIS TIME, BIG BROTHER, YOU'RE NOT GETTING AWAY WITH JUST ONE LESS ARM!
SHHHHH
WHOOOO
DUNK

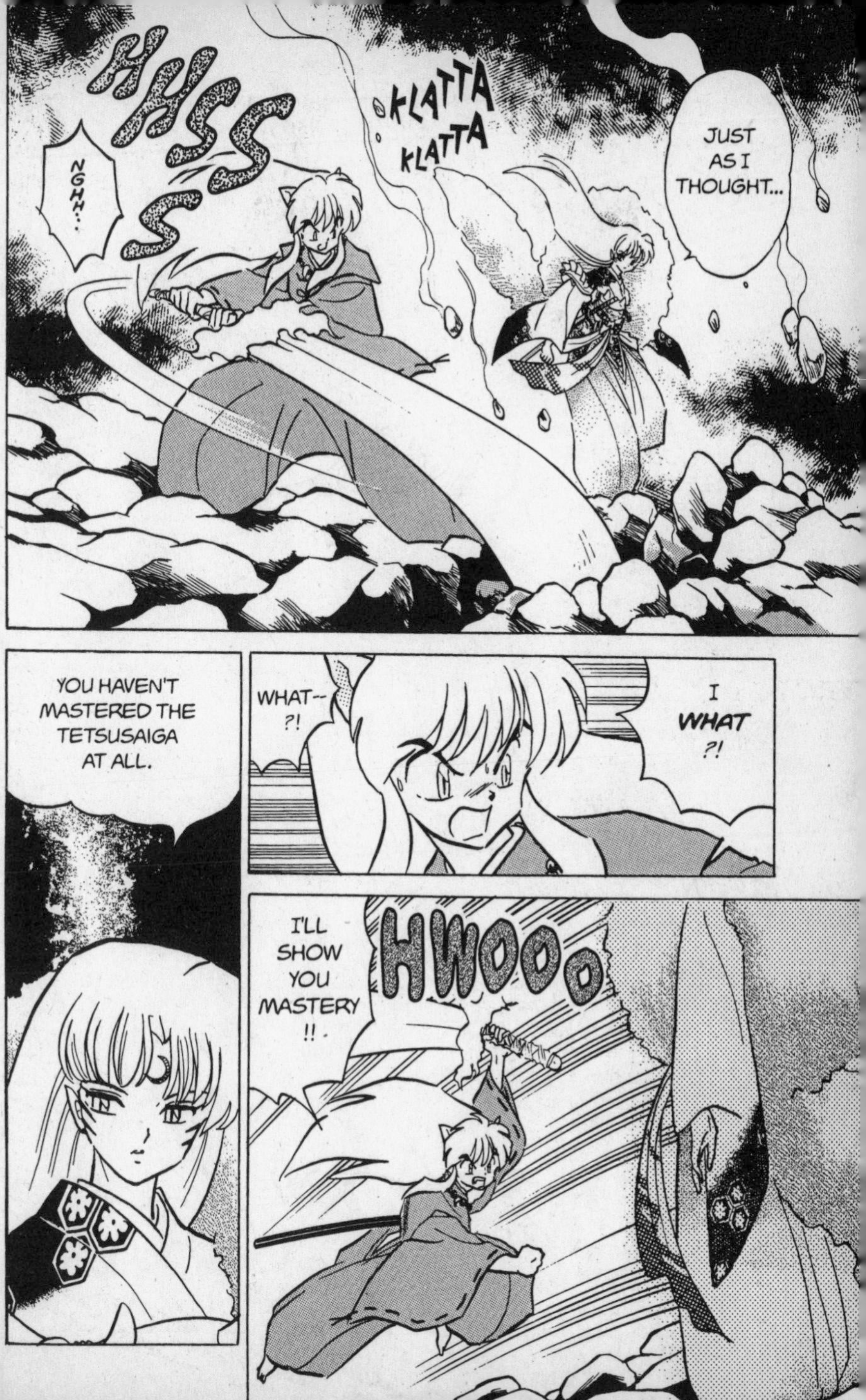
HHSSS
NGHH...
KLATTA KLATTA
JUST AS I THOUGHT...
YOU HAVEN'T MASTERED THE TETSUSAIGA AT ALL.
WHAT--?!
I WHAT?!
I'LL SHOW YOU MASTERY!!
HWOOO

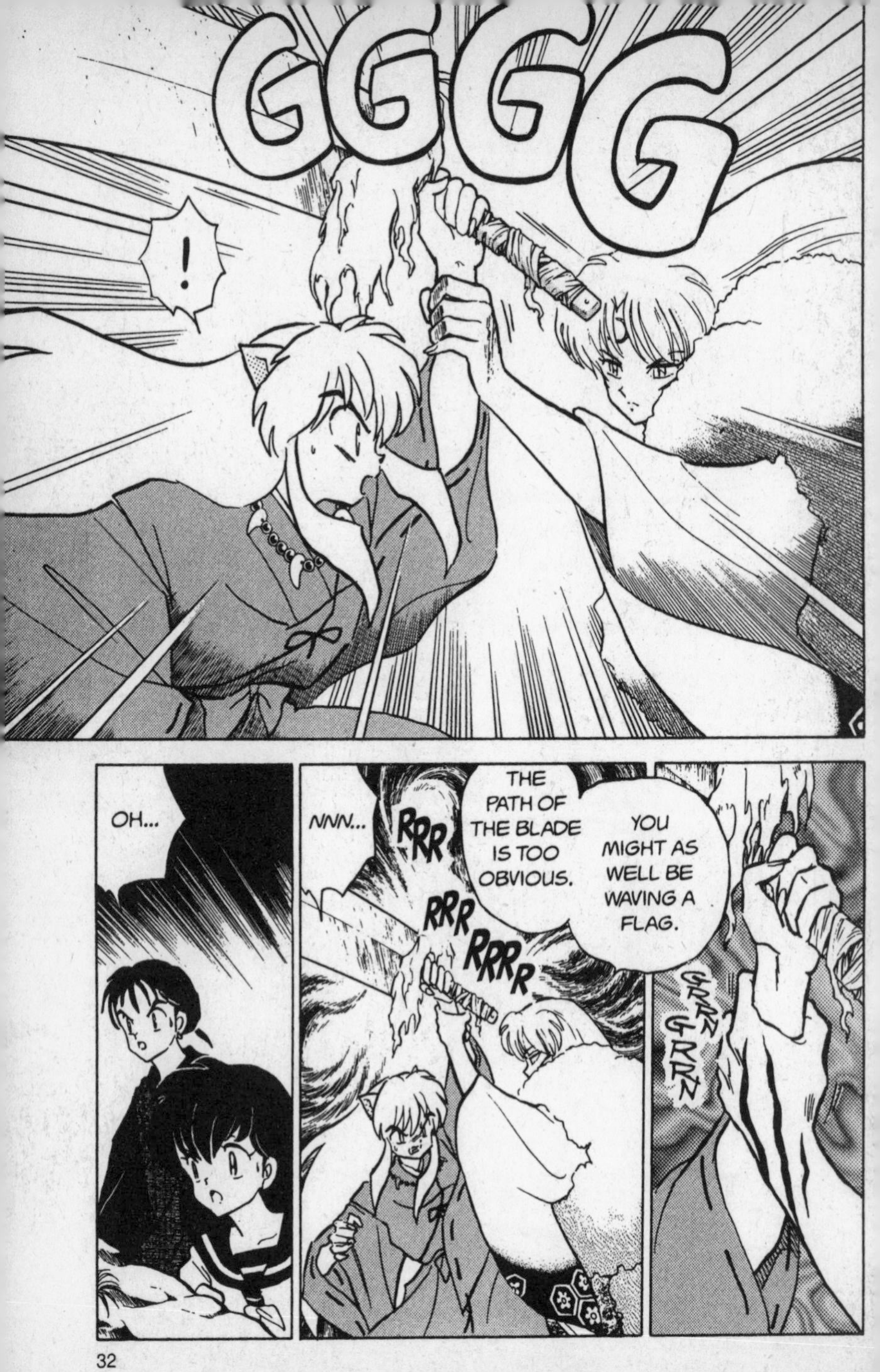
GGGG
!
OH...
NNN...
RRR
RRR
RRRR
THE PATH OF THE BLADE IS TOO OBVIOUS.
YOU MIGHT AS WELL BE WAVING A FLAG.
GRRN GRRN

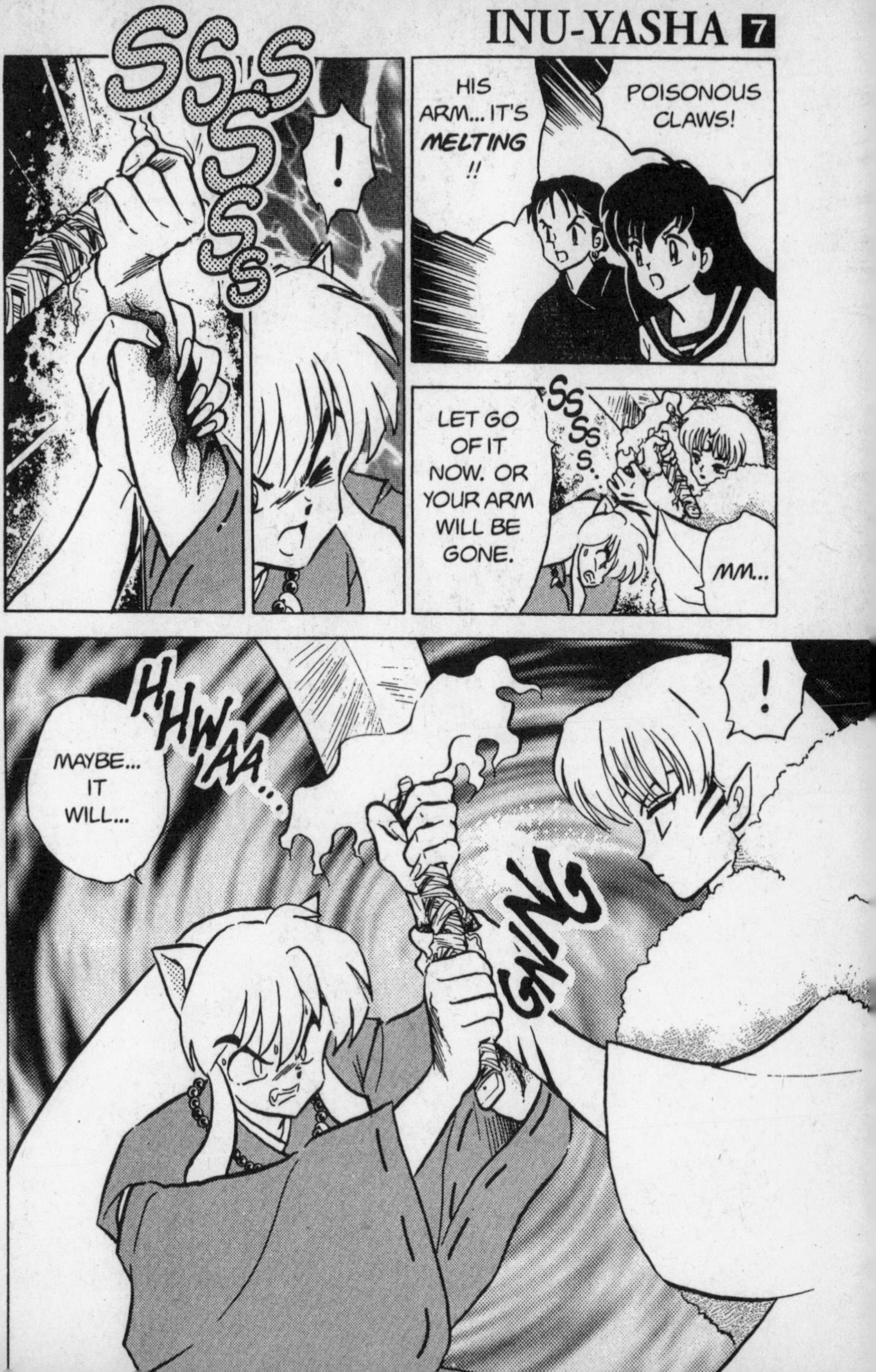
SSSSSSSS
!
HIS ARM... IT'S MELTING !!
POISONOUS CLAWS!
LET GO OF IT NOW. OR YOUR ARM WILL BE GONE.
SSSSS...
MM...
MAYBE... IT WILL...
HHWAAA...
!
GNNG

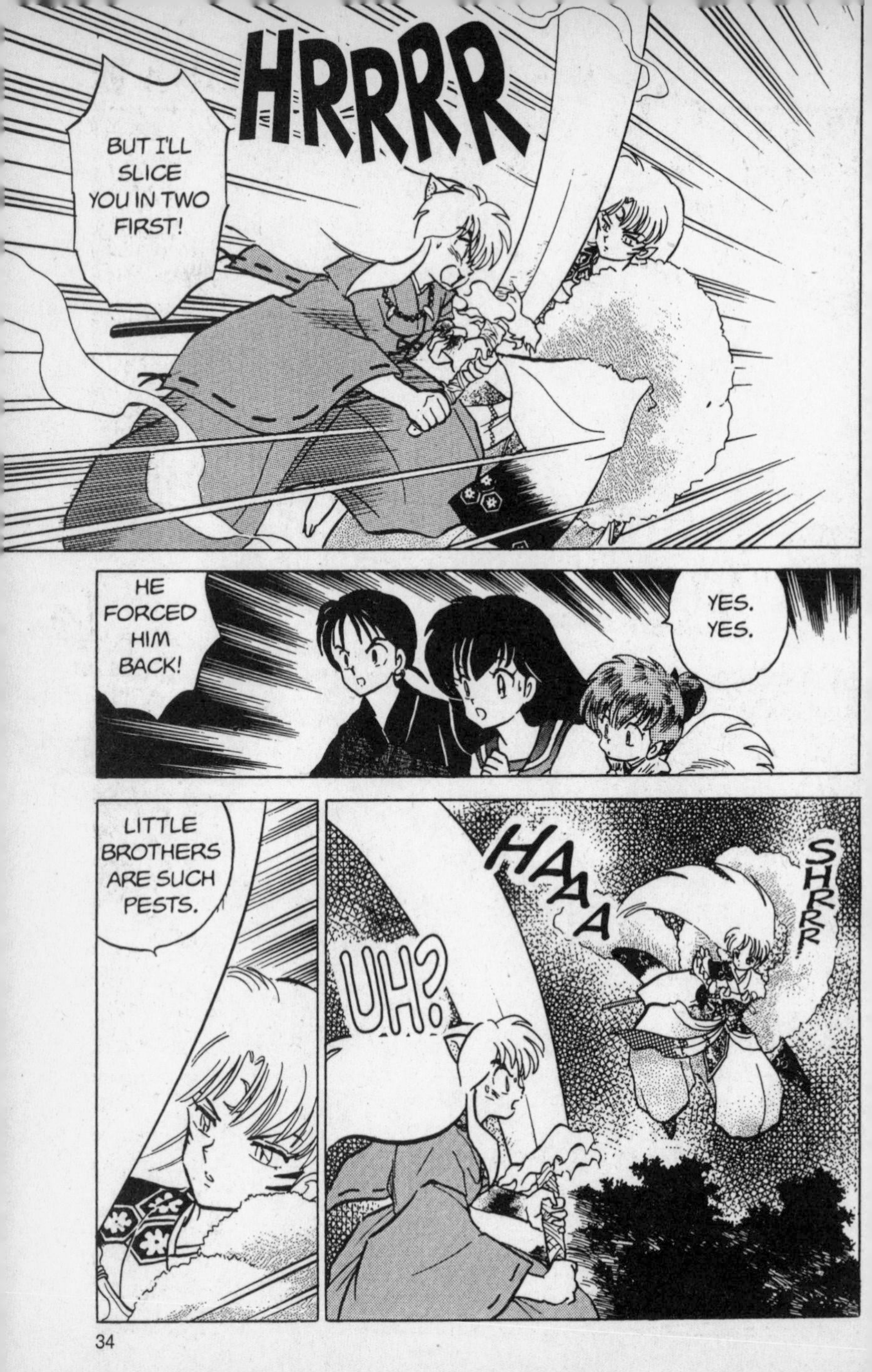
HRRRR
BUT I'LL SLICE YOU IN TWO FIRST!
HE FORCED HIM BACK!
YES. YES.
LITTLE BROTHERS ARE SUCH PESTS.
HAAAA
SHRRR
UH?

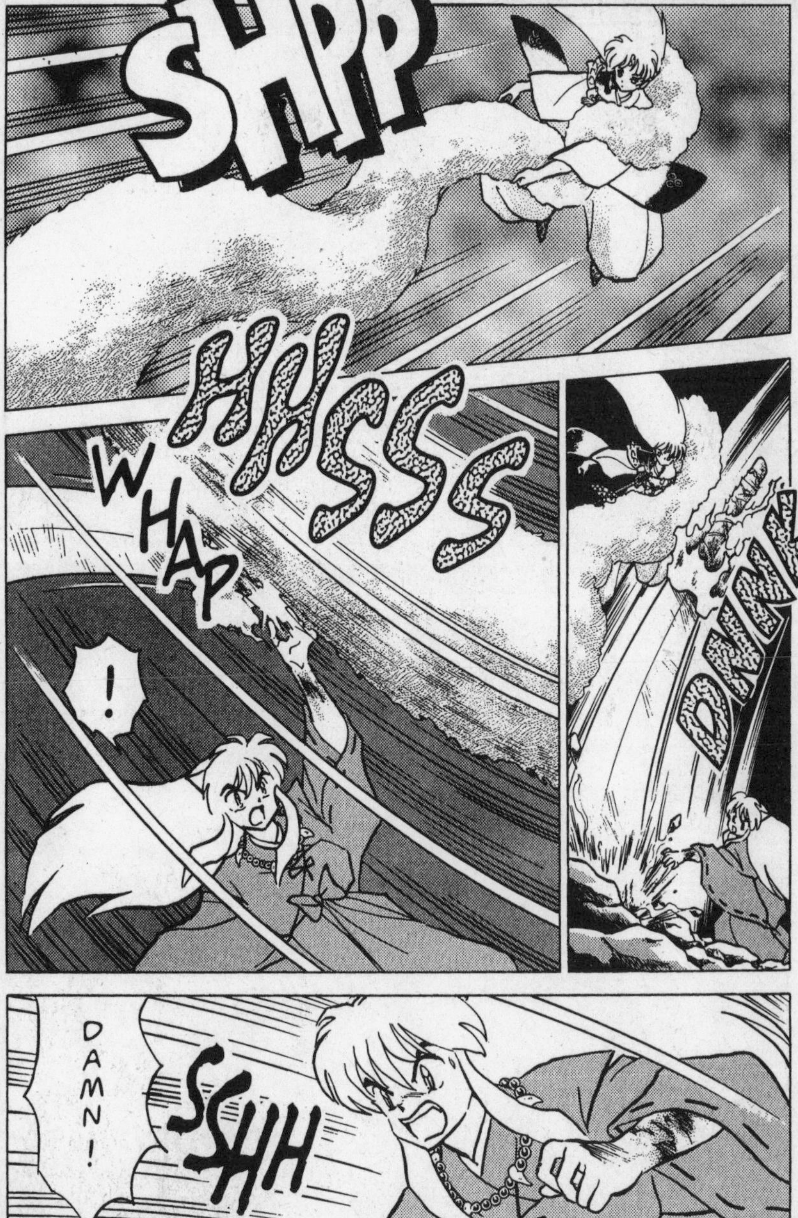
SHPP
HYSSSS
WHAP
!
DWMNK
SSHH
DAMN!

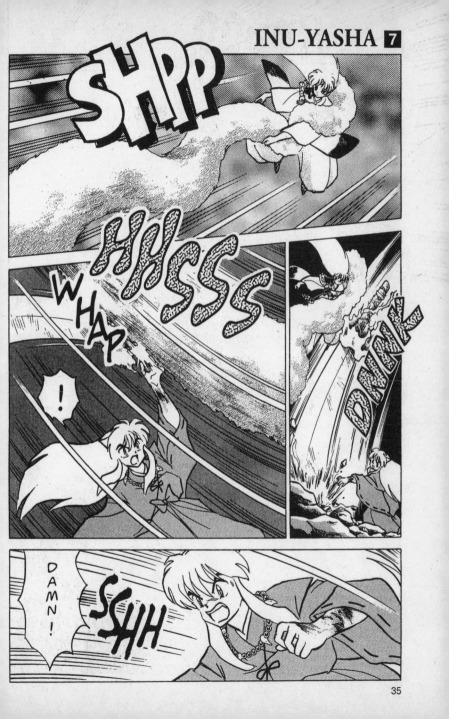

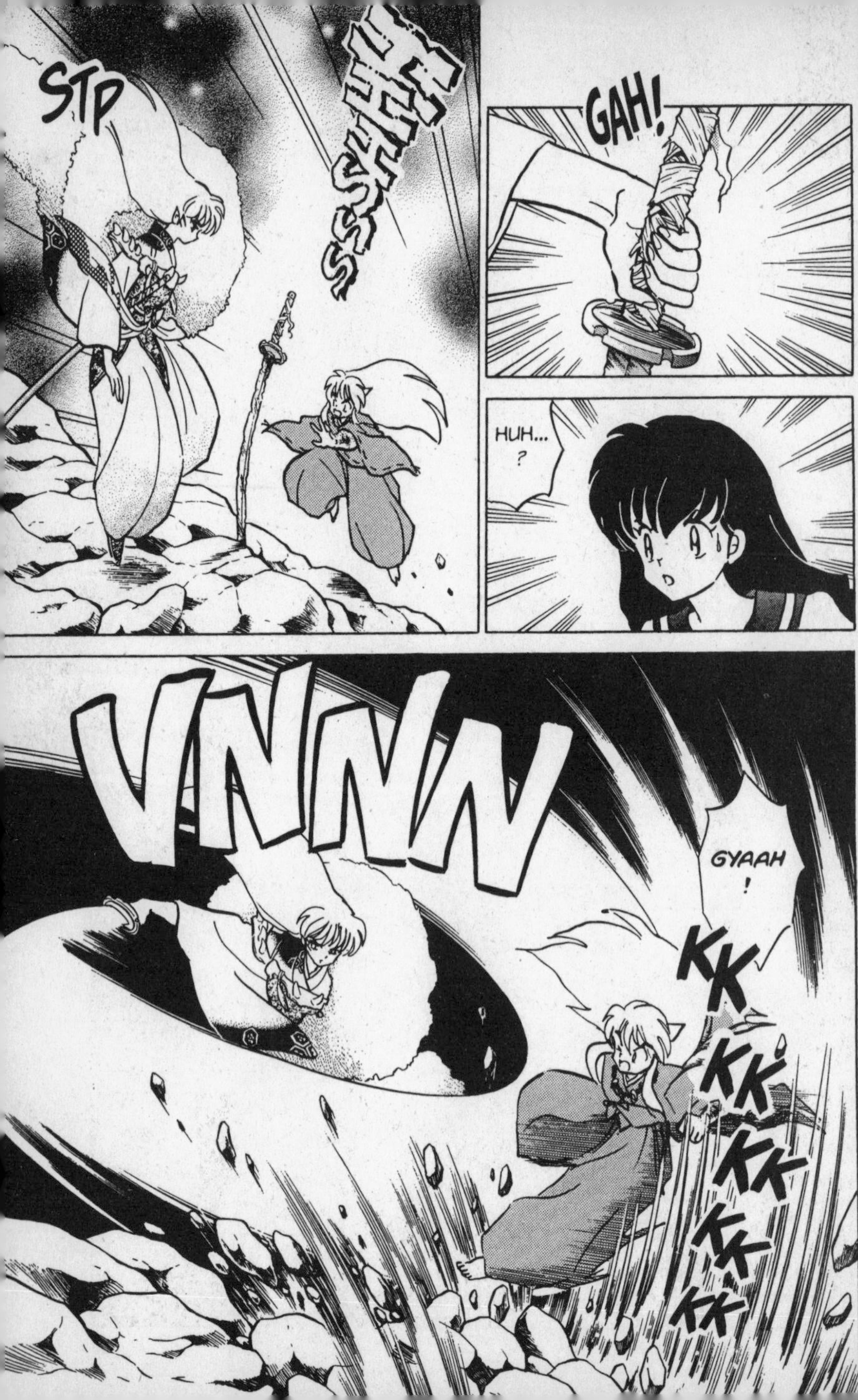
STP
SSSHHH
GAH!
HUH...?
VNNN
GYAAH!
KKKKKKKKKK

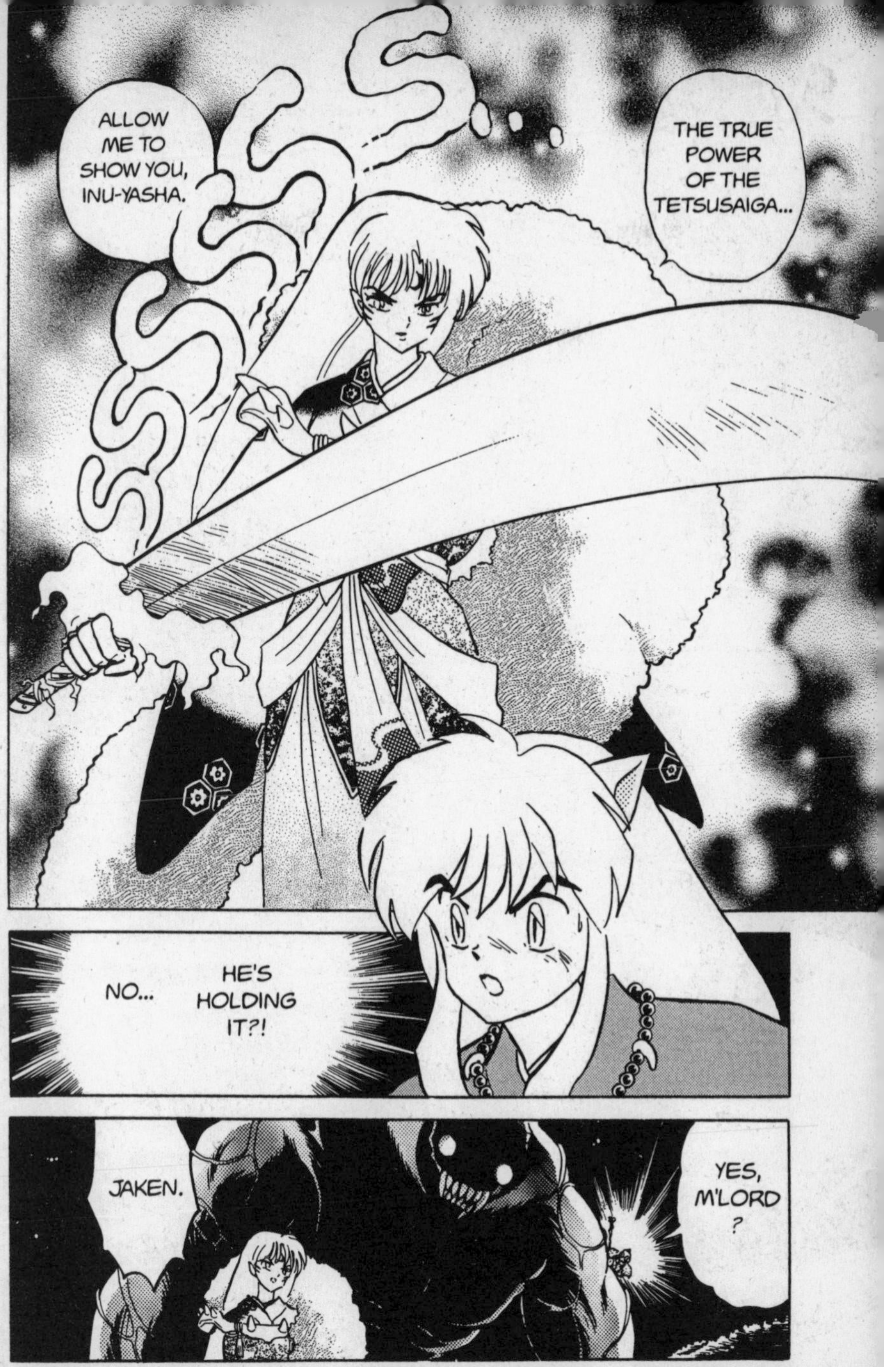
ALLOW ME TO SHOW YOU, INU-YASHA.
THE TRUE POWER OF THE TETSUSAIGA...
NO...
HE'S HOLDING IT?!
JAKEN.
YES, M'LORD ?

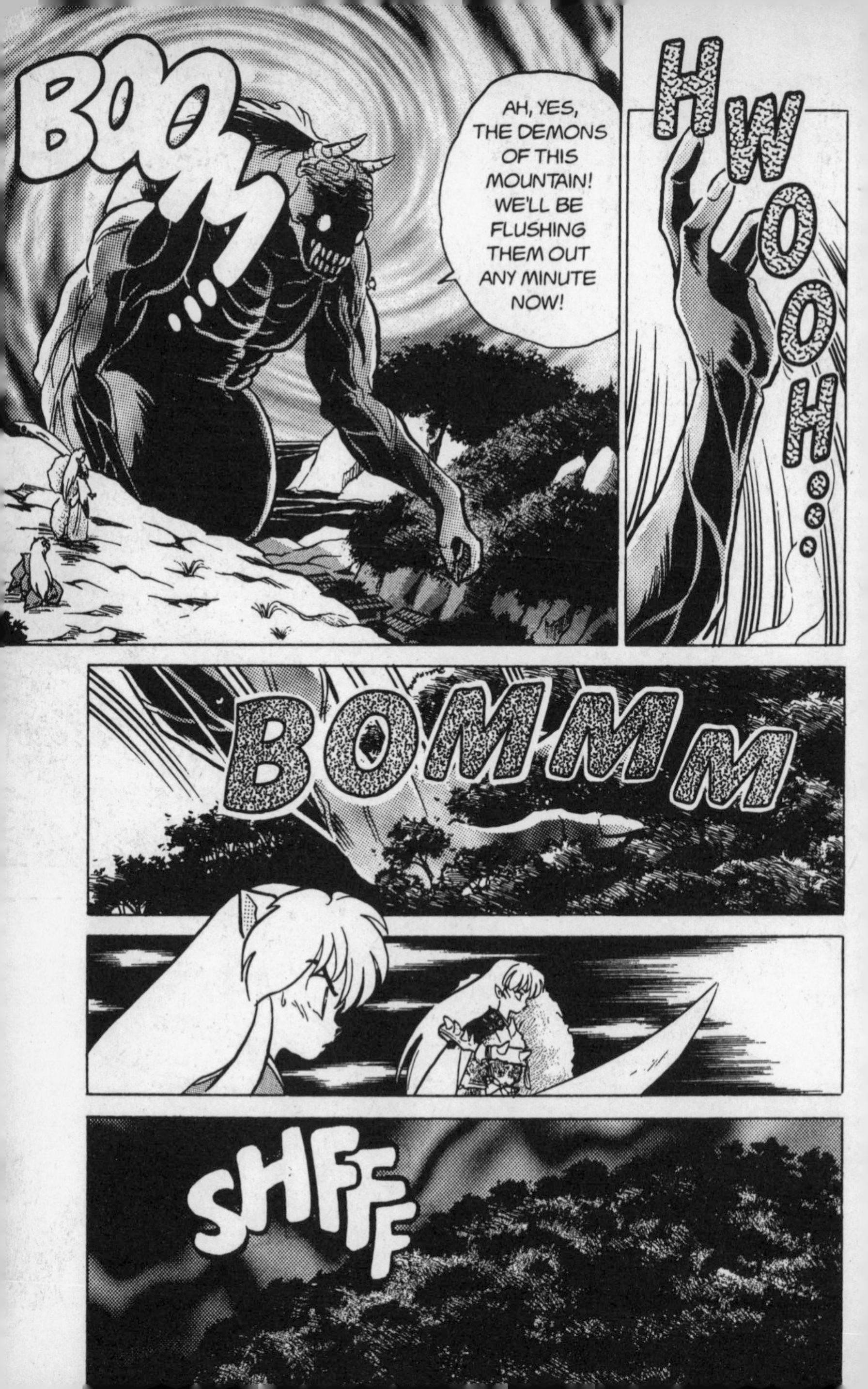
BOOM...
AH, YES, THE DEMONS OF THIS MOUNTAIN! WE'LL BE FLUSHING THEM OUT ANY MINUTE NOW!
HWOOOH...
BOMMM
SHFFF

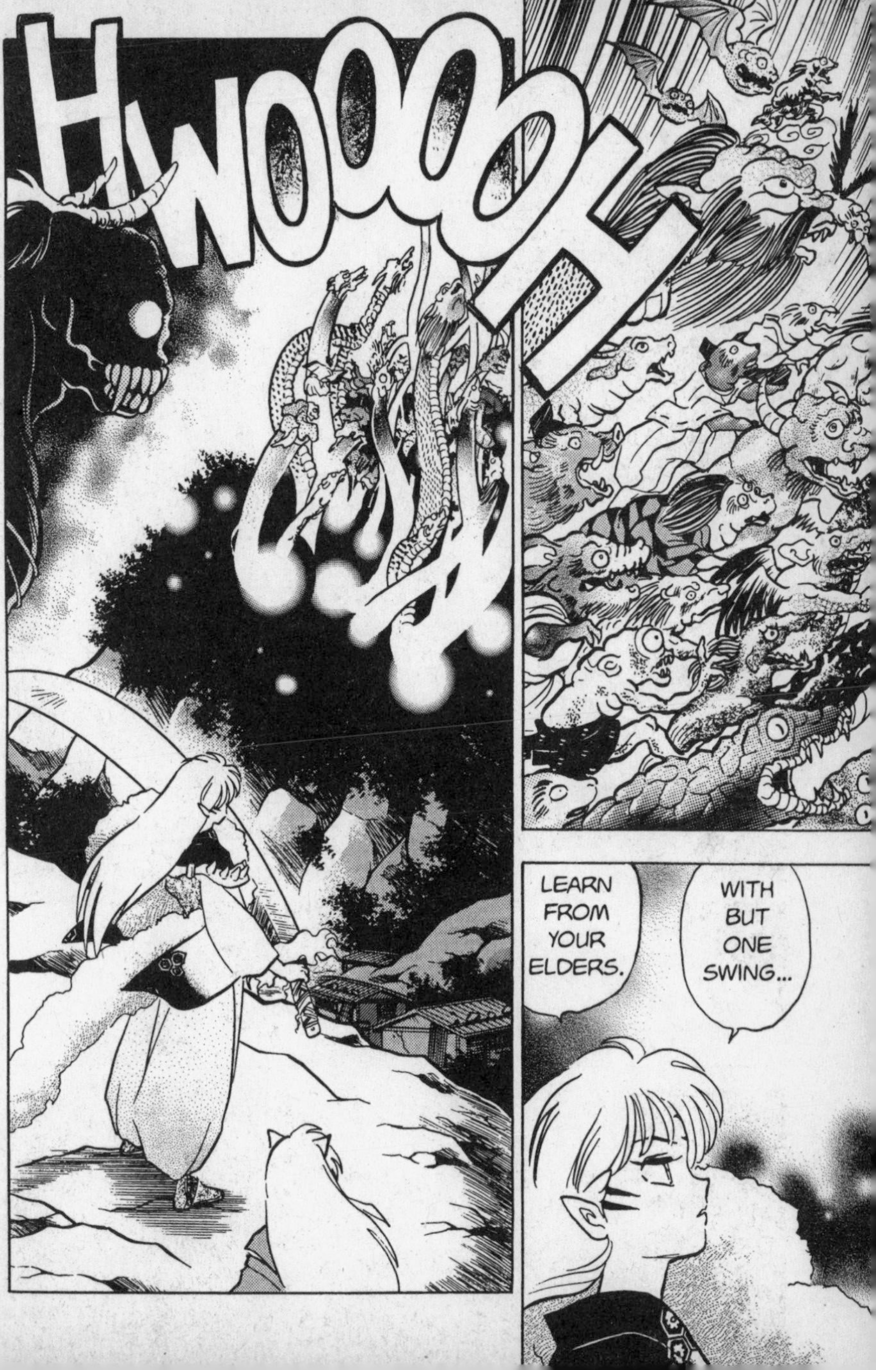
HWOOOH
LEARN FROM YOUR ELDERS.
WITH BUT ONE SWING...

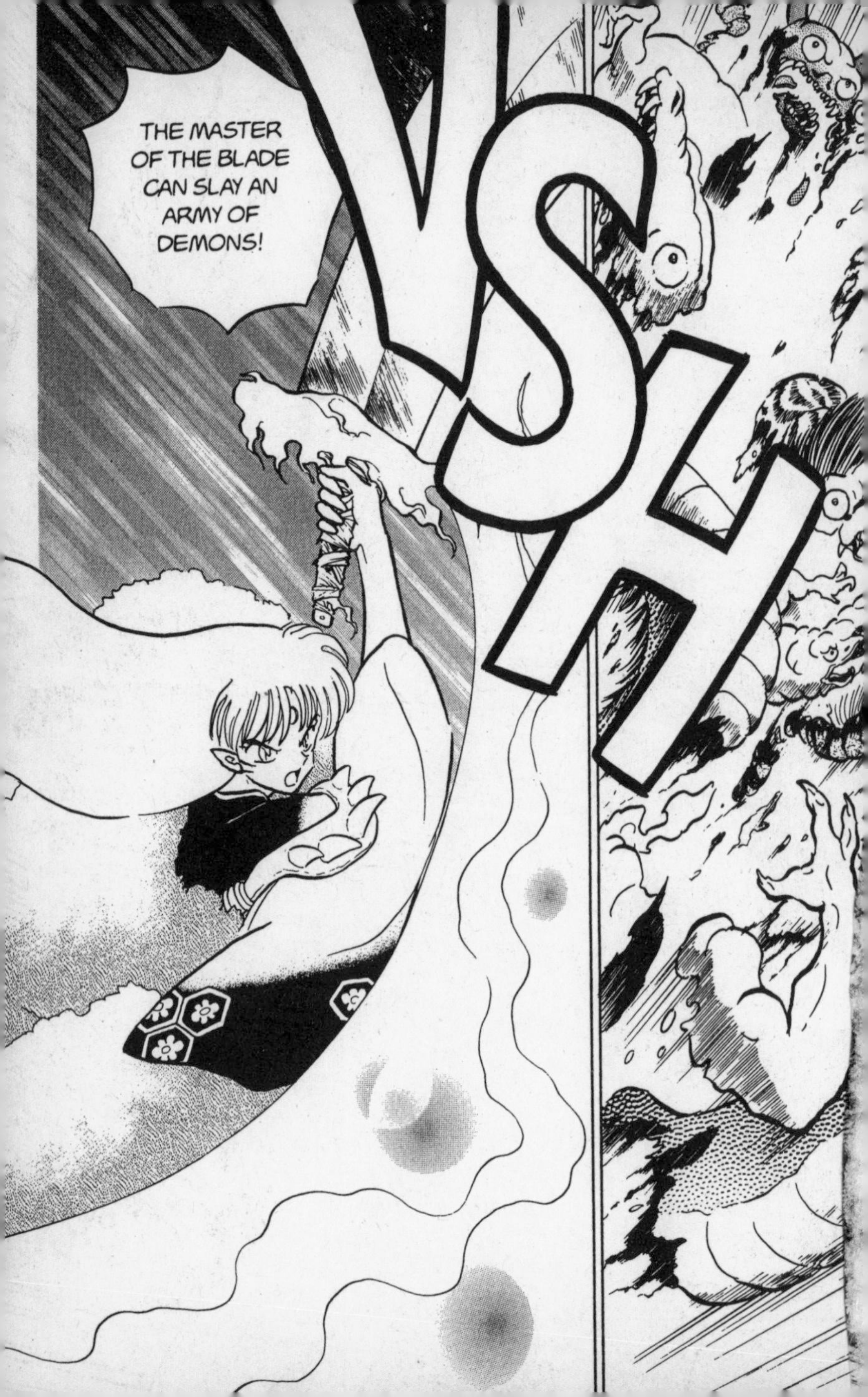
THE MASTER OF THE BLADE CAN SLAY AN ARMY OF DEMONS!
VSH

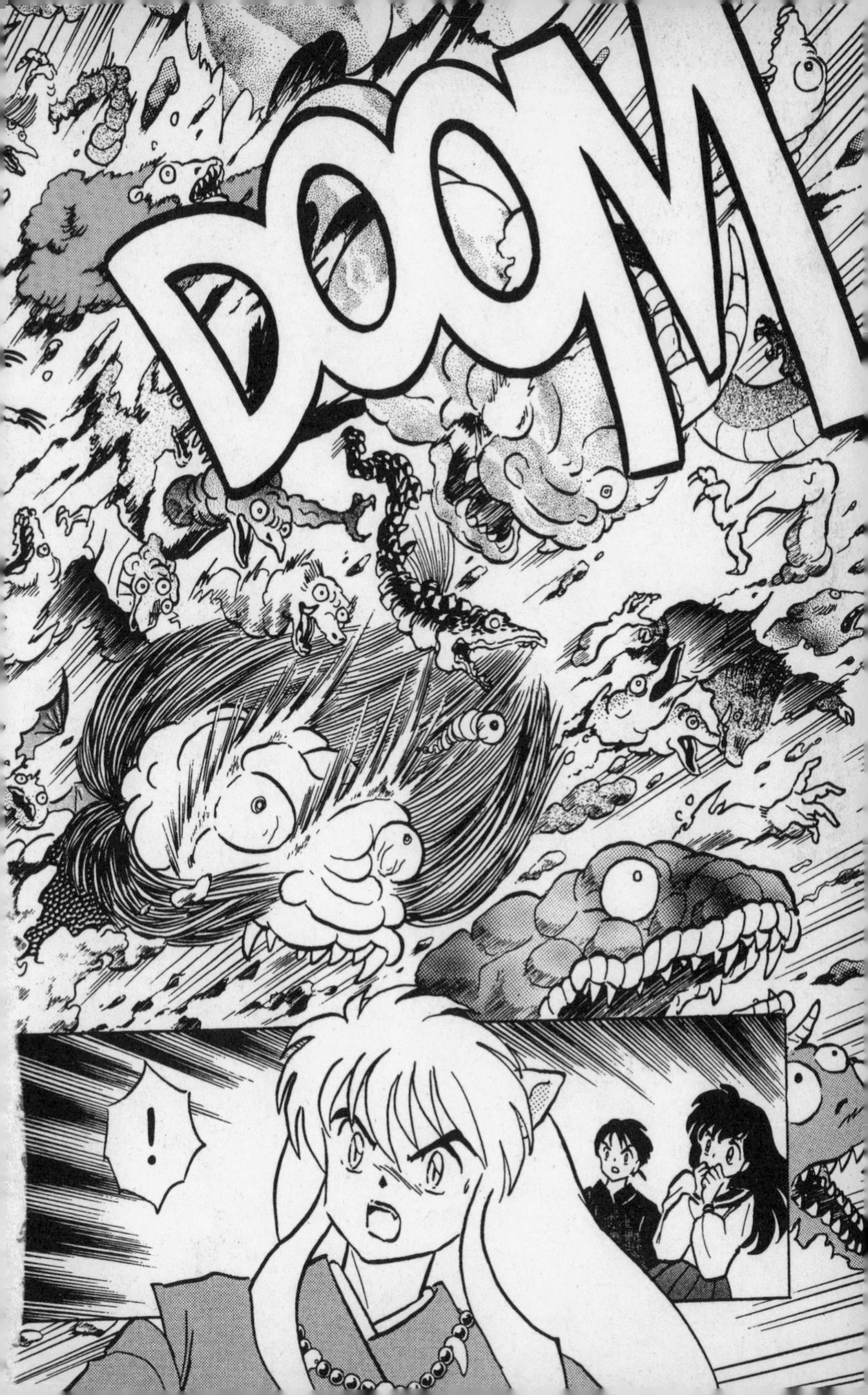
DOOM
!

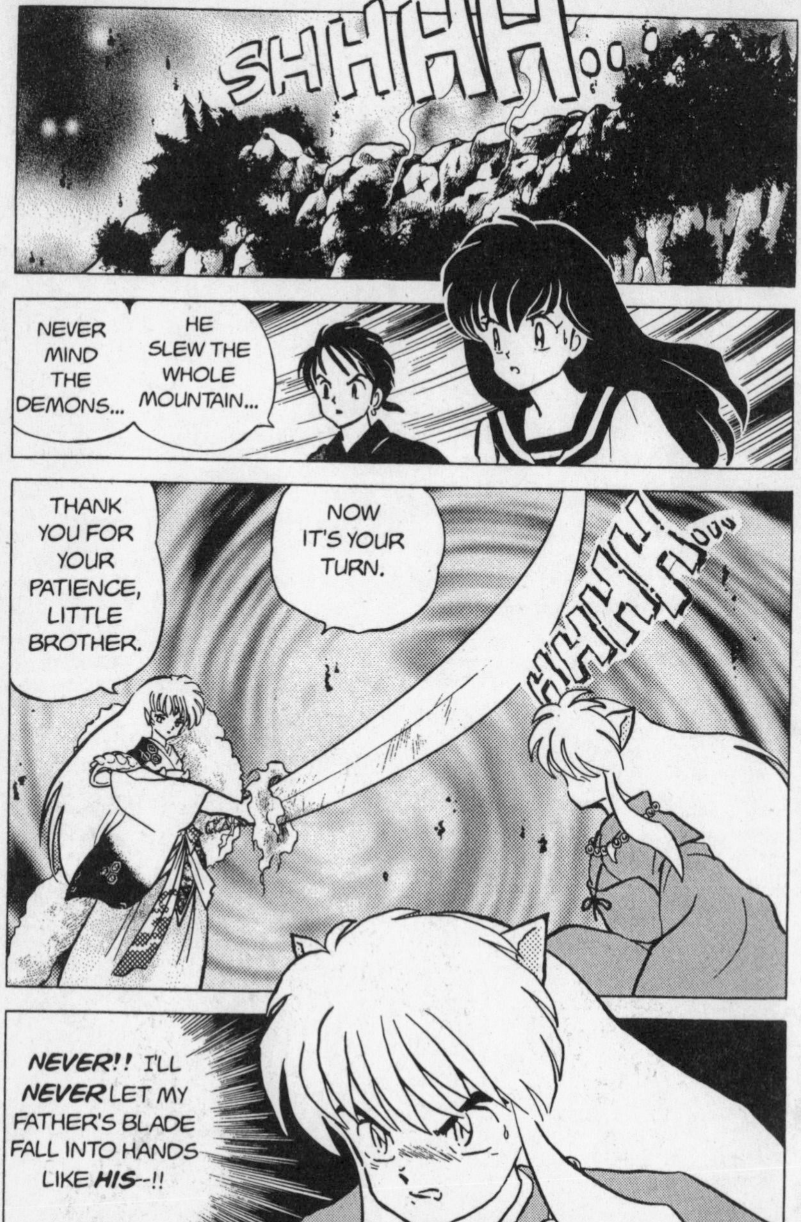
SHHHH...
NEVER MIND THE DEMONS...
HE SLEW THE WHOLE MOUNTAIN...
THANK YOU FOR YOUR PATIENCE, LITTLE BROTHER.
NOW IT'S YOUR TURN.
NEVER!! I'LL NEVER LET MY FATHER'S BLADE FALL INTO HANDS LIKE HIS--!!

SCROLL THREE

THE STING OF VICTORY

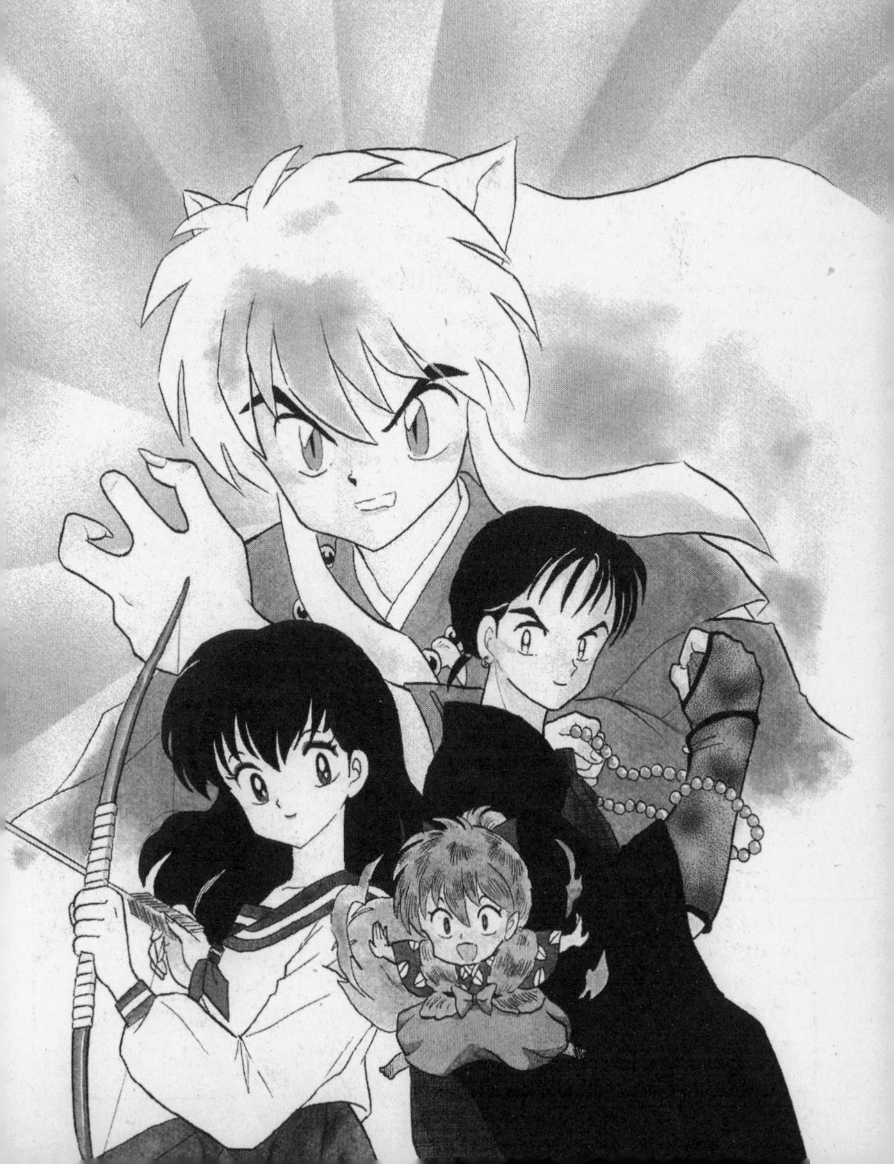

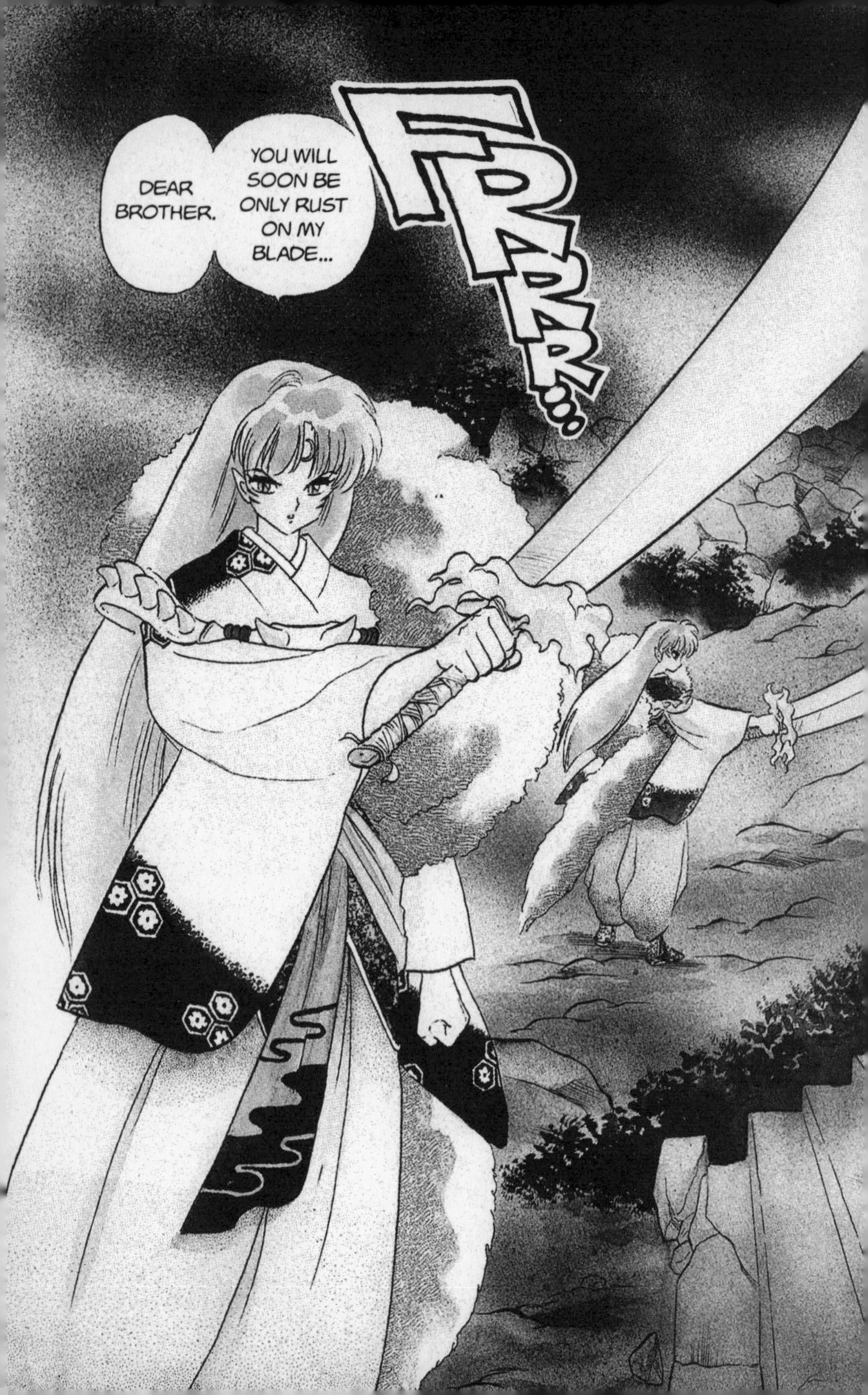
DEAR BROTHER.
YOU WILL SOON BE ONLY RUST ON MY BLADE...
FRRRR...

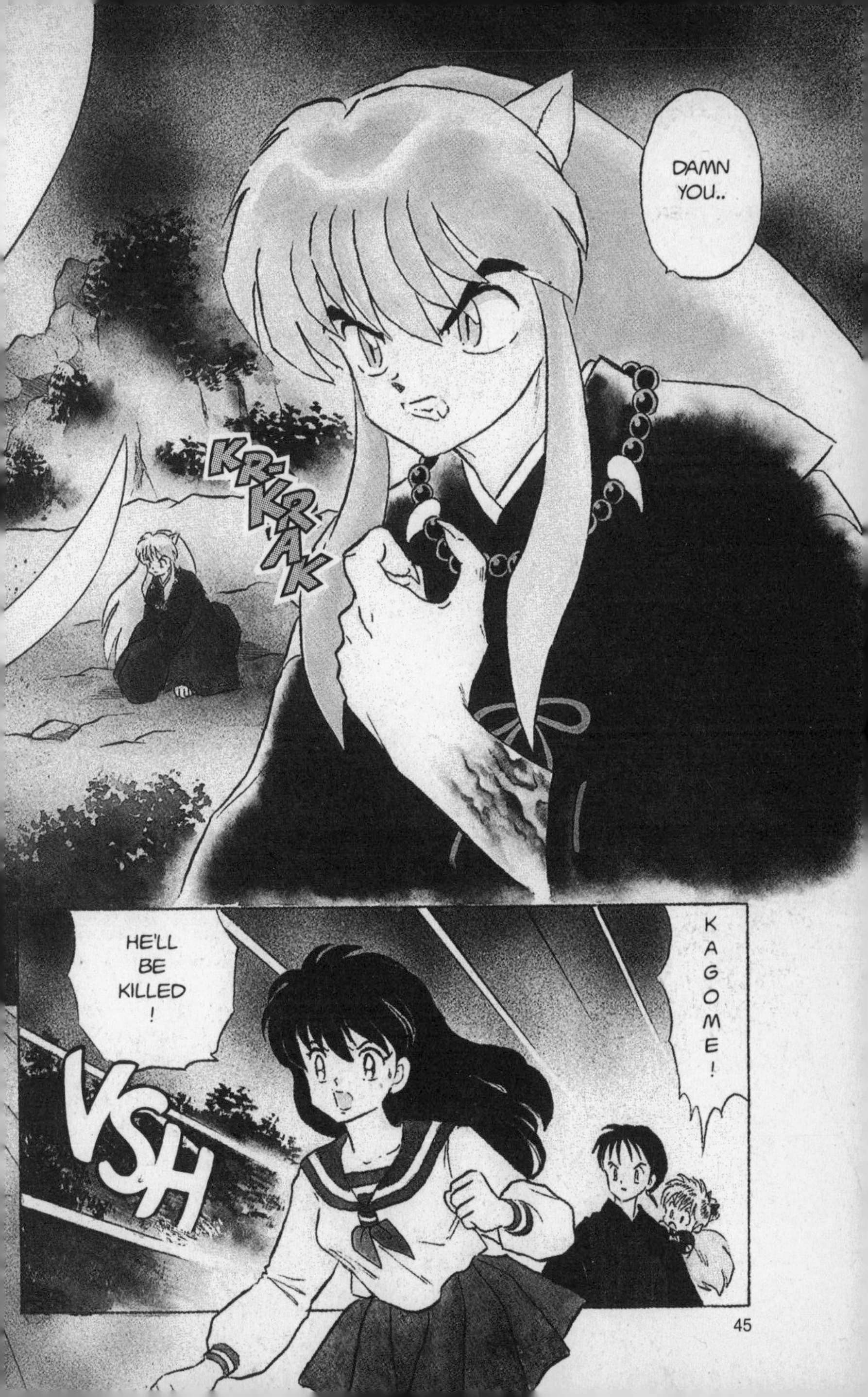
DAMN YOU..
KR-KR-KRAK
HE'LL BE KILLED !
VSH
KAGOME!

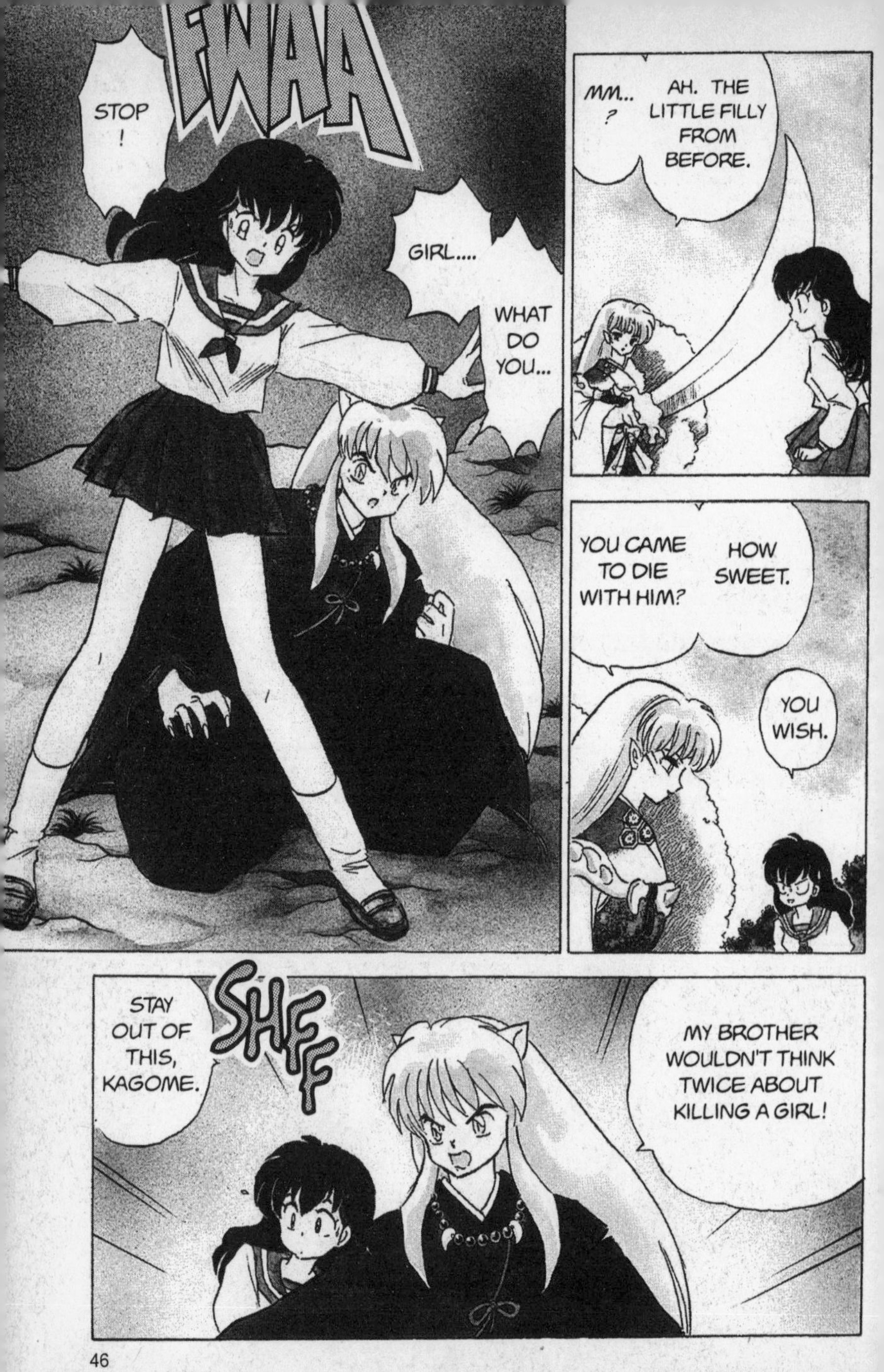
FWAA
STOP !
GIRL....
WHAT DO YOU...
MM... ?
AH. THE LITTLE FILLY FROM BEFORE.
YOU CAME TO DIE WITH HIM?
HOW SWEET.
YOU WISH.
STAY OUT OF THIS, KAGOME.
SHFF
MY BROTHER WOULDN'T THINK TWICE ABOUT KILLING A GIRL!

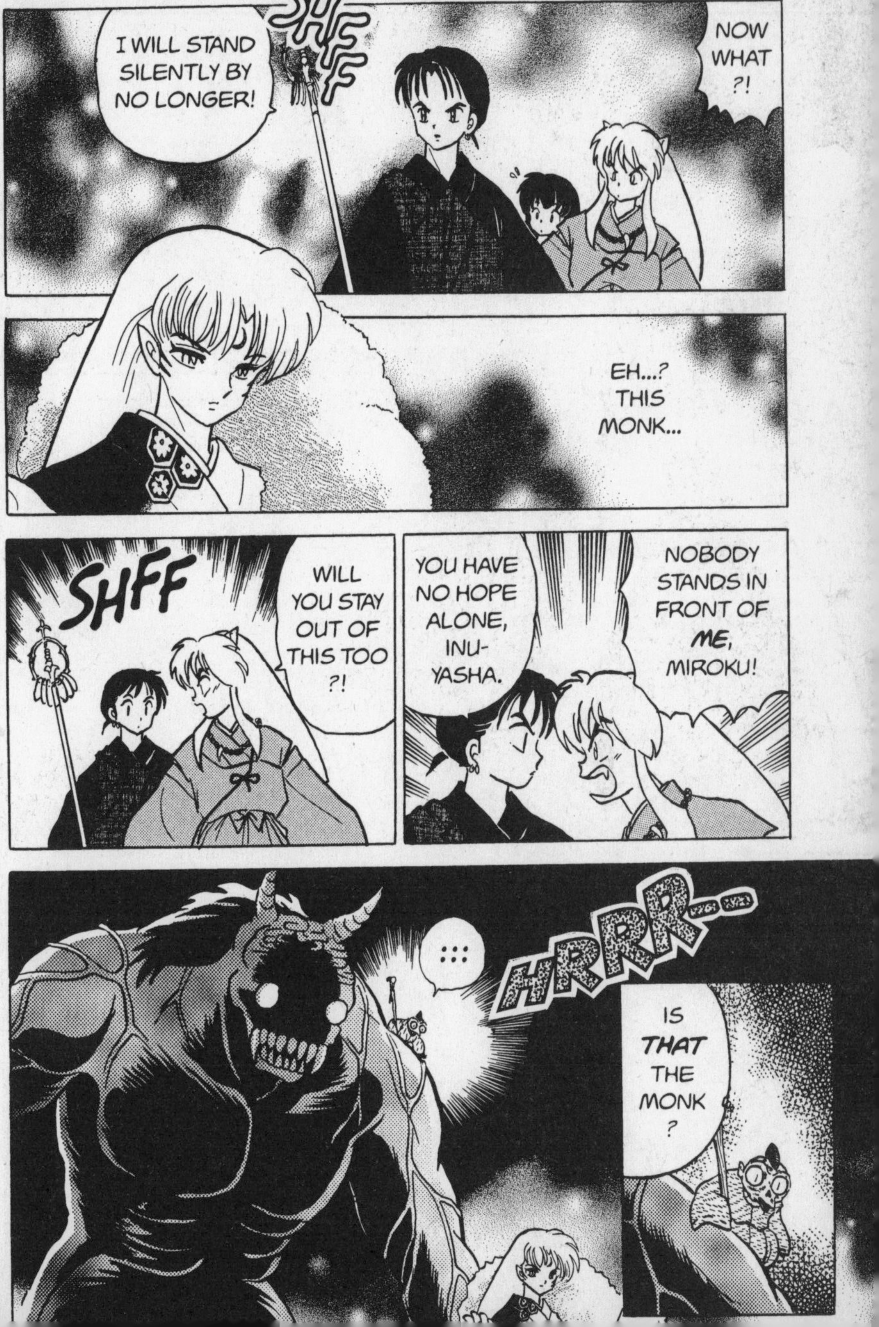
I WILL STAND SILENTLY BY NO LONGER!
SHFF
NOW WHAT ?!
EH...? THIS MONK...
SHFF
WILL YOU STAY OUT OF THIS TOO ?!
YOU HAVE NO HOPE ALONE, INU-YASHA.
NOBODY STANDS IN FRONT OF *ME*, MIROKU!
......
HRRR--
IS *THAT* THE MONK ?

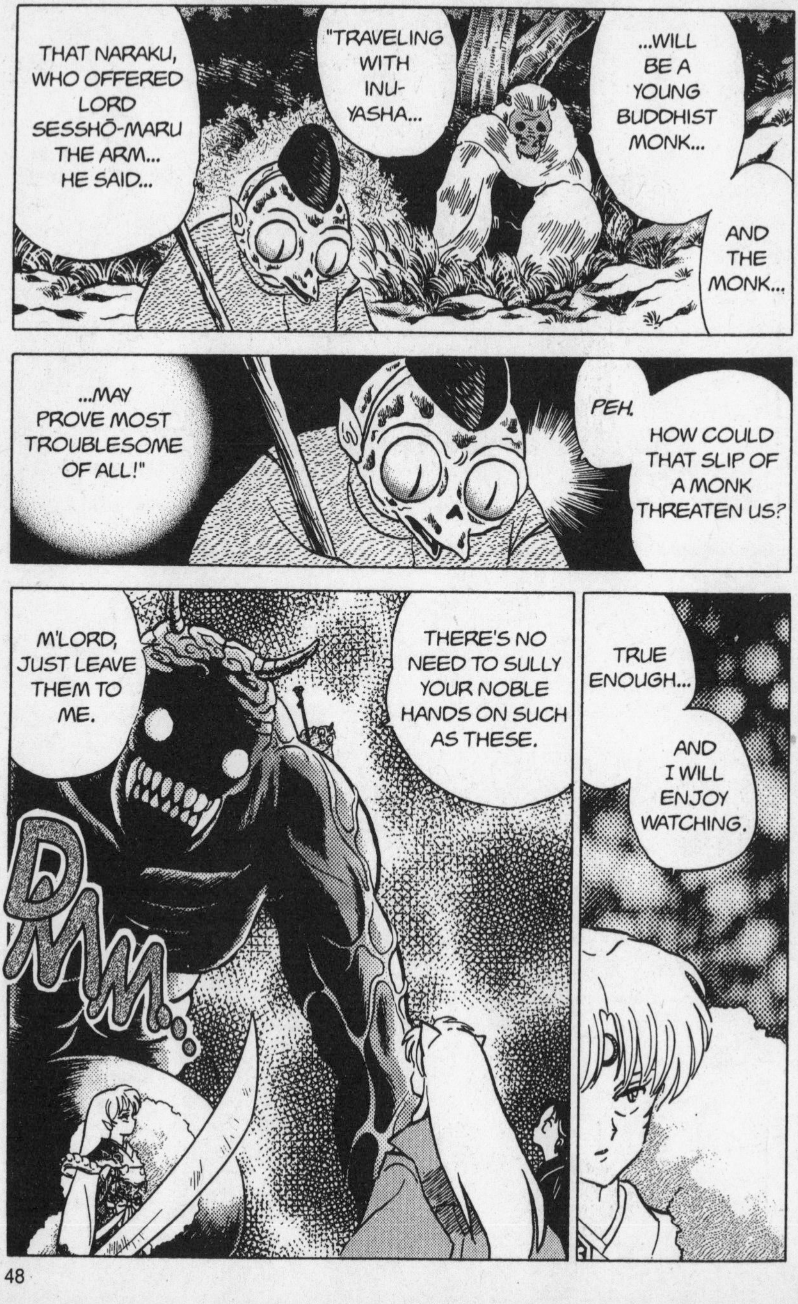
THAT NARAKU, WHO OFFERED LORD SESSHŌ-MARU THE ARM... HE SAID...
"TRAVELING WITH INU-YASHA...
...WILL BE A YOUNG BUDDHIST MONK...
AND THE MONK...
...MAY PROVE MOST TROUBLESOME OF ALL!"
PEH.
HOW COULD THAT SLIP OF A MONK THREATEN US?
M'LORD, JUST LEAVE THEM TO ME.
THERE'S NO NEED TO SULLY YOUR NOBLE HANDS ON SUCH AS THESE.
DMM...
TRUE ENOUGH...
AND I WILL ENJOY WATCHING.

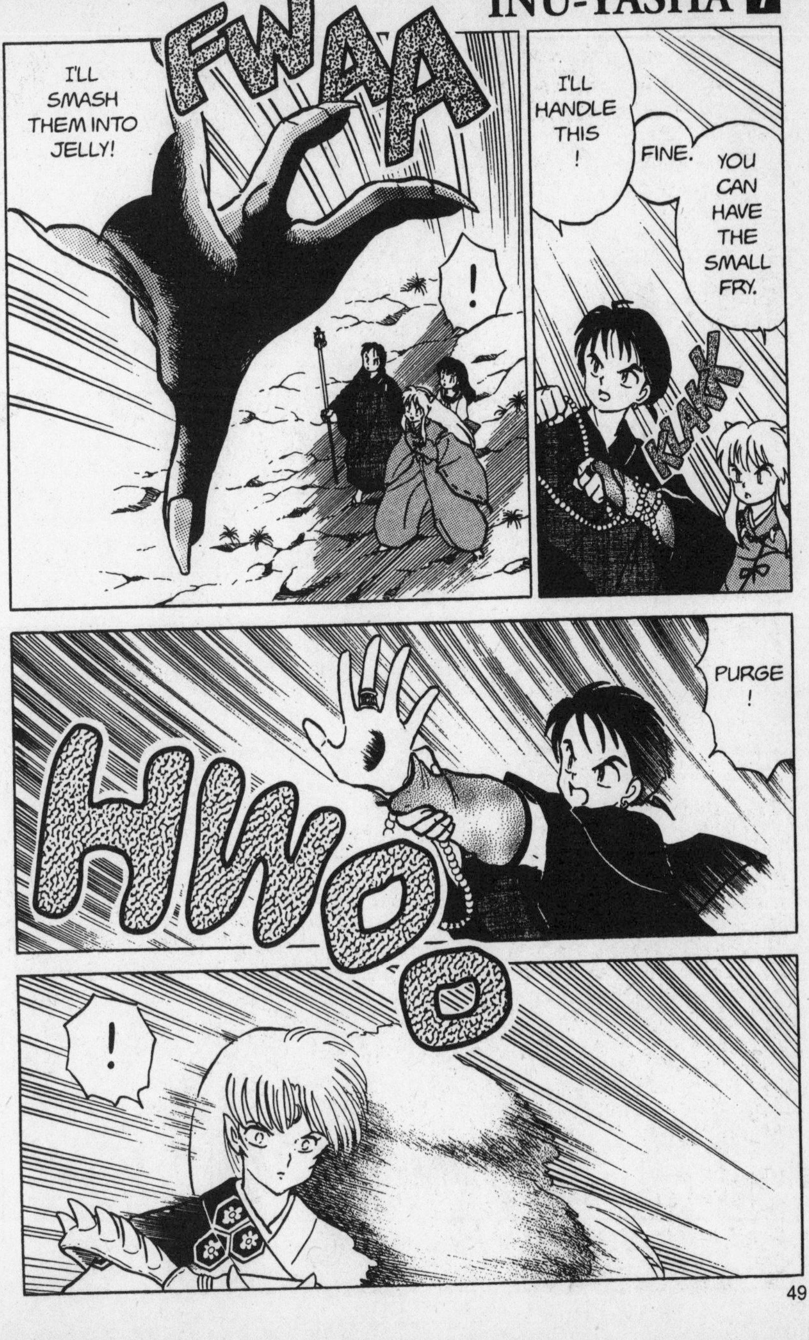
I'LL SMASH THEM INTO JELLY!
FWAA
!
I'LL HANDLE THIS!
FINE.
YOU CAN HAVE THE SMALL FRY.
HWOO
PURGE!
!

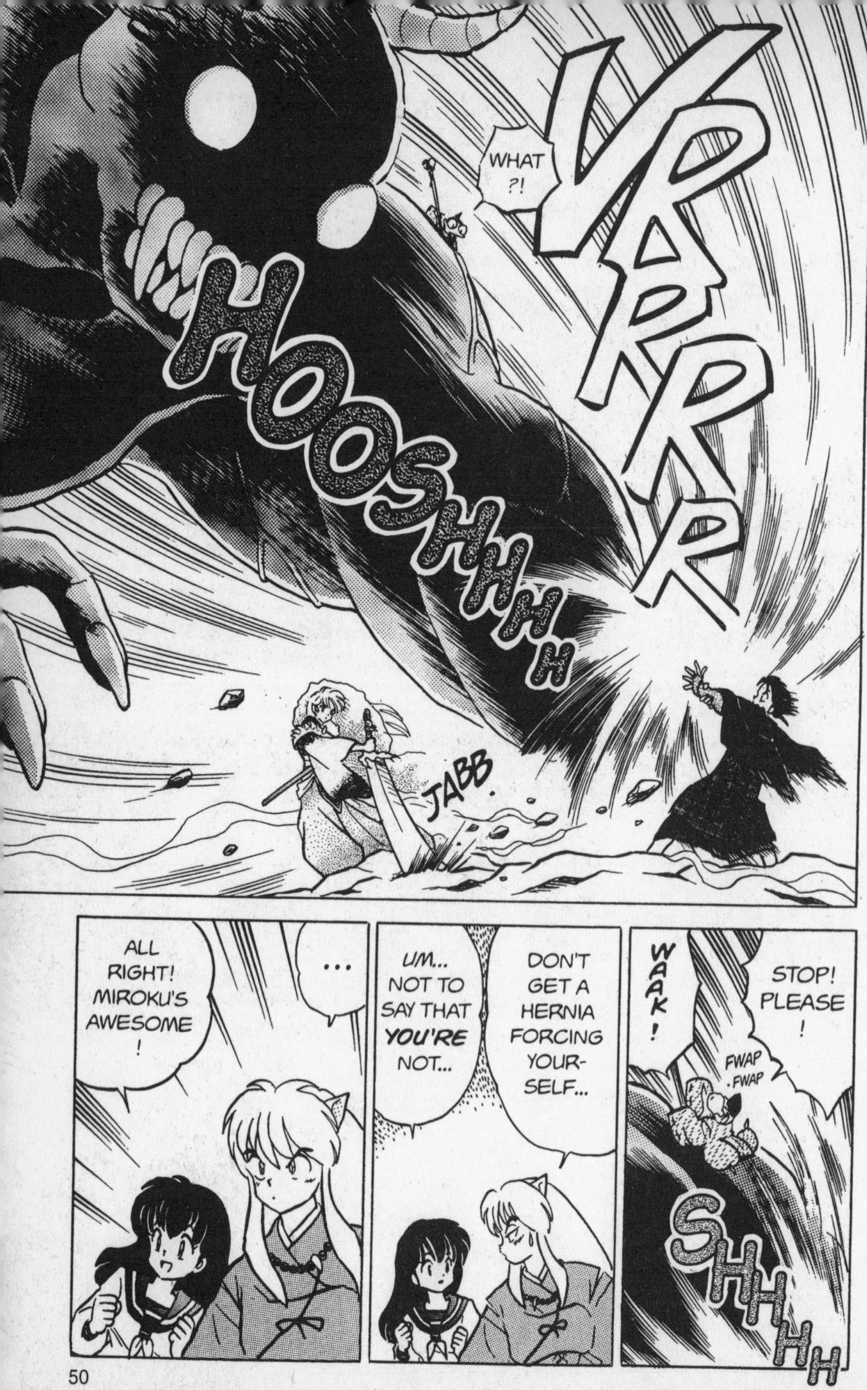
WHAT ?!
VRRRR
HOOSHHHHHH
JABB.
ALL RIGHT! MIROKU'S AWESOME!
...
UM... NOT TO SAY THAT YOU'RE NOT...
DON'T GET A HERNIA FORCING YOURSELF...
WAAK!
STOP! PLEASE!
FWAP FWAP
SHHHHH

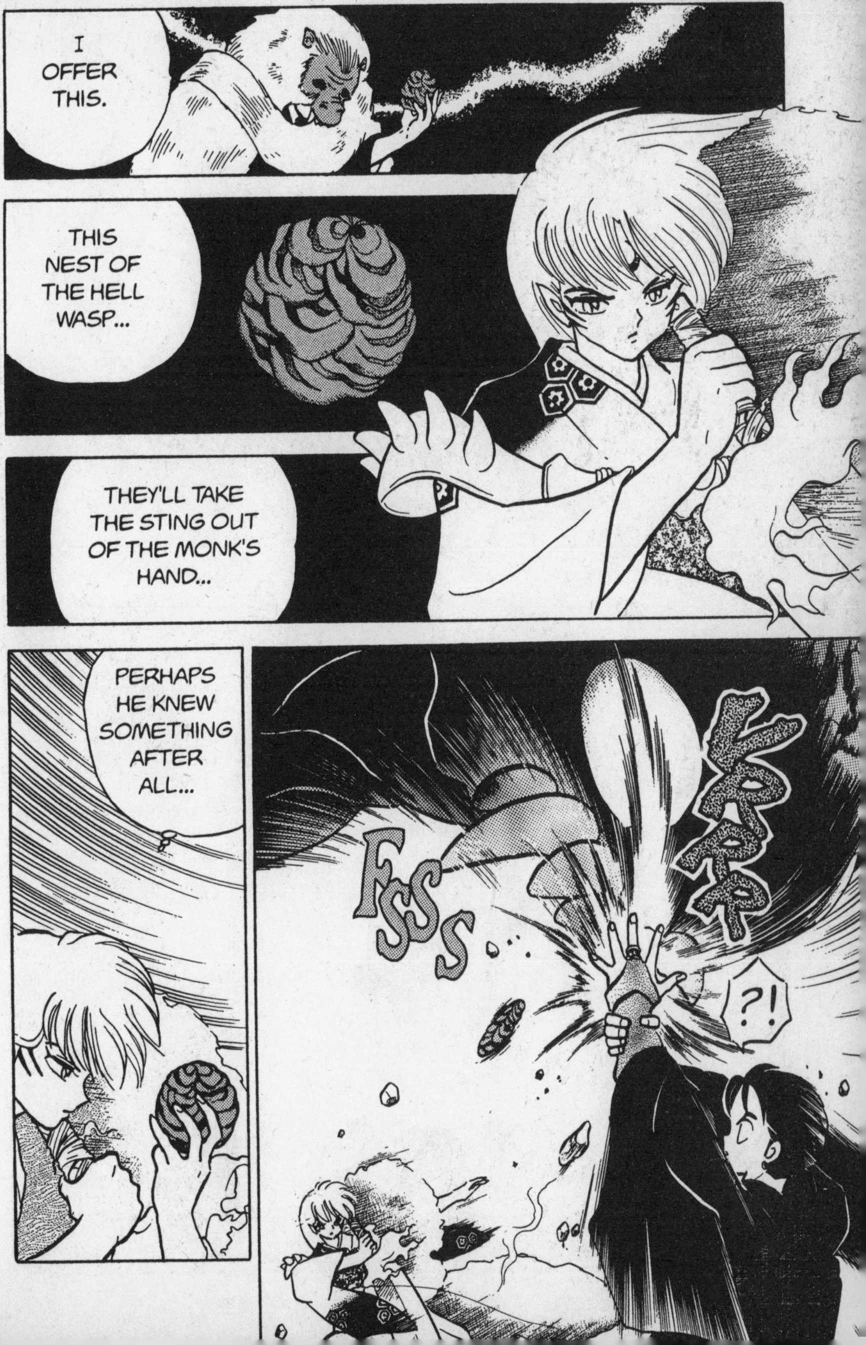
I OFFER THIS.
THIS NEST OF THE HELL WASP...
THEY'LL TAKE THE STING OUT OF THE MONK'S HAND...
PERHAPS HE KNEW SOMETHING AFTER ALL...
FSSS
KRRR
?!

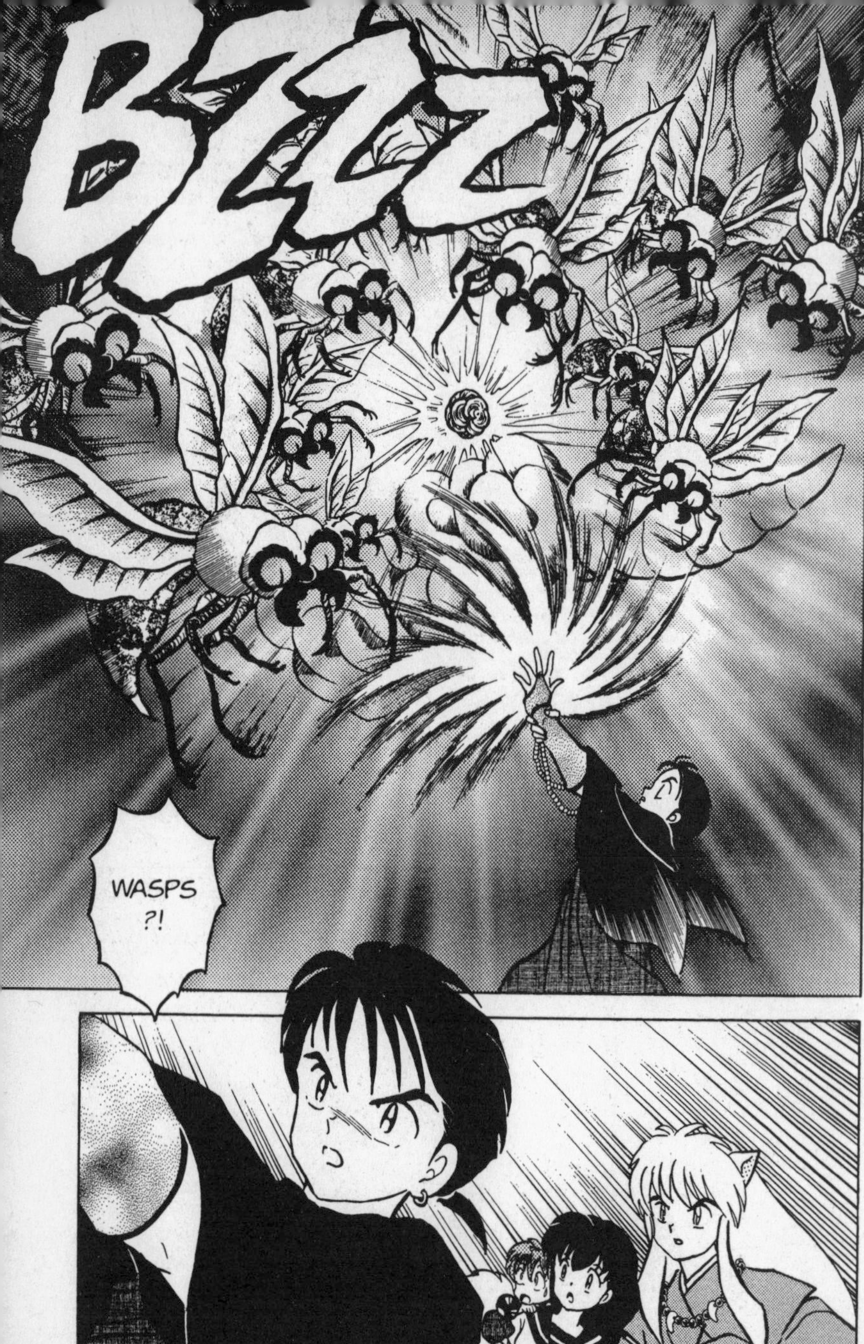
BZZZ
WASPS ?!

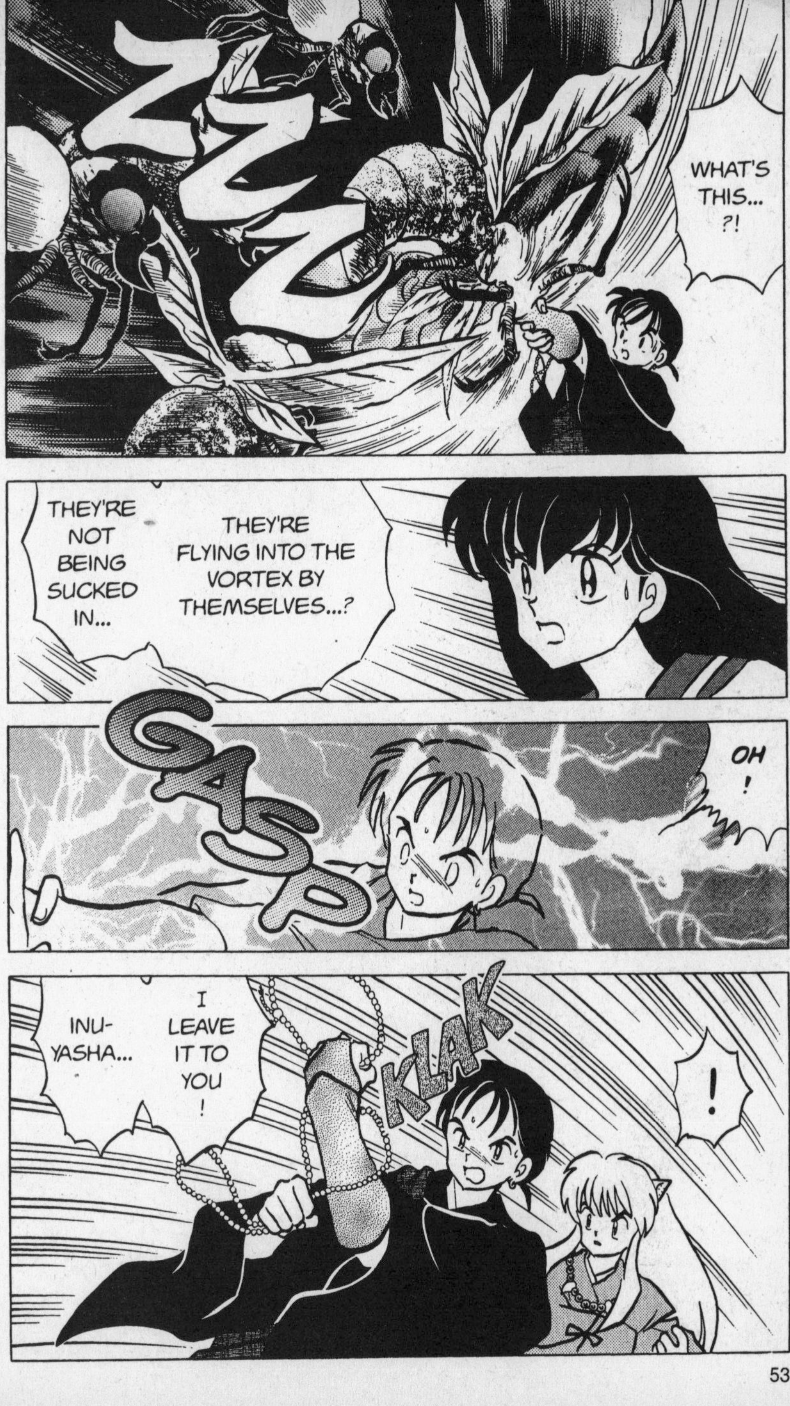
WHAT'S THIS... ?!
THEY'RE NOT BEING SUCKED IN...
THEY'RE FLYING INTO THE VORTEX BY THEMSELVES...?
GASP
OH !
INU-YASHA...
I LEAVE IT TO YOU !
KLAK
!

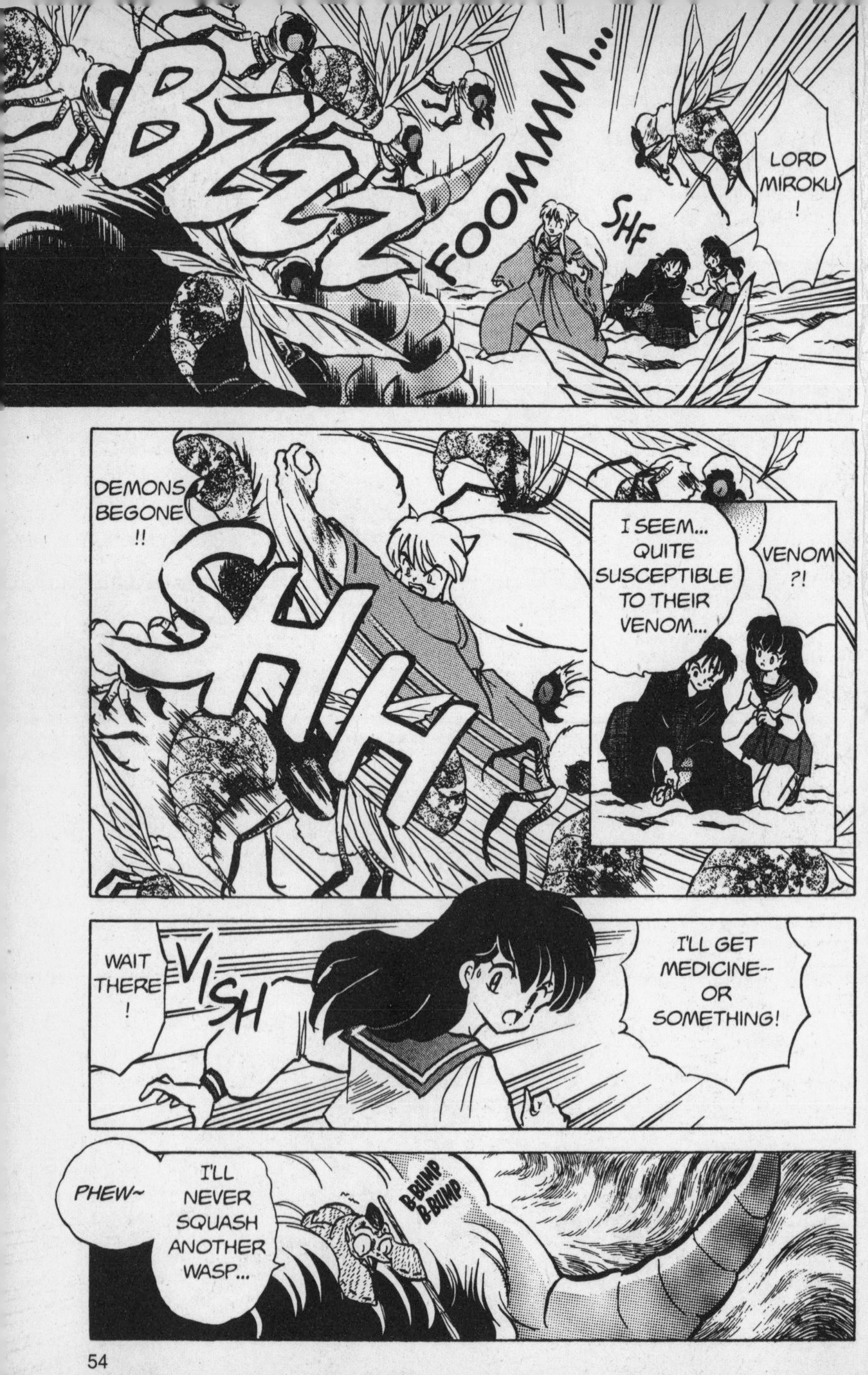
BZZZ
FOOMMM...
SHF
LORD MIROKU!
DEMONS BEGONE!!
SHH
I SEEM... QUITE SUSCEPTIBLE TO THEIR VENOM...
VENOM?!
WAIT THERE!
VISH
I'LL GET MEDICINE-- OR SOMETHING!
PHEW~
I'LL NEVER SQUASH ANOTHER WASP...
B-BUMP B-BUMP

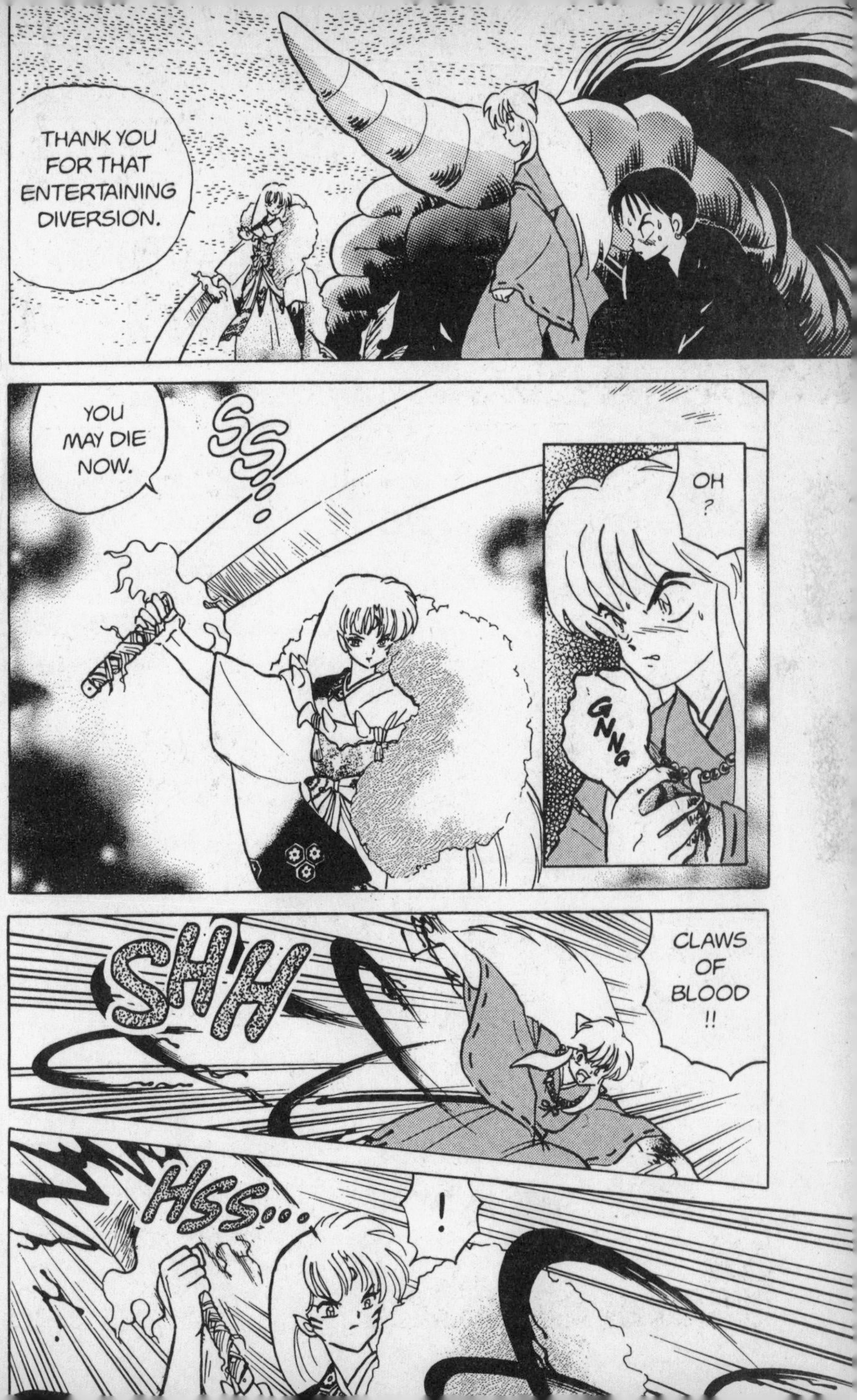
THANK YOU FOR THAT ENTERTAINING DIVERSION.
YOU MAY DIE NOW.
SS...
OH ?
GNNG
SHH
CLAWS OF BLOOD !!
HSS...
!

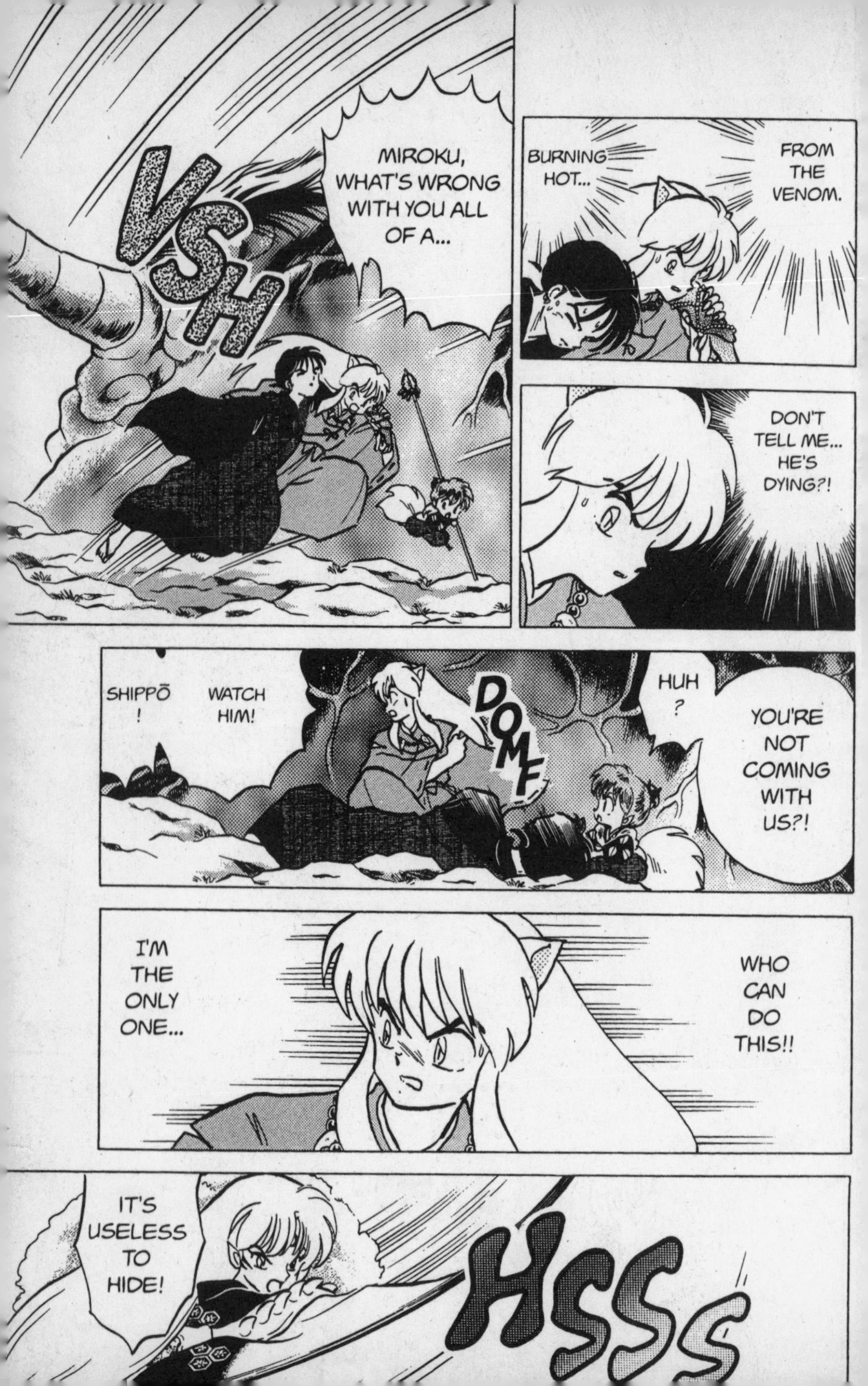
VSH
MIROKU, WHAT'S WRONG WITH YOU ALL OF A...
BURNING HOT...
FROM THE VENOM.
DON'T TELL ME... HE'S DYING?!
SHIPPŌ!
WATCH HIM!
DOMF
HUH?
YOU'RE NOT COMING WITH US?!
I'M THE ONLY ONE...
WHO CAN DO THIS!!
IT'S USELESS TO HIDE!
HSSS

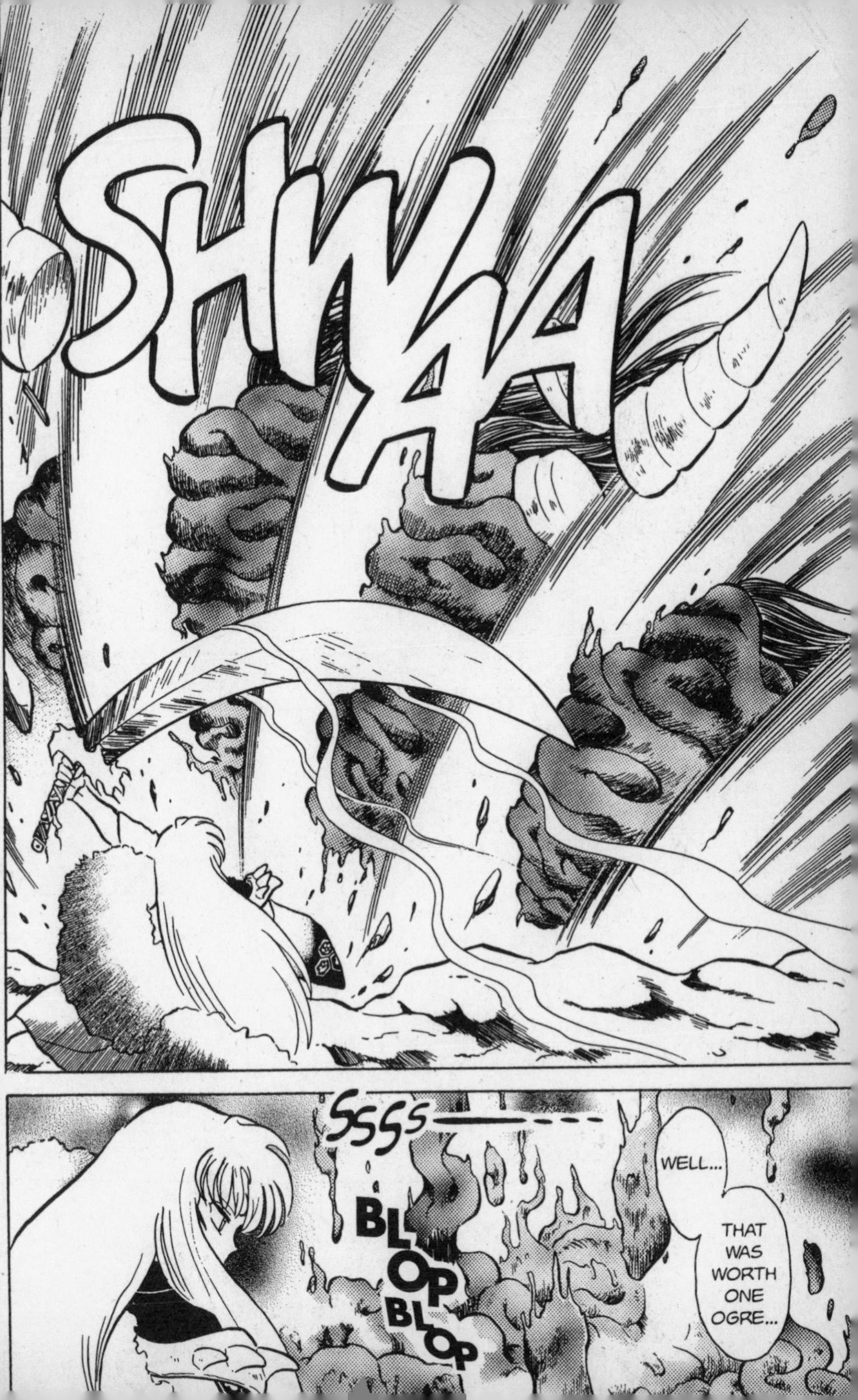
SHWA
SSSS
BLOP BLOP
BLOP BLOP
WELL...
THAT WAS WORTH ONE OGRE...

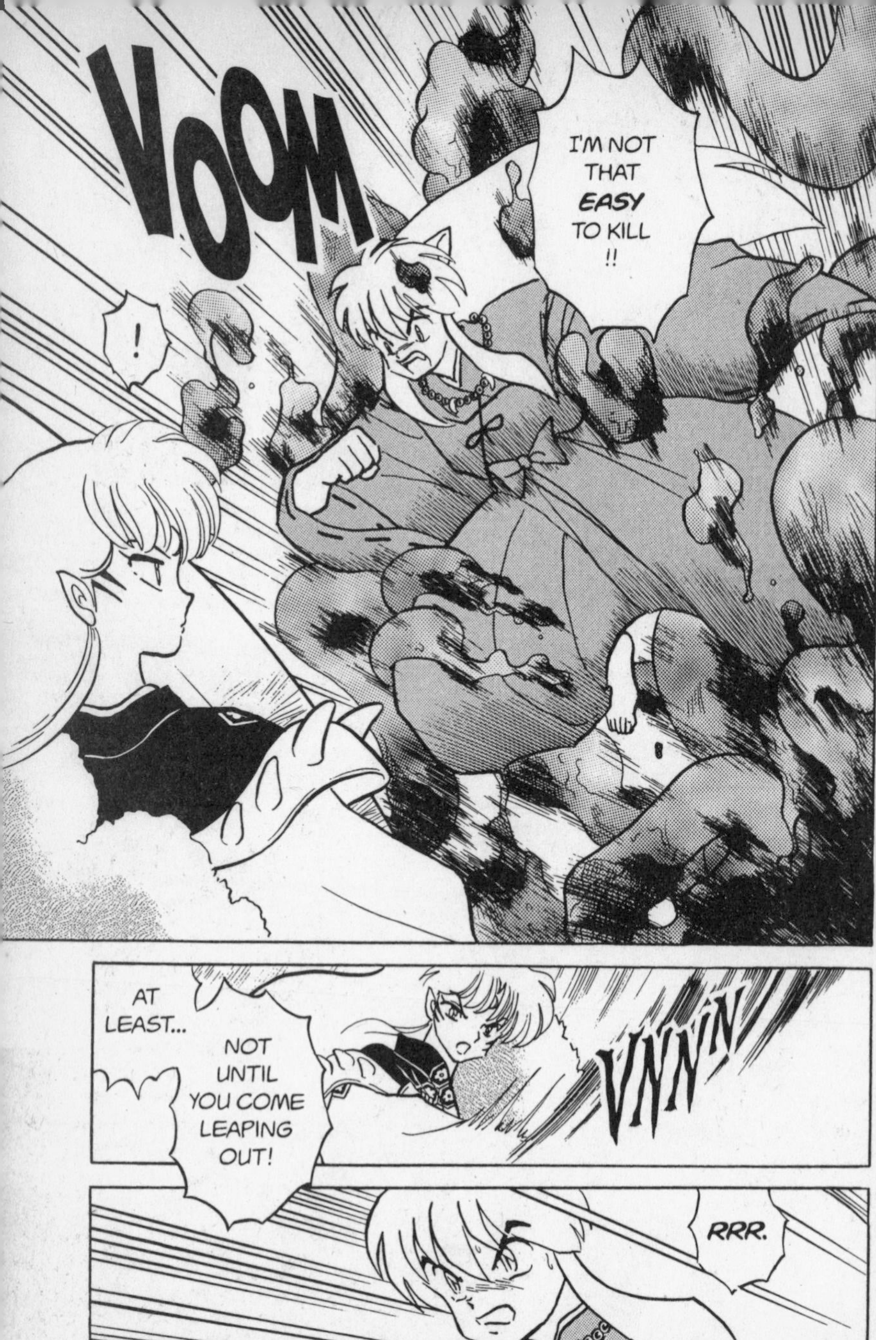
I'M NOT THAT *EASY* TO KILL !!
VOOM
!
VNNN
AT LEAST...
NOT UNTIL YOU COME LEAPING OUT!
RRR.

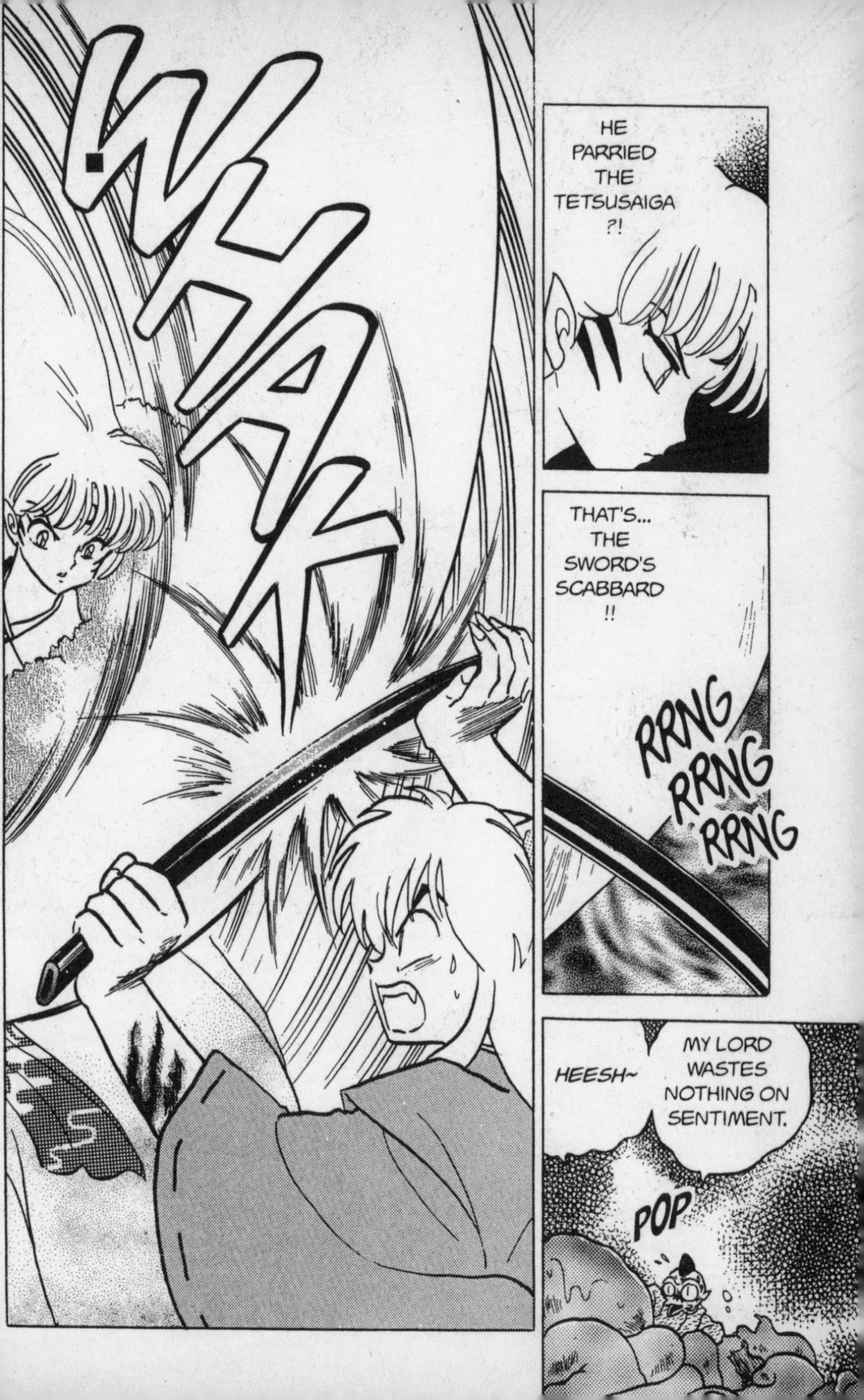
HE PARRIED THE TETSUSAIGA ?!
THAT'S... THE SWORD'S SCABBARD !!
RRNG RRNG RRNG
MY LORD WASTES NOTHING ON SENTIMENT.
HEESH~
POP
WHAK

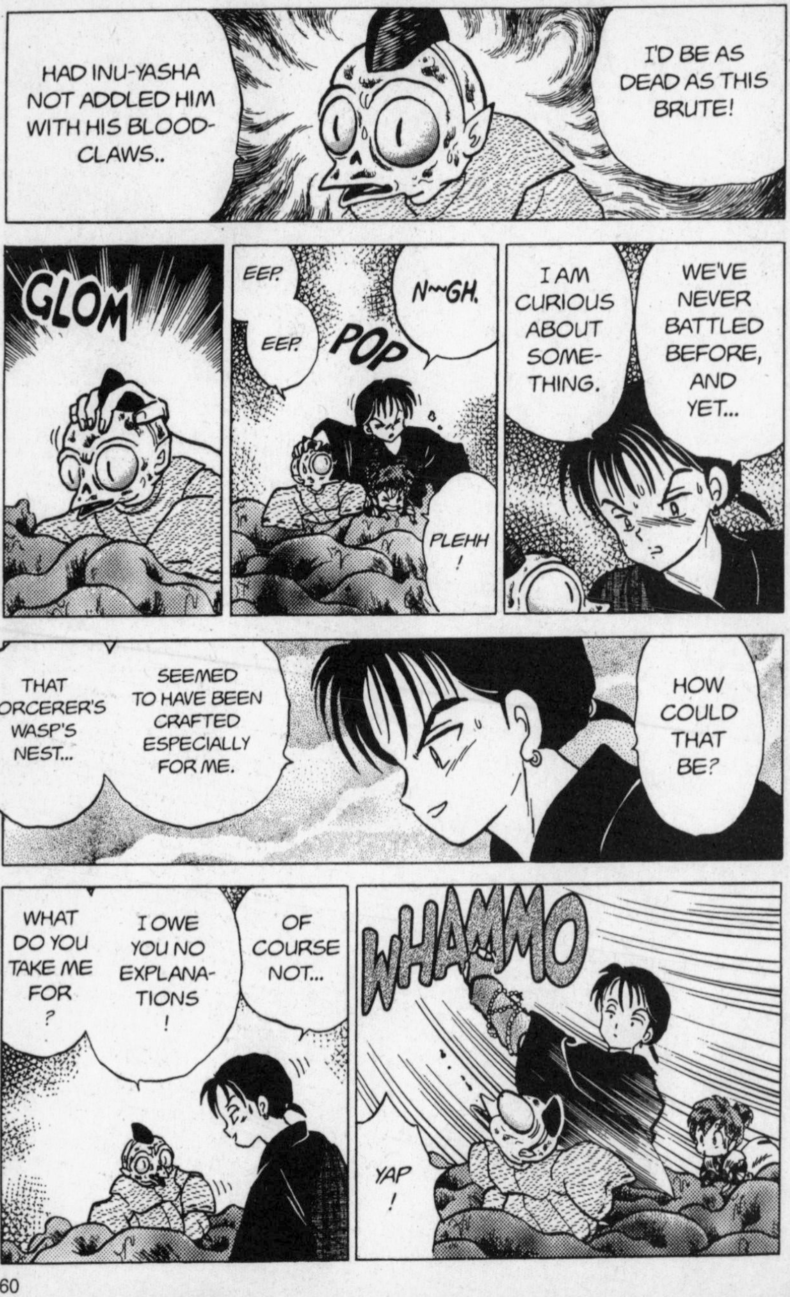
HAD INU-YASHA NOT ADDLED HIM WITH HIS BLOOD-CLAWS..
I'D BE AS DEAD AS THIS BRUTE!
GLOM
EEP.
EEP.
POP
N~~GH.
PLEHH!
I AM CURIOUS ABOUT SOME-THING.
WE'VE NEVER BATTLED BEFORE, AND YET...
THAT SORCERER'S WASP'S NEST...
SEEMED TO HAVE BEEN CRAFTED ESPECIALLY FOR ME.
HOW COULD THAT BE?
WHAT DO YOU TAKE ME FOR?
I OWE YOU NO EXPLANA-TIONS!
OF COURSE NOT...
WHAMMO
YAP!

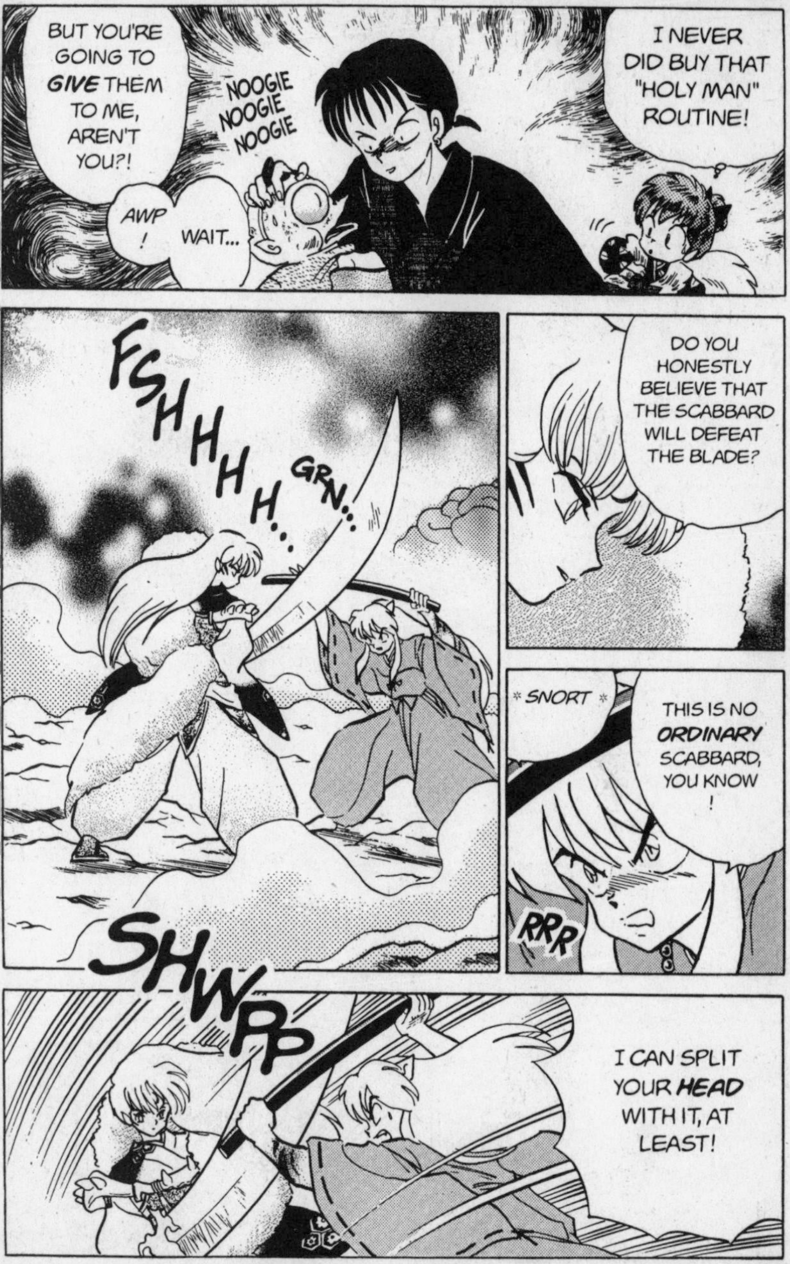
BUT YOU'RE GOING TO GIVE THEM TO ME, AREN'T YOU?!
NOOGIE NOOGIE NOOGIE
AWP!
WAIT...
I NEVER DID BUY THAT "HOLY MAN" ROUTINE!
FSHHHH...
GRN...
SHWPP
DO YOU HONESTLY BELIEVE THAT THE SCABBARD WILL DEFEAT THE BLADE?
* SNORT *
THIS IS NO ORDINARY SCABBARD, YOU KNOW!
RRR
I CAN SPLIT YOUR HEAD WITH IT, AT LEAST!

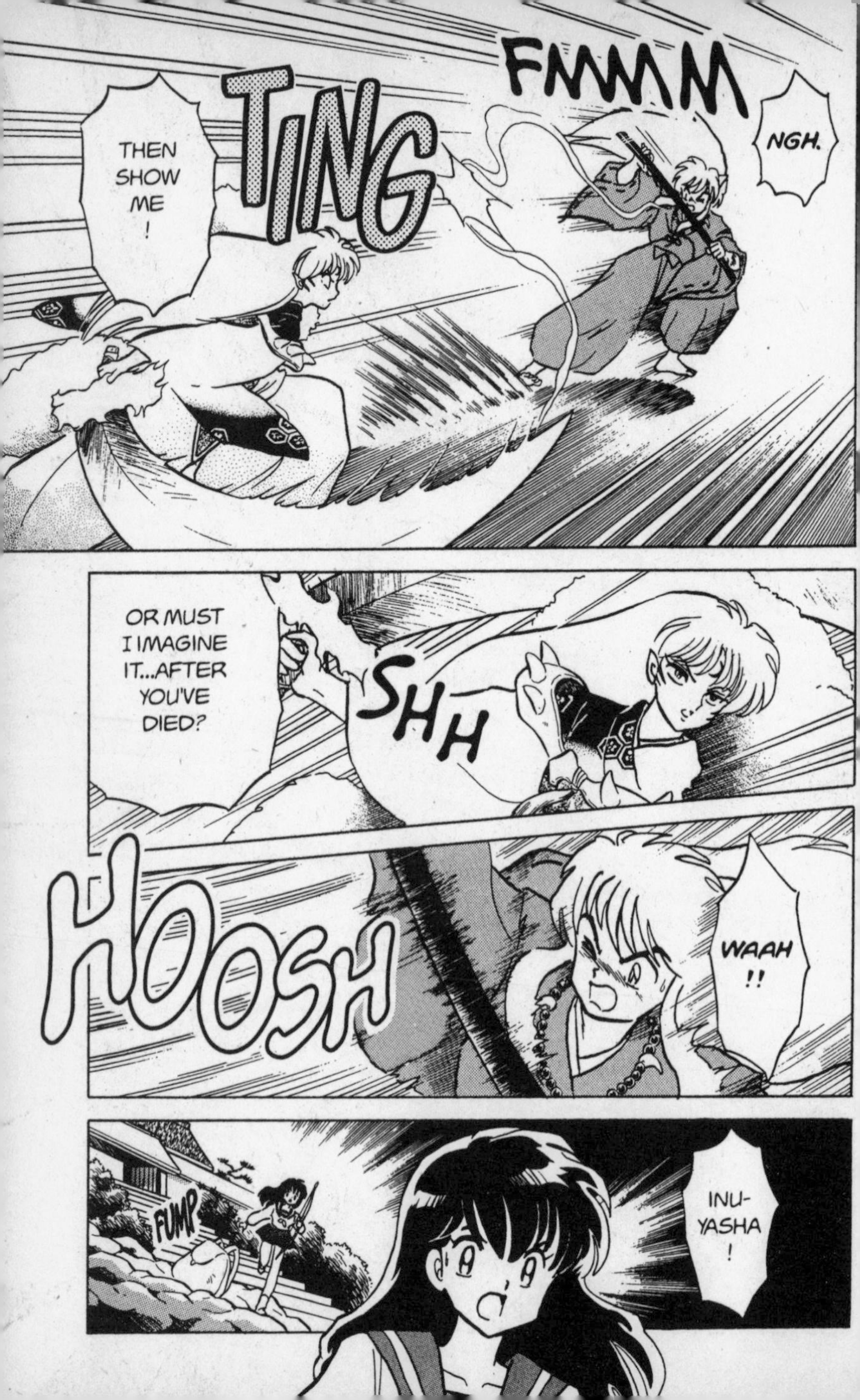
THEN SHOW ME !
TING
FMMM
NGH.
OR MUST I IMAGINE IT...AFTER YOU'VE DIED?
SHH
WHOOSH
WAAH !!
FUMP
INU-YASHA !

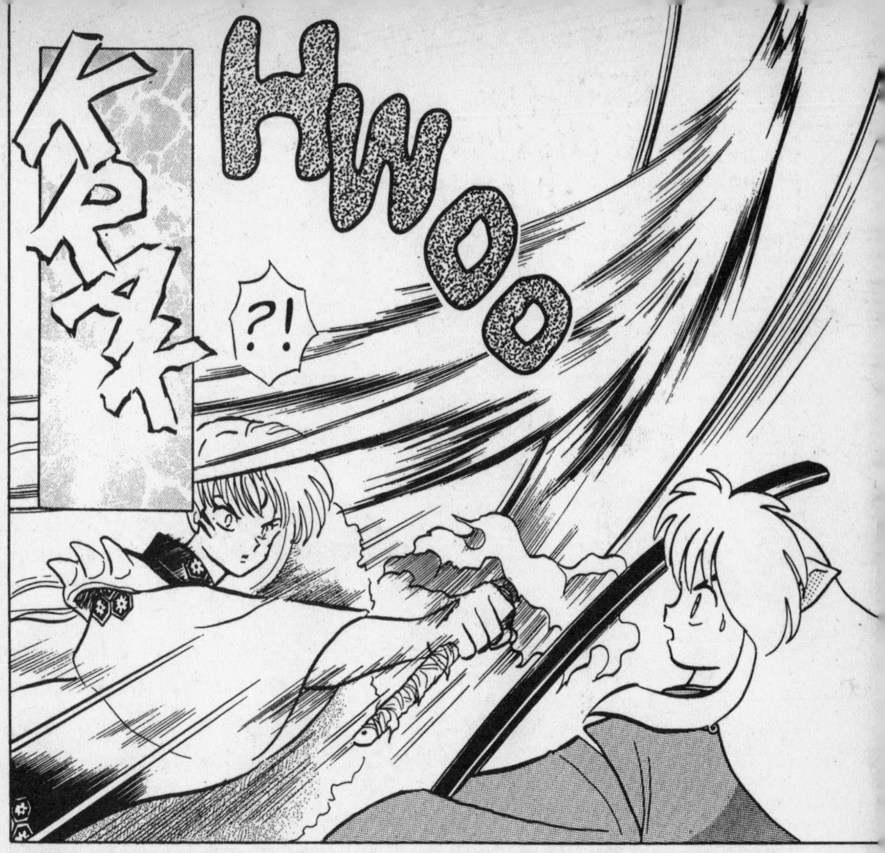
KRAK
HWOOO
?!
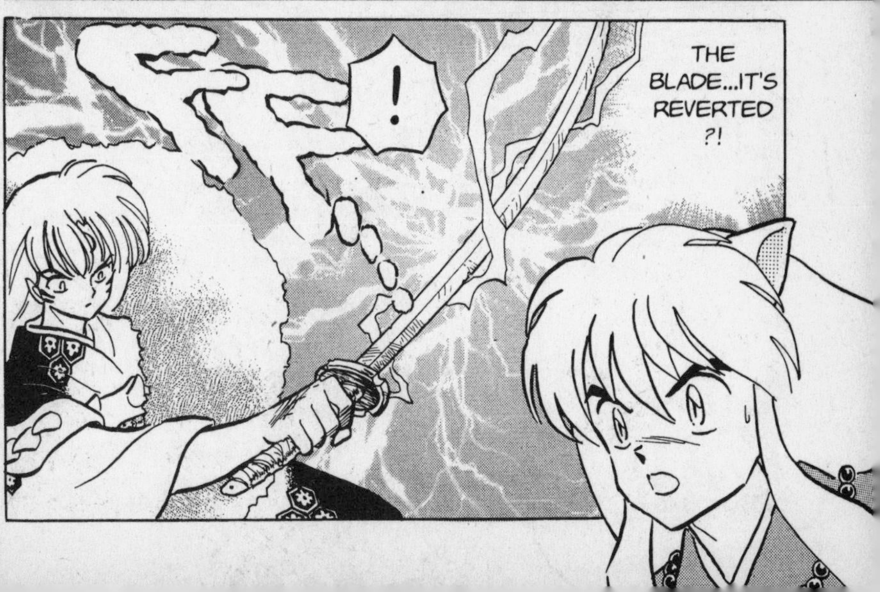
!
THE BLADE...IT'S REVERTED ?!

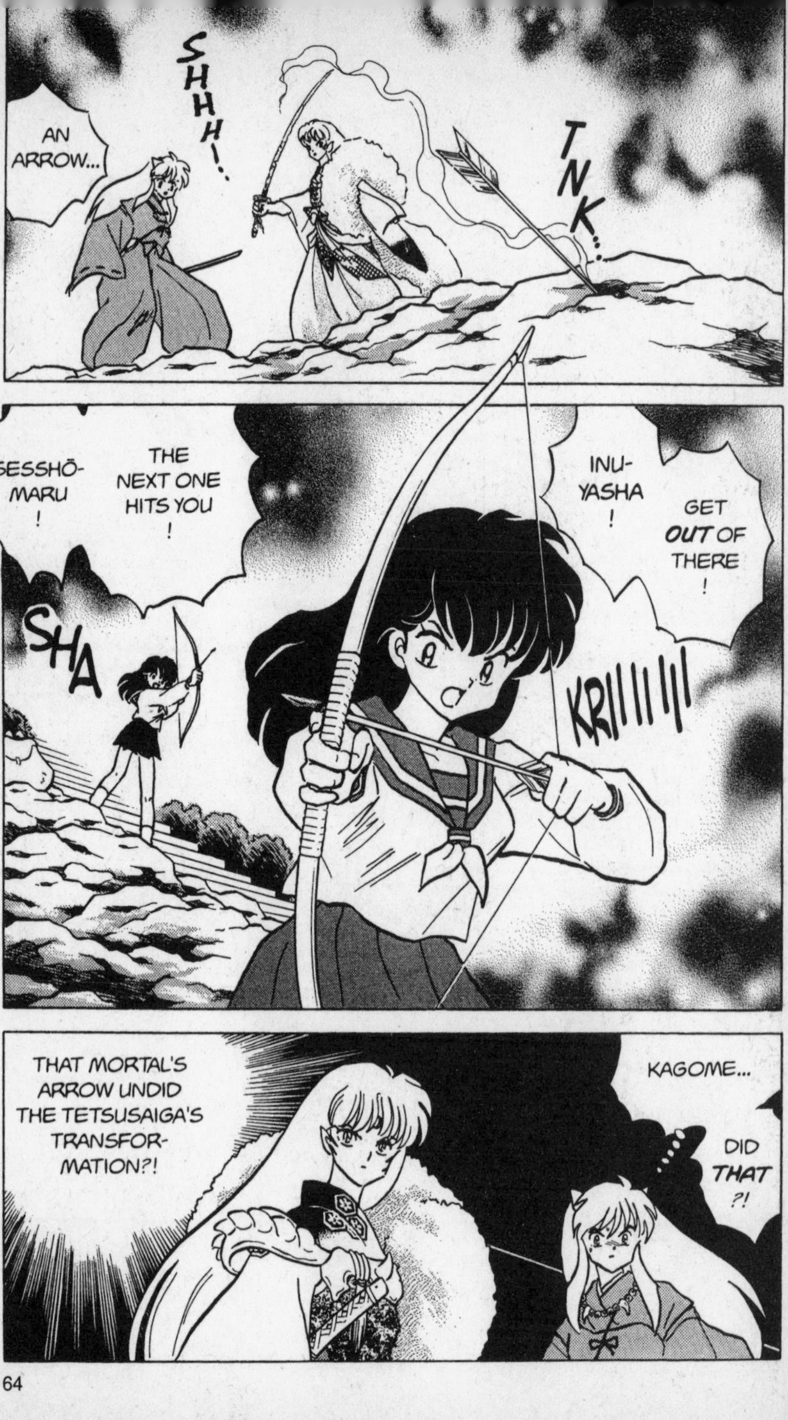
AN ARROW...
SHHH!...
TNK...
SESSHŌ-MARU!
THE NEXT ONE HITS YOU!
INU-YASHA!
GET OUT OF THERE!
SHA
KRIIIIII
THAT MORTAL'S ARROW UNDID THE TETSUSAIGA'S TRANSFORMATION?!
KAGOME...
DID THAT?!

SCROLL FOUR

ARM ROBBERY

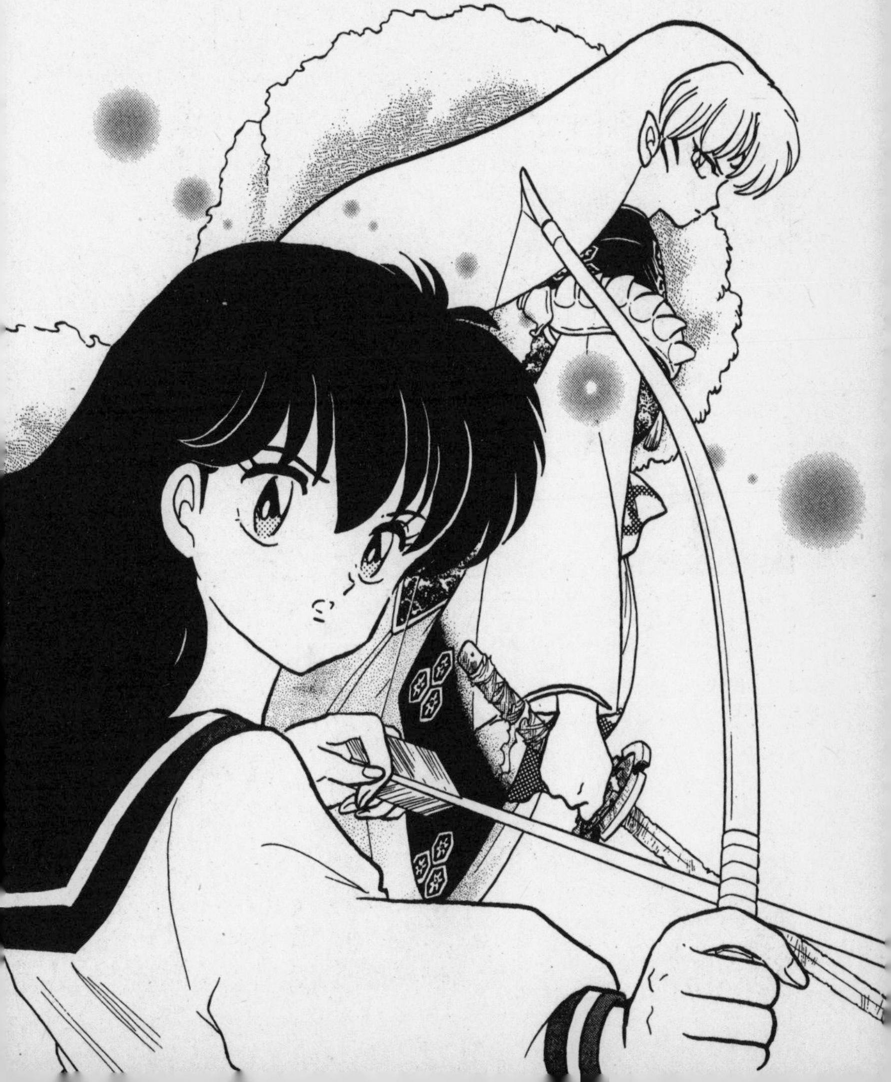

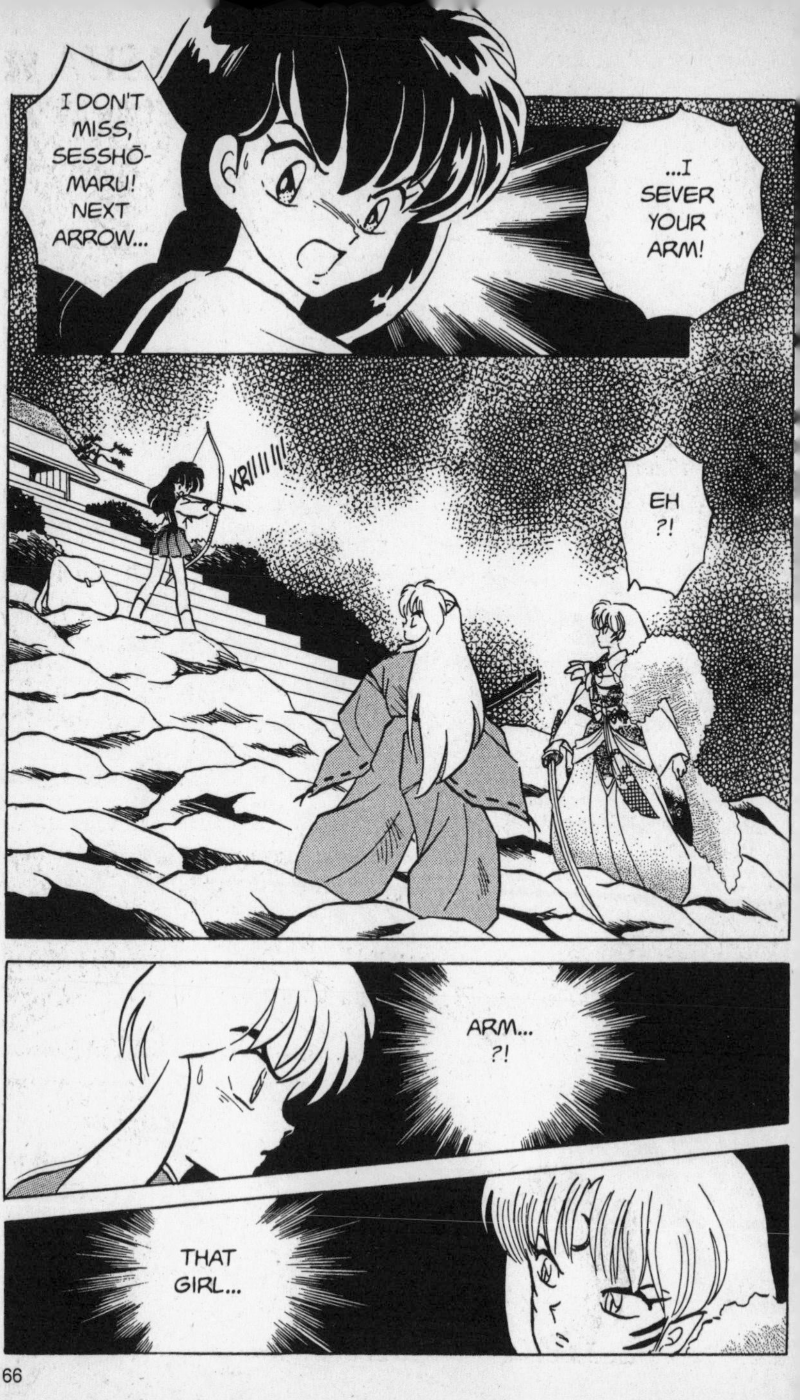
I DON'T MISS, SESSHŌ-MARU! NEXT ARROW...
...I SEVER YOUR ARM!
KRIIIIII
EH ?!
ARM... ?!
THAT GIRL...

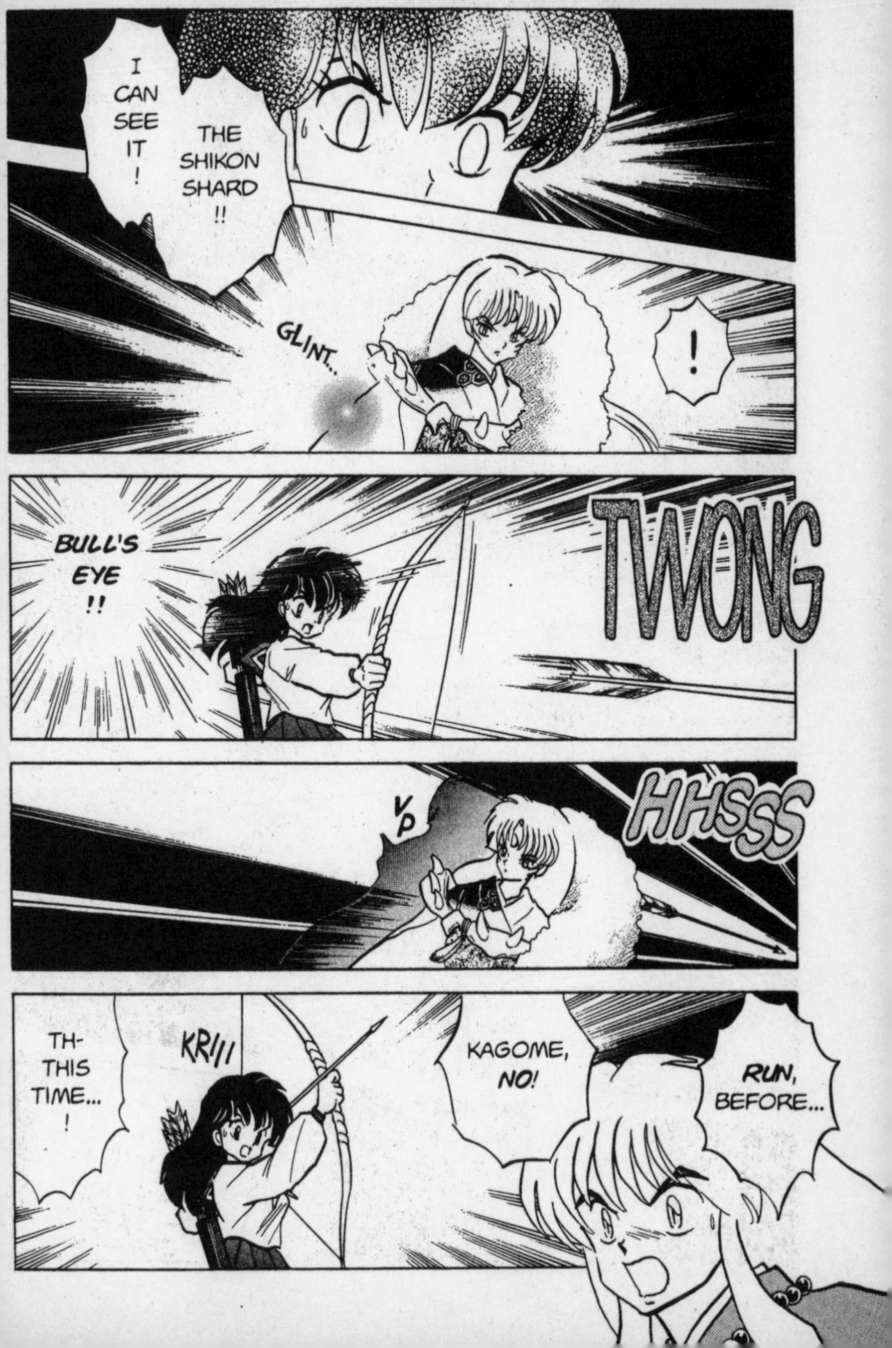
I CAN SEE IT !
THE SHIKON SHARD !!
GLINT...
!
BULL'S EYE !!
TWONG
VP
HHSSS
TH- THIS TIME... !
KRIII
KAGOME, NO!
RUN, BEFORE...

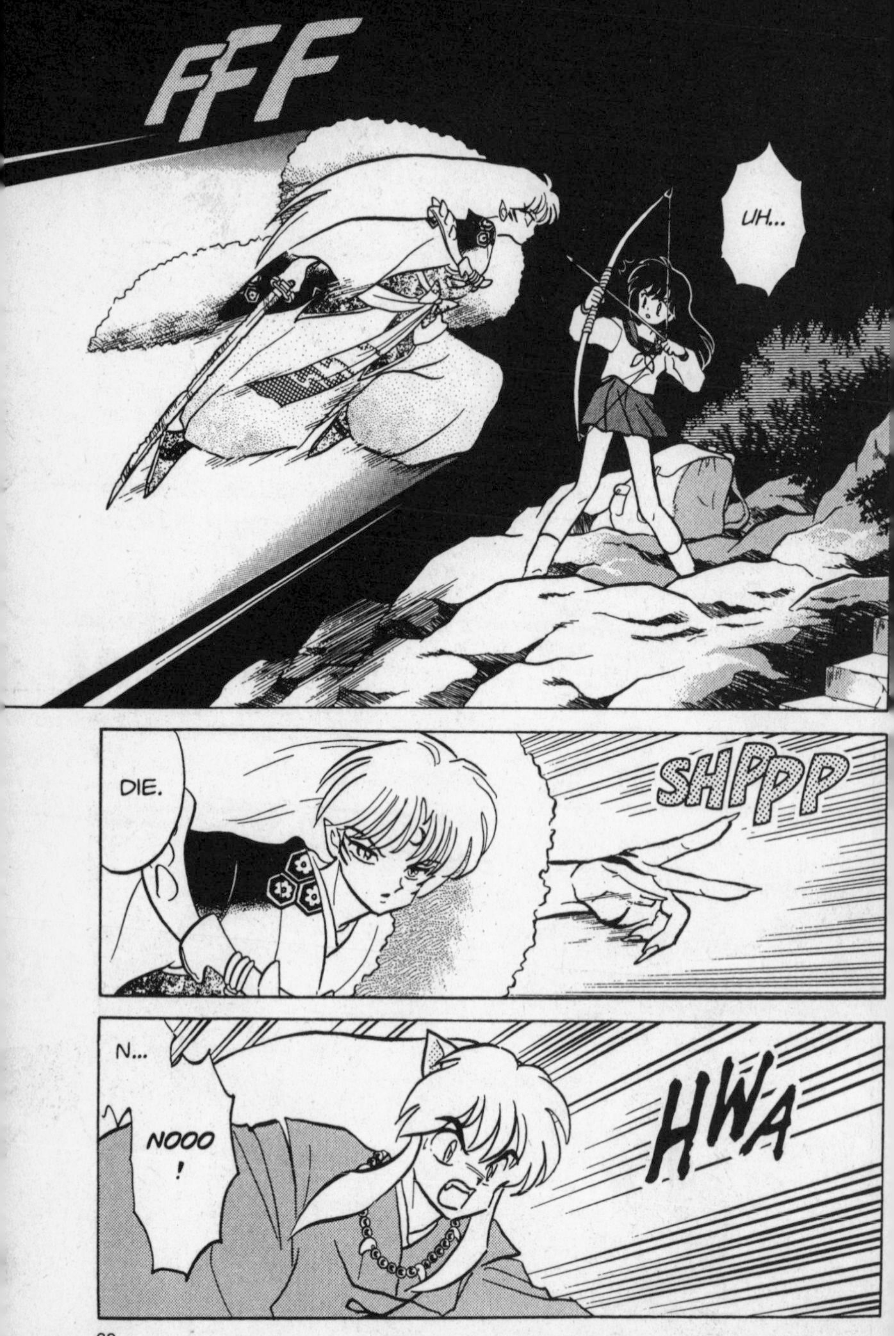
FFF
UH...
DIE.
SHPPP
N...
NOOO
!
HWA

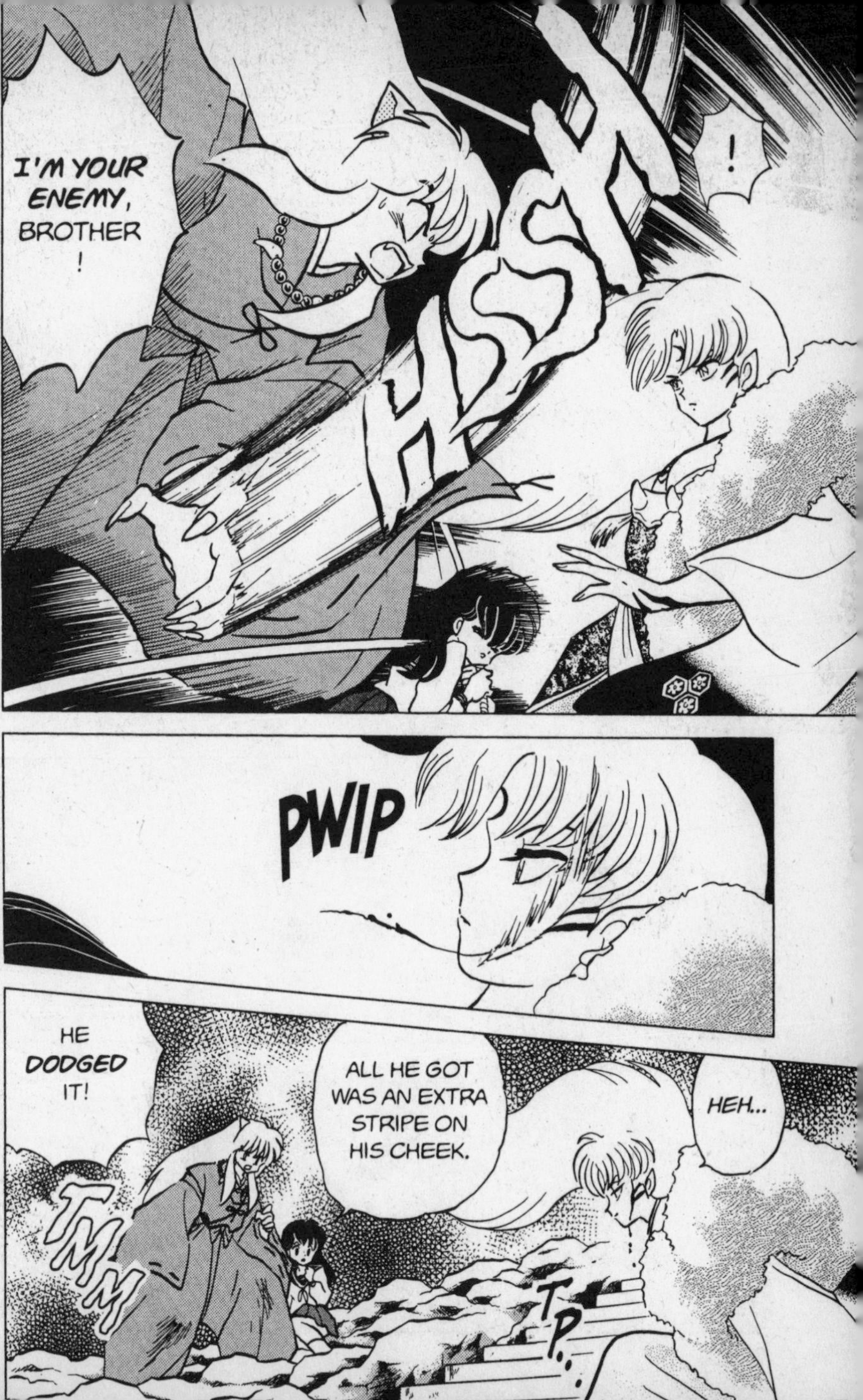
I'M YOUR ENEMY, BROTHER!
HISSH
!
PWIP
HE DODGED IT!
TMMM
ALL HE GOT WAS AN EXTRA STRIPE ON HIS CHEEK.
HEH...
TP...

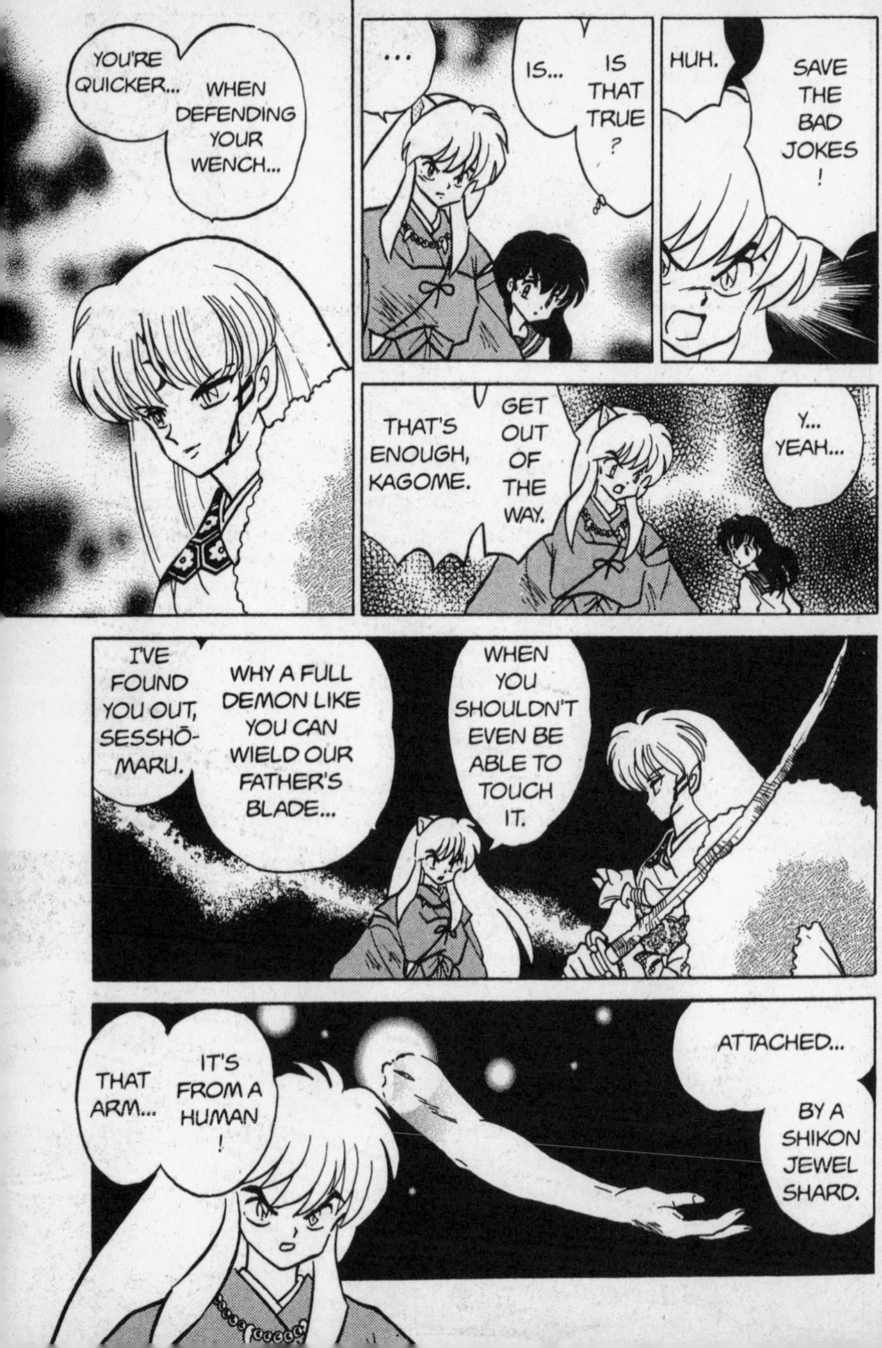

YOU'RE QUICKER... WHEN DEFENDING YOUR WENCH...
...
IS... IS THAT TRUE?
HUH.
SAVE THE BAD JOKES!
THAT'S ENOUGH, KAGOME.
GET OUT OF THE WAY.
Y... YEAH...
I'VE FOUND YOU OUT, SESSHŌ-MARU.
WHY A FULL DEMON LIKE YOU CAN WIELD OUR FATHER'S BLADE...
WHEN YOU SHOULDN'T EVEN BE ABLE TO TOUCH IT.
THAT ARM...
IT'S FROM A HUMAN!
ATTACHED...
BY A SHIKON JEWEL SHARD.

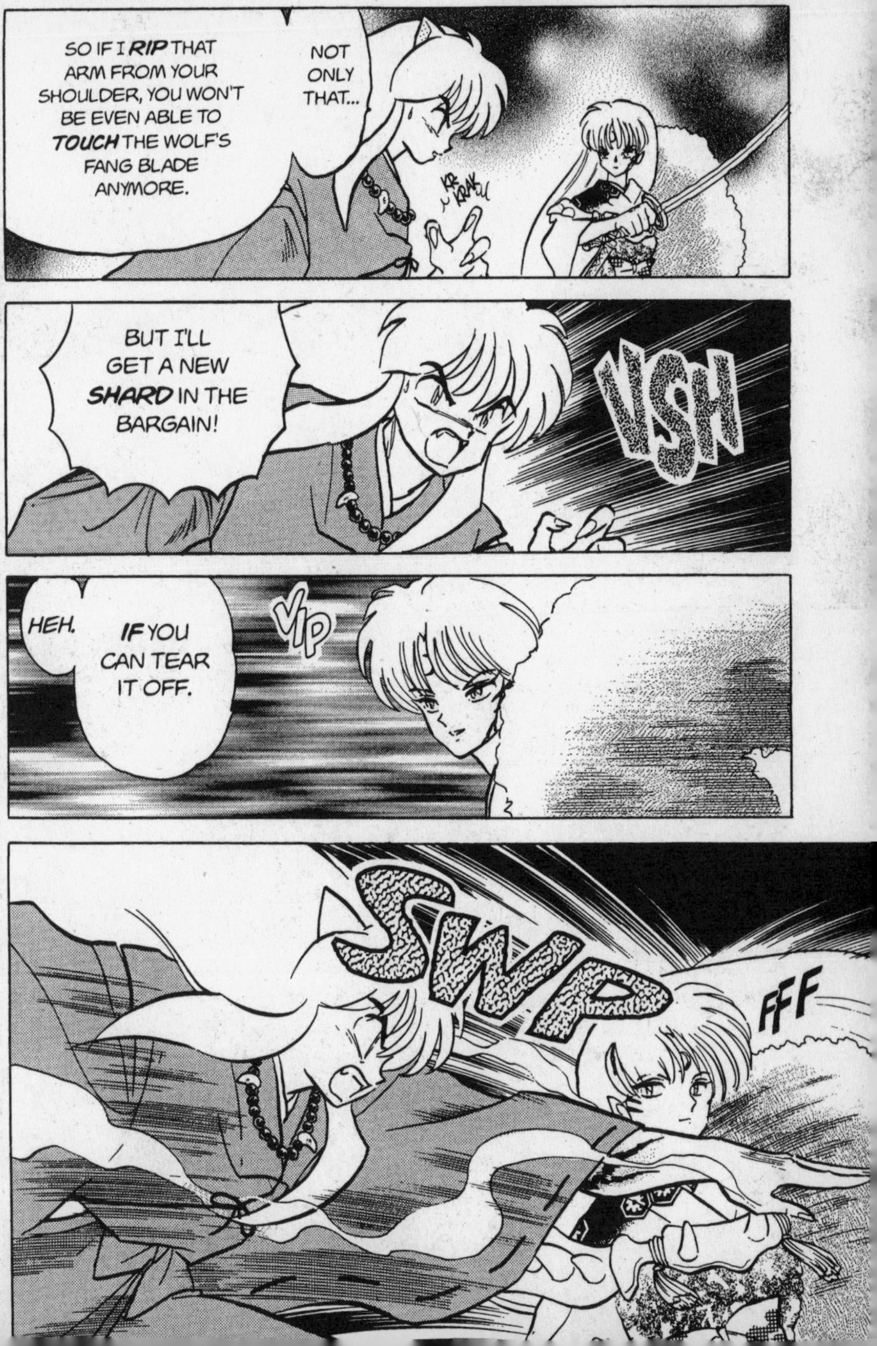
SO IF I RIP THAT ARM FROM YOUR SHOULDER, YOU WON'T BE EVEN ABLE TO TOUCH THE WOLF'S FANG BLADE ANYMORE.
NOT ONLY THAT...
KR KRAK
BUT I'LL GET A NEW SHARD IN THE BARGAIN!
VSH
HEH.
IF YOU CAN TEAR IT OFF.
VIP
SWP
FFF

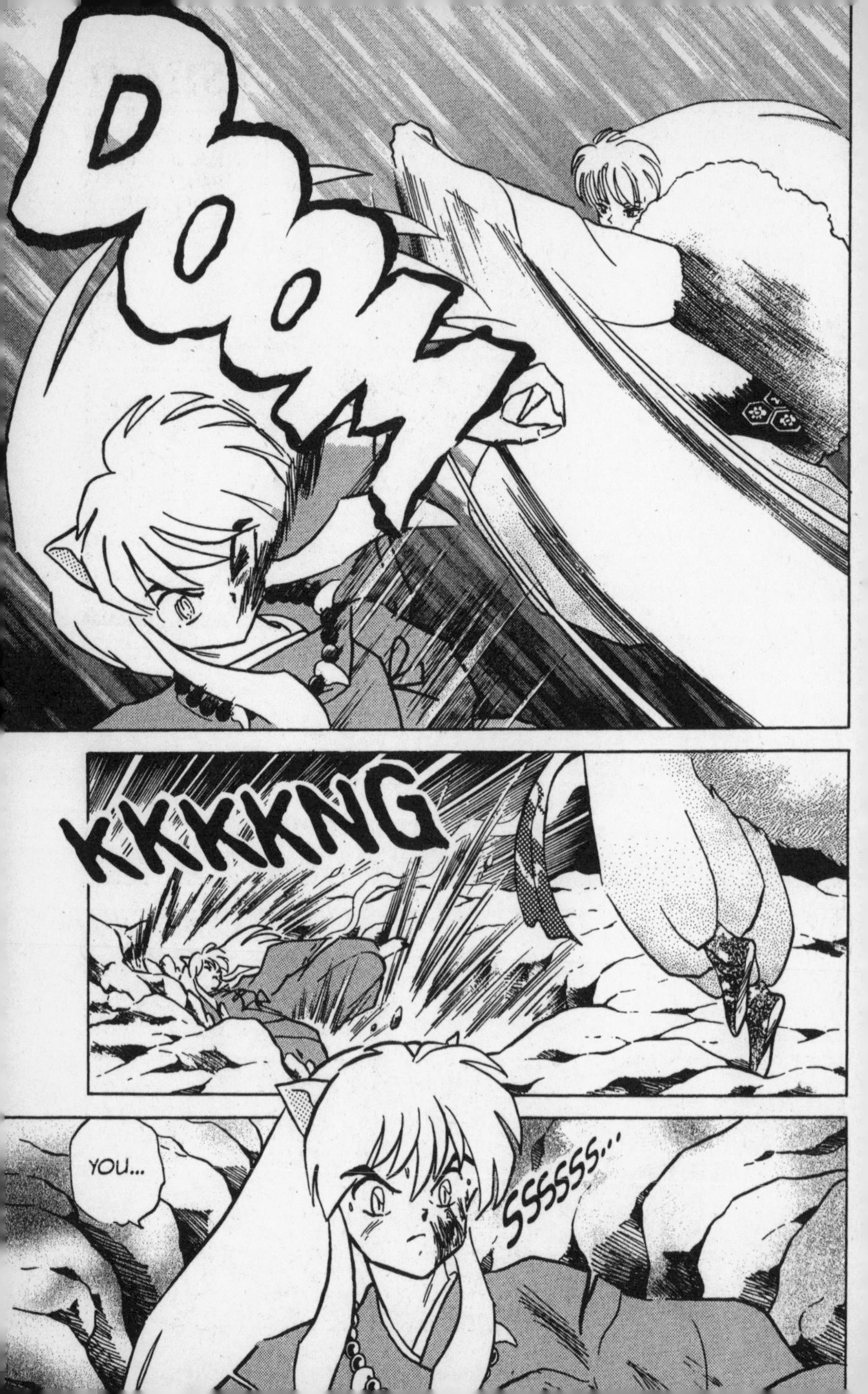
DOOOM
KKKKNG
YOU...
SSSSSS...

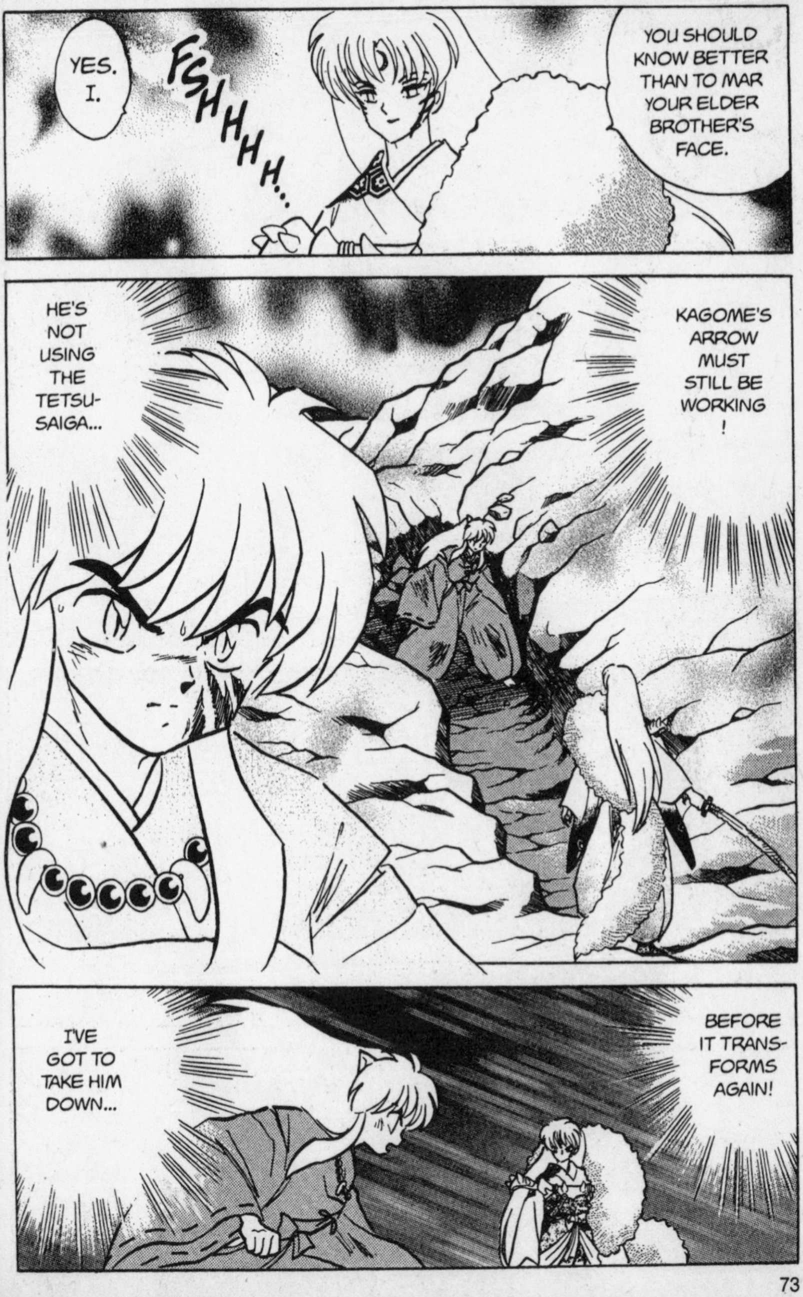
YES. I.
FSHHHH...
YOU SHOULD KNOW BETTER THAN TO MAR YOUR ELDER BROTHER'S FACE.
HE'S NOT USING THE TETSU-SAIGA...
KAGOME'S ARROW MUST STILL BE WORKING!
I'VE GOT TO TAKE HIM DOWN...
BEFORE IT TRANS-FORMS AGAIN!

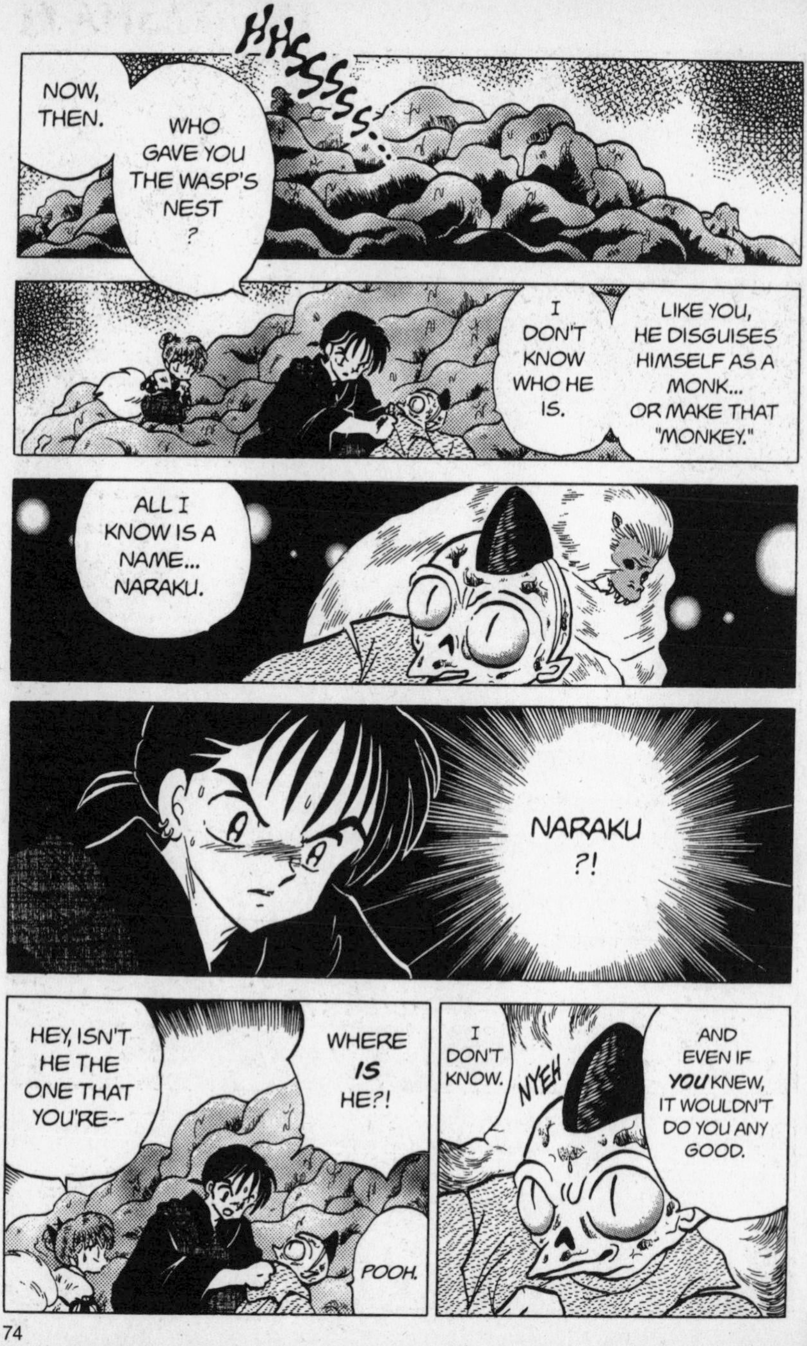
HHSSSSS...
NOW, THEN.
WHO GAVE YOU THE WASP'S NEST ?
I DON'T KNOW WHO HE IS.
LIKE YOU, HE DISGUISES HIMSELF AS A MONK... OR MAKE THAT "MONKEY."
ALL I KNOW IS A NAME... NARAKU.
NARAKU ?!
HEY, ISN'T HE THE ONE THAT YOU'RE--
WHERE *IS* HE?!
POOH.
I DON'T KNOW.
NYEH
AND EVEN IF *YOU* KNEW, IT WOULDN'T DO YOU ANY GOOD.

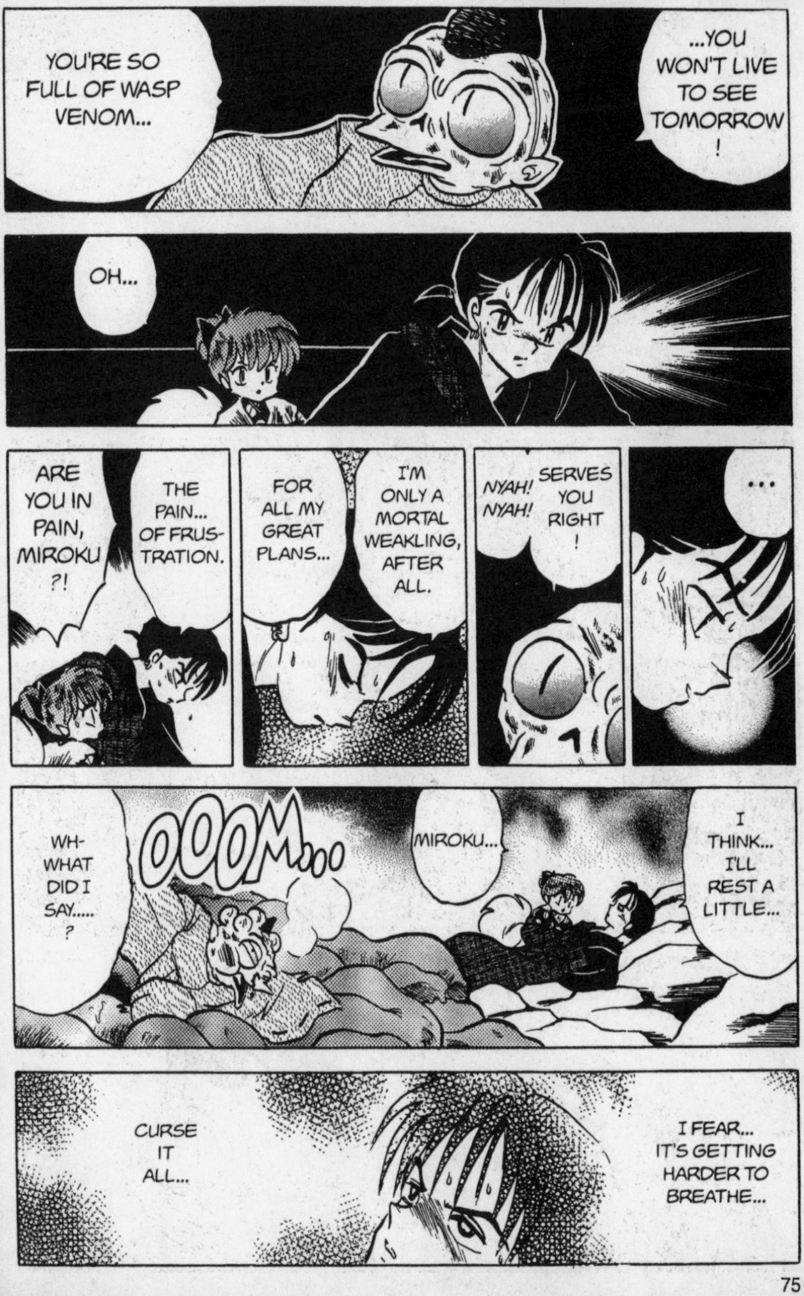
YOU'RE SO FULL OF WASP VENOM...
...YOU WON'T LIVE TO SEE TOMORROW!
OH...
ARE YOU IN PAIN, MIROKU?!
THE PAIN... OF FRUS-TRATION.
FOR ALL MY GREAT PLANS...
I'M ONLY A MORTAL WEAKLING, AFTER ALL.
NYAH! NYAH!
SERVES YOU RIGHT!
...
WH-WHAT DID I SAY.....?
OOOMooo
MIROKU...
I THINK... I'LL REST A LITTLE...
CURSE IT ALL...
I FEAR... IT'S GETTING HARDER TO BREATHE...

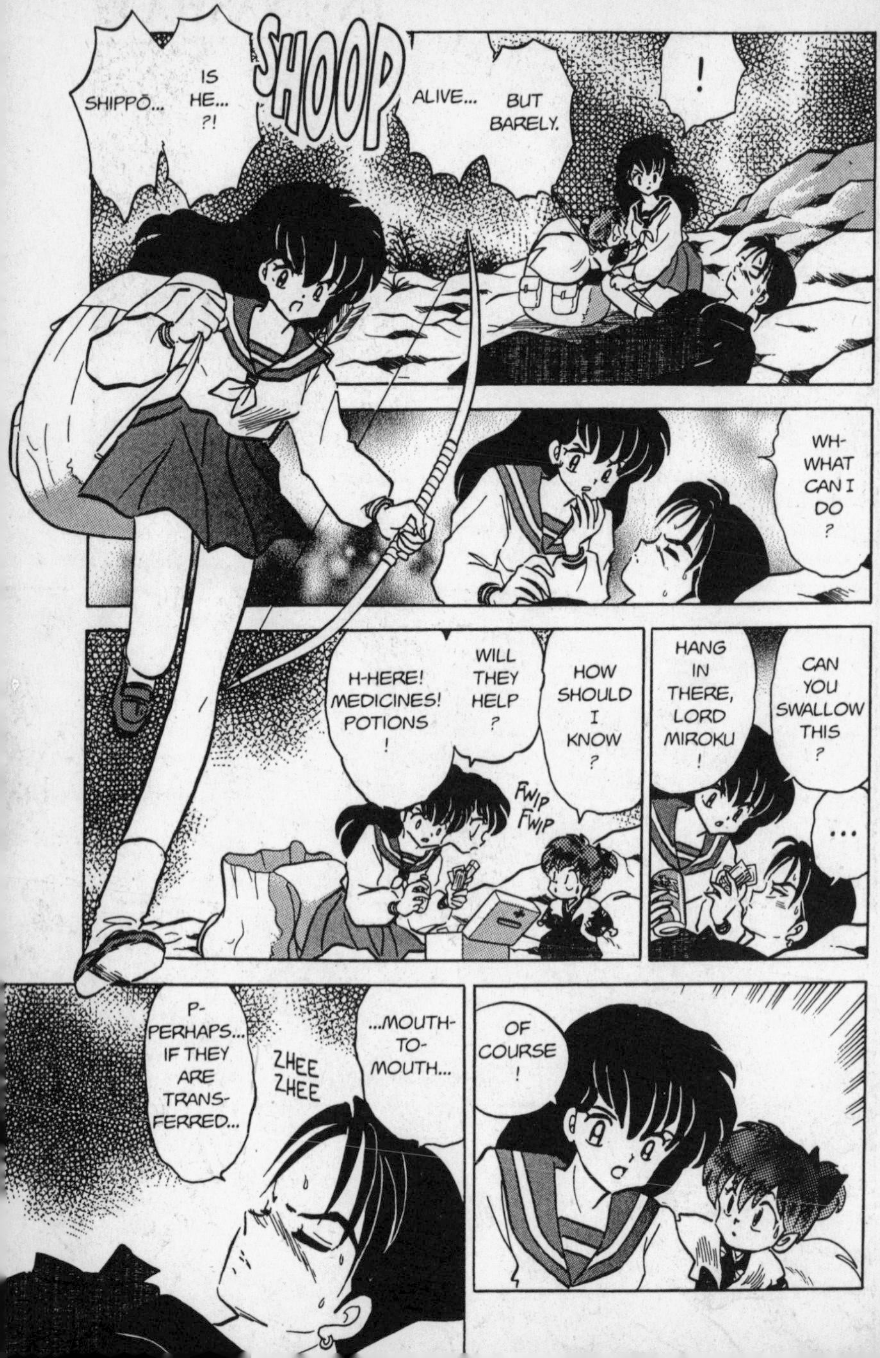
SHIPPŌ... IS HE...?!
SHOOP
ALIVE... BUT BARELY.
!
WH-WHAT CAN I DO?
H-HERE! MEDICINES! POTIONS!
WILL THEY HELP?
HOW SHOULD I KNOW?
FWIP FWIP
HANG IN THERE, LORD MIROKU!
CAN YOU SWALLOW THIS?
...
P-PERHAPS... IF THEY ARE TRANS-FERRED...
ZHEE ZHEE
...MOUTH-TO-MOUTH...
OF COURSE!

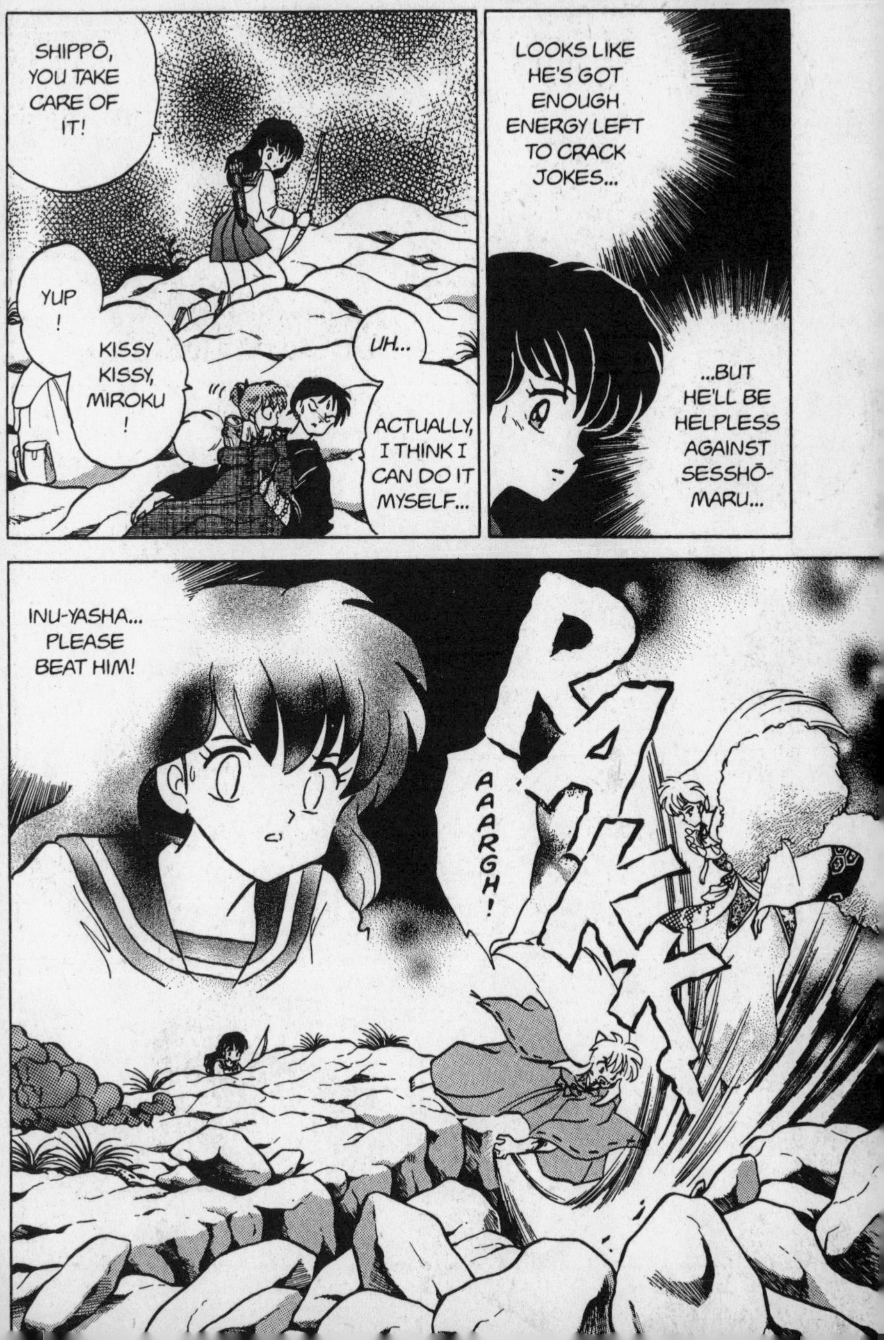
SHIPPŌ, YOU TAKE CARE OF IT!
YUP!
KISSY KISSY, MIROKU!
UH...
ACTUALLY, I THINK I CAN DO IT MYSELF...
LOOKS LIKE HE'S GOT ENOUGH ENERGY LEFT TO CRACK JOKES...
...BUT HE'LL BE HELPLESS AGAINST SESSHŌ-MARU...
INU-YASHA... PLEASE BEAT HIM!
RAK
AAARGH!

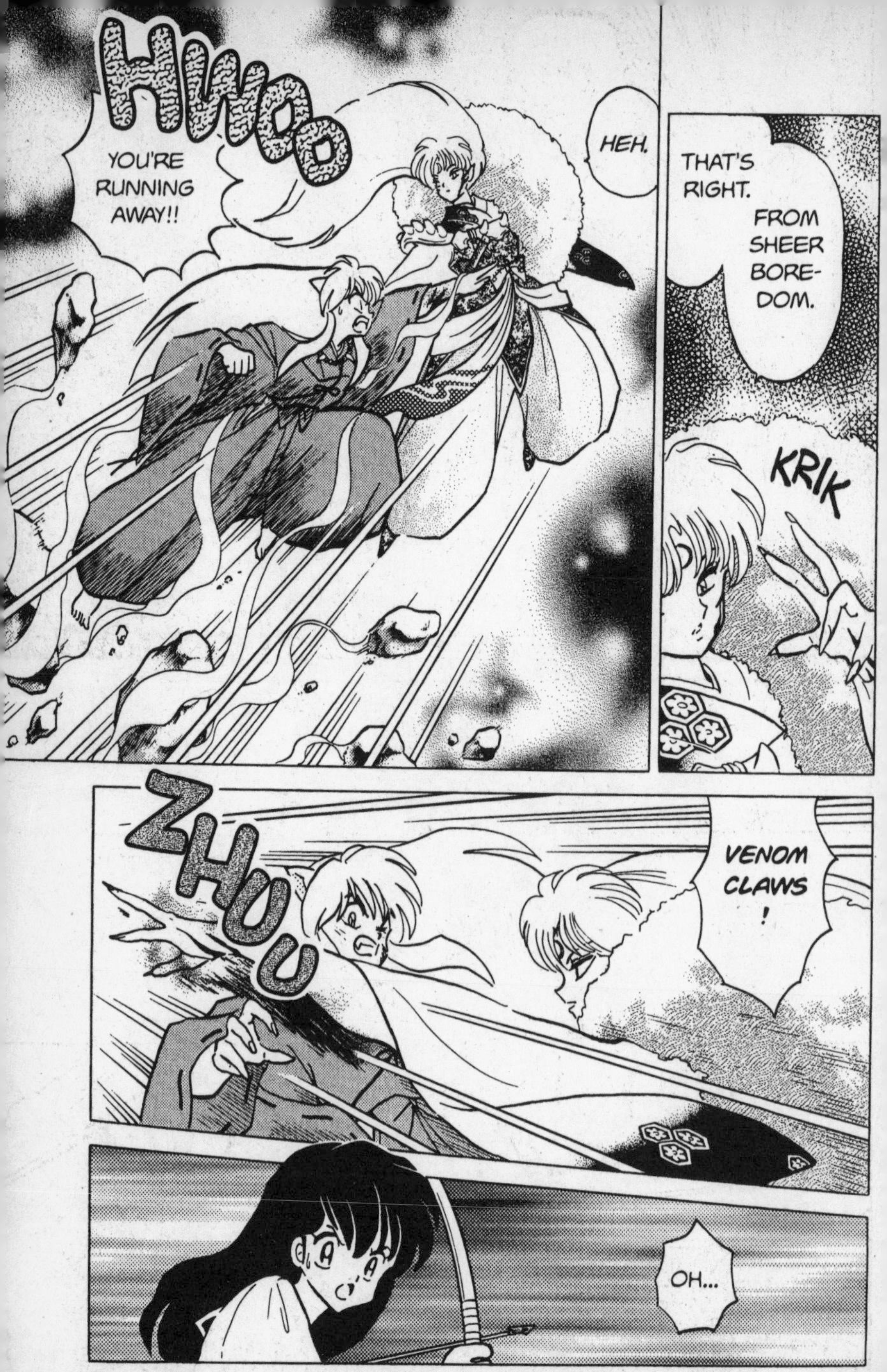
HWOO
YOU'RE RUNNING AWAY!!
HEH.
THAT'S RIGHT.
FROM SHEER BORE-DOM.
KRIK
ZHUU
VENOM CLAWS !
OH...

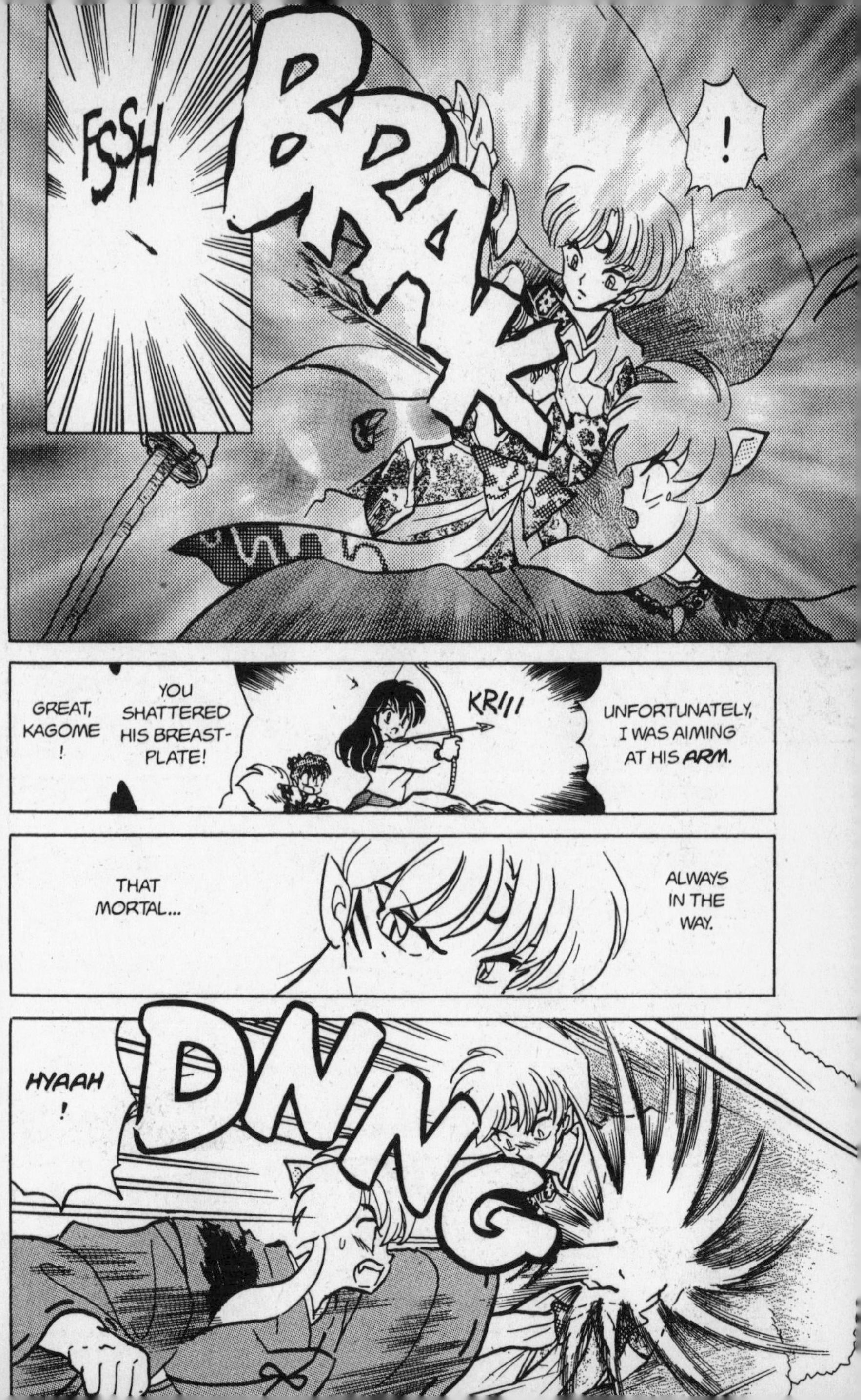
FSSH
BRAK
!
GREAT, KAGOME!
YOU SHATTERED HIS BREAST-PLATE!
KRI
UNFORTUNATELY, I WAS AIMING AT HIS ARM.
THAT MORTAL...
ALWAYS IN THE WAY.
HYAAH!
DNNG

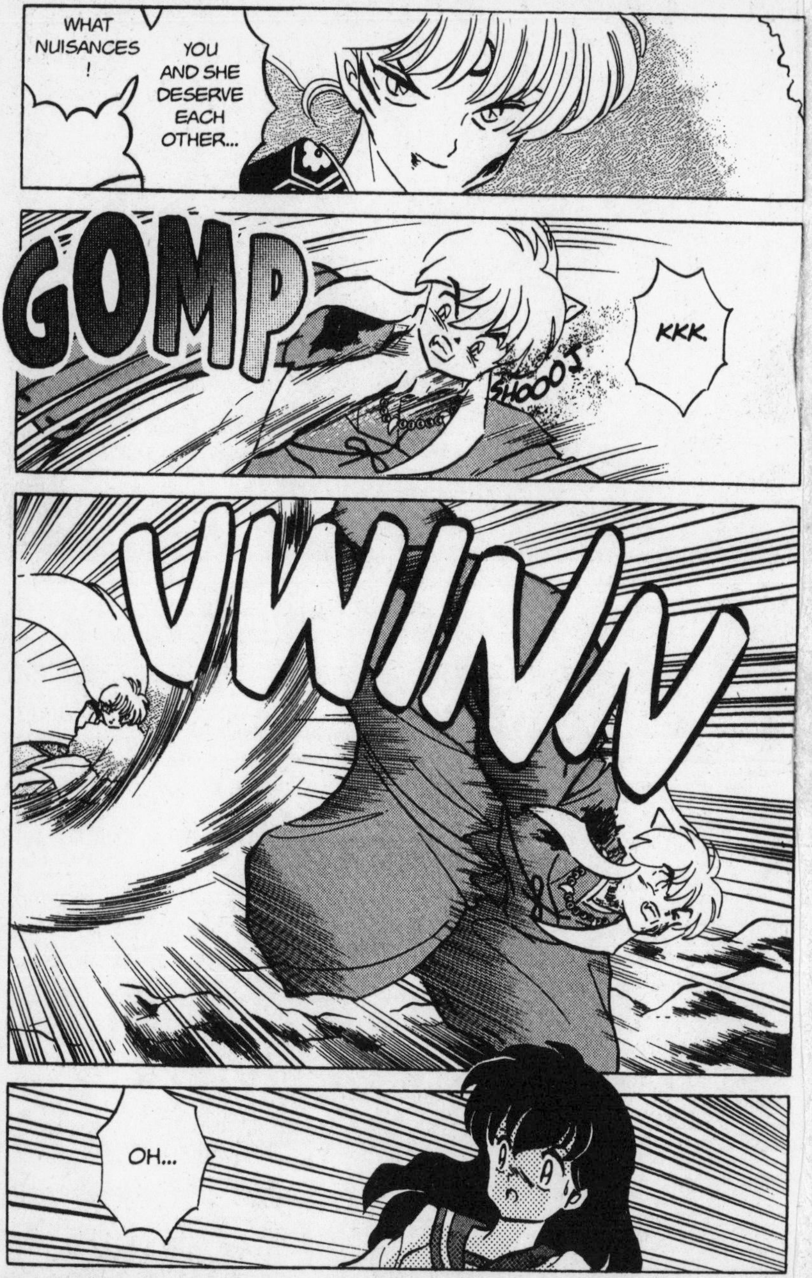
WHAT NUISANCES !
YOU AND SHE DESERVE EACH OTHER...
GOMP
SHOOOJ
KKK.
VWINN
OH...

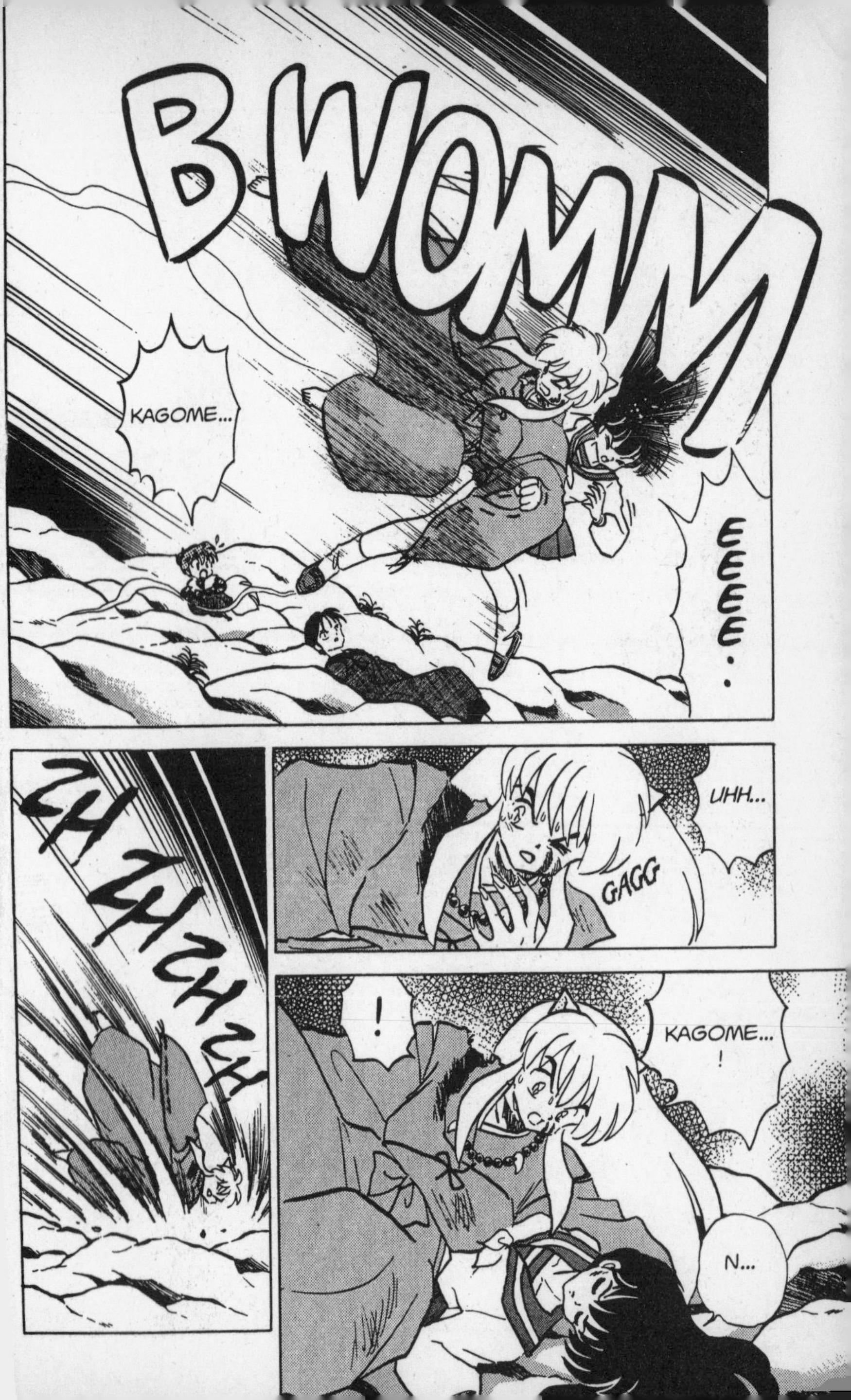
BWOMM
KAGOME...
EEEE...
UHH...
GAGG
!
KAGOME... !
N...

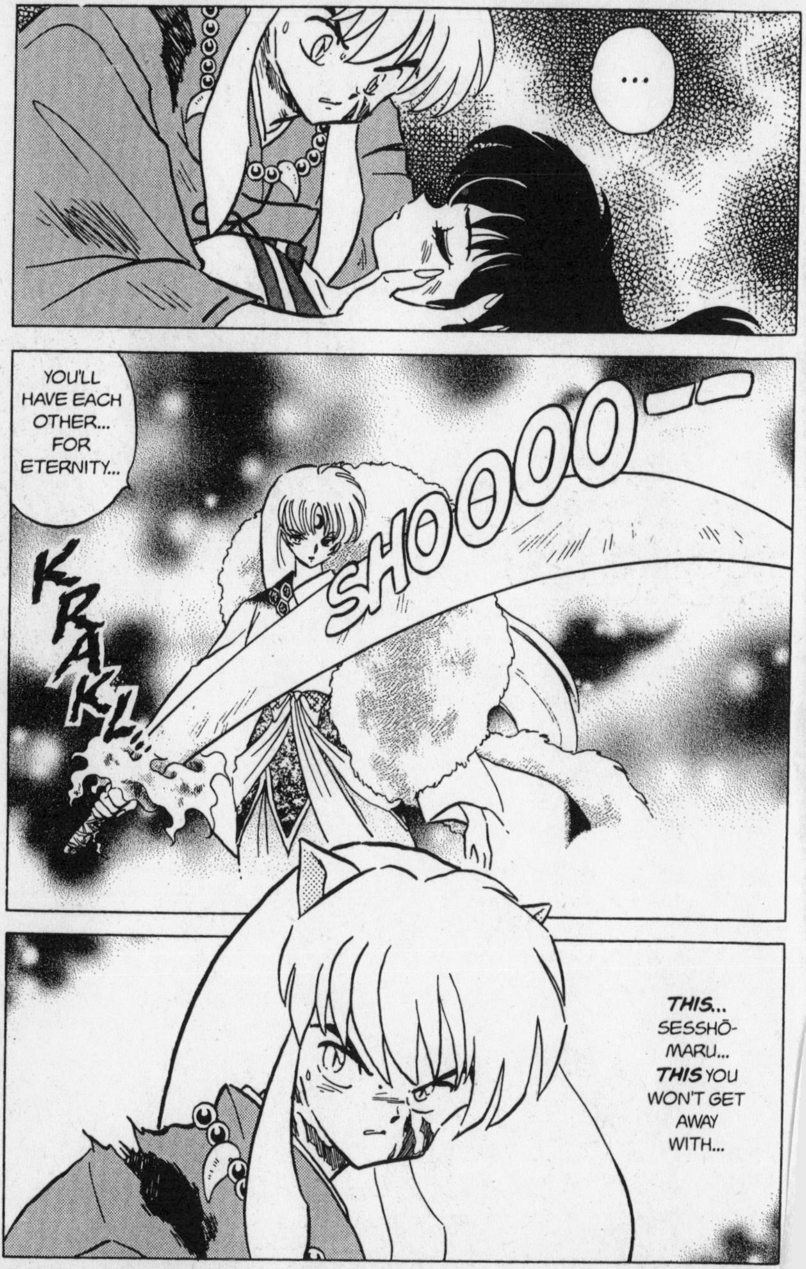
...
YOU'LL HAVE EACH OTHER... FOR ETERNITY...
KRAKL
SHOOOO--
THIS... SESSHŌ-MARU... THIS YOU WON'T GET AWAY WITH...

SCROLL FIVE
RECLAMATION

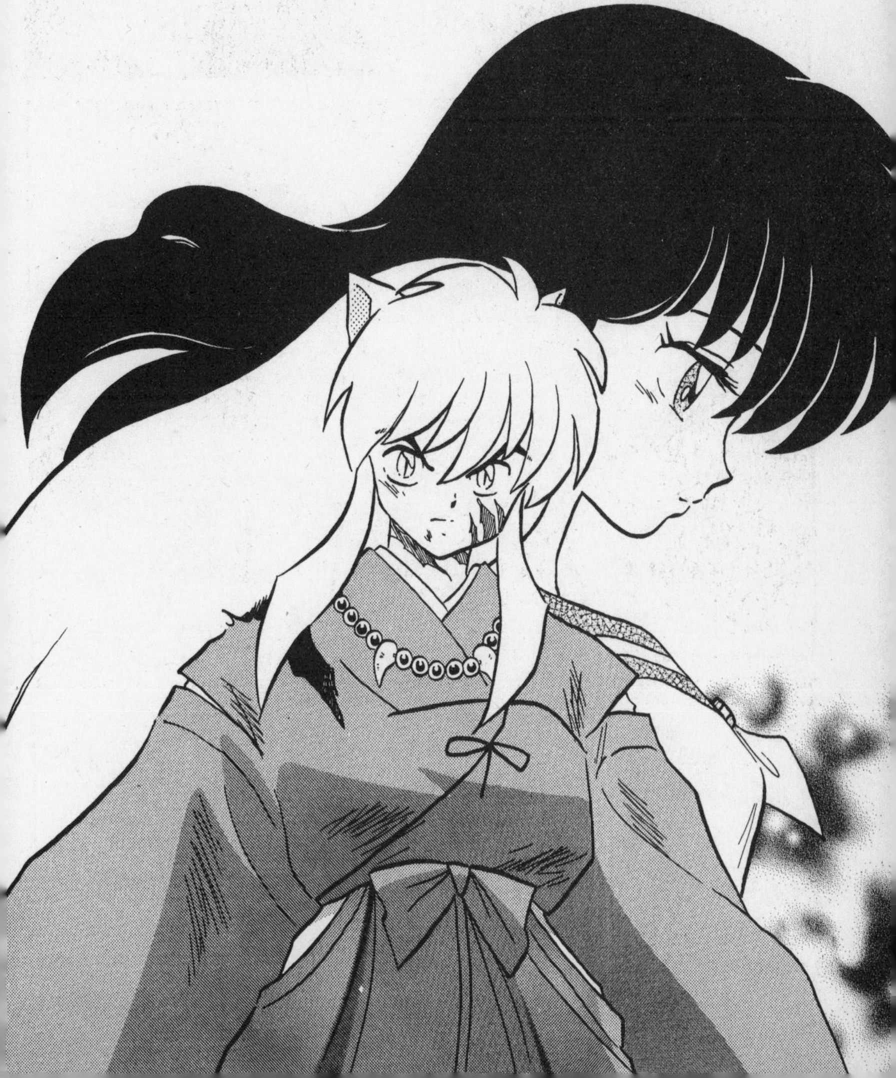

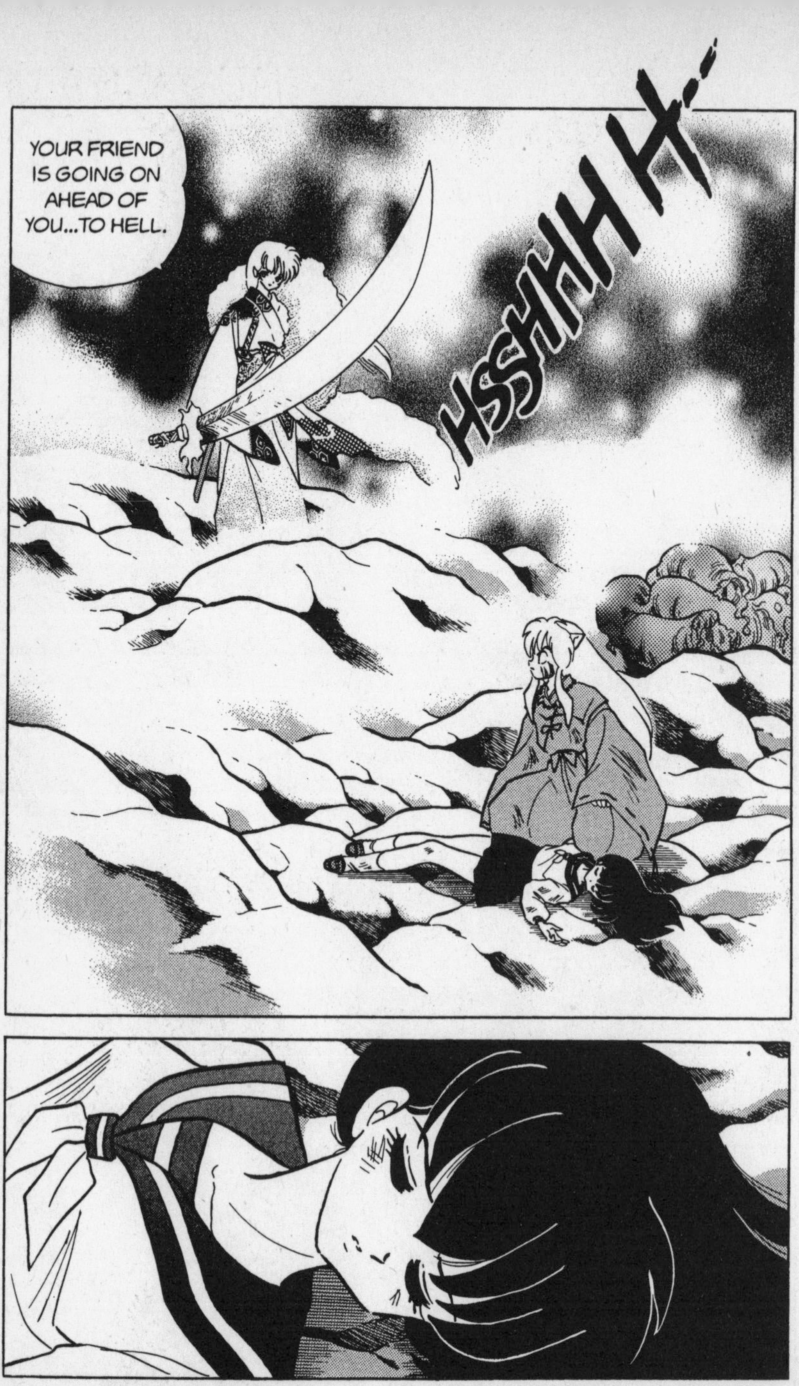
YOUR FRIEND IS GOING ON AHEAD OF YOU...TO HELL.
HSSHHHH...

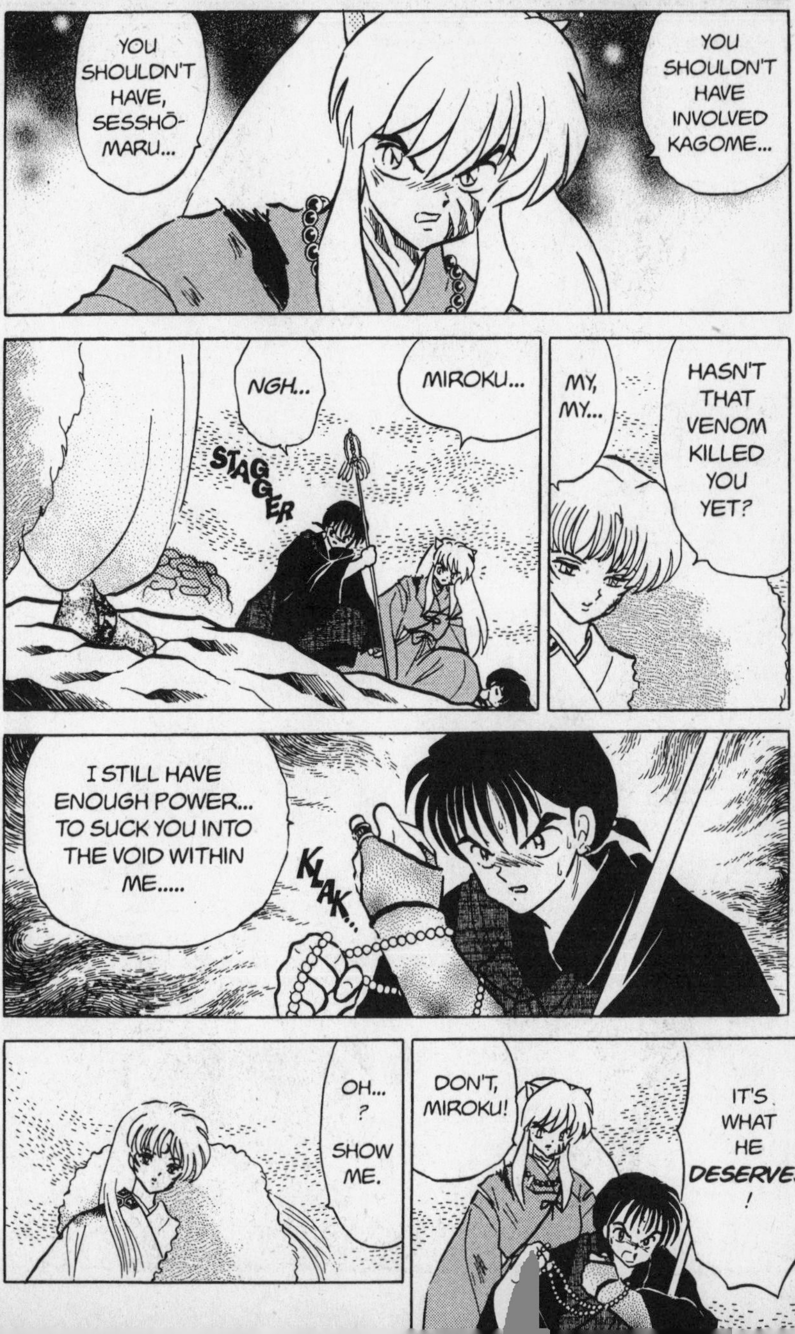
YOU SHOULDN'T HAVE, SESSHŌ-MARU...
YOU SHOULDN'T HAVE INVOLVED KAGOME...
NGH...
STAGGER
MIROKU...
MY, MY...
HASN'T THAT VENOM KILLED YOU YET?
I STILL HAVE ENOUGH POWER... TO SUCK YOU INTO THE VOID WITHIN ME.....
KLAK...
OH...?
SHOW ME.
DON'T, MIROKU!
IT'S WHAT HE **DESERVES**!

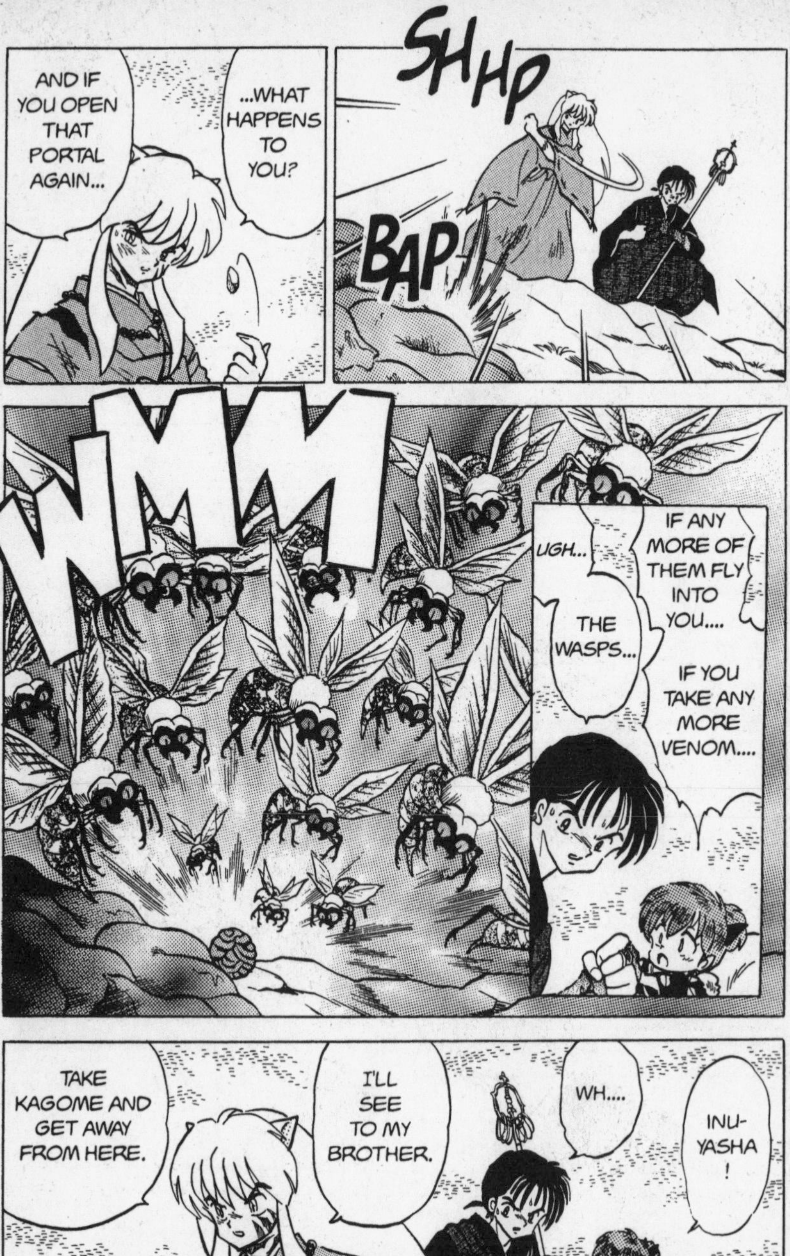
AND IF YOU OPEN THAT PORTAL AGAIN...
...WHAT HAPPENS TO YOU?
SHHP
BAP
WMM
UGH...
THE WASPS...
IF ANY MORE OF THEM FLY INTO YOU....
IF YOU TAKE ANY MORE VENOM....
TAKE KAGOME AND GET AWAY FROM HERE.
I'LL SEE TO MY BROTHER.
WH....
INU-YASHA!

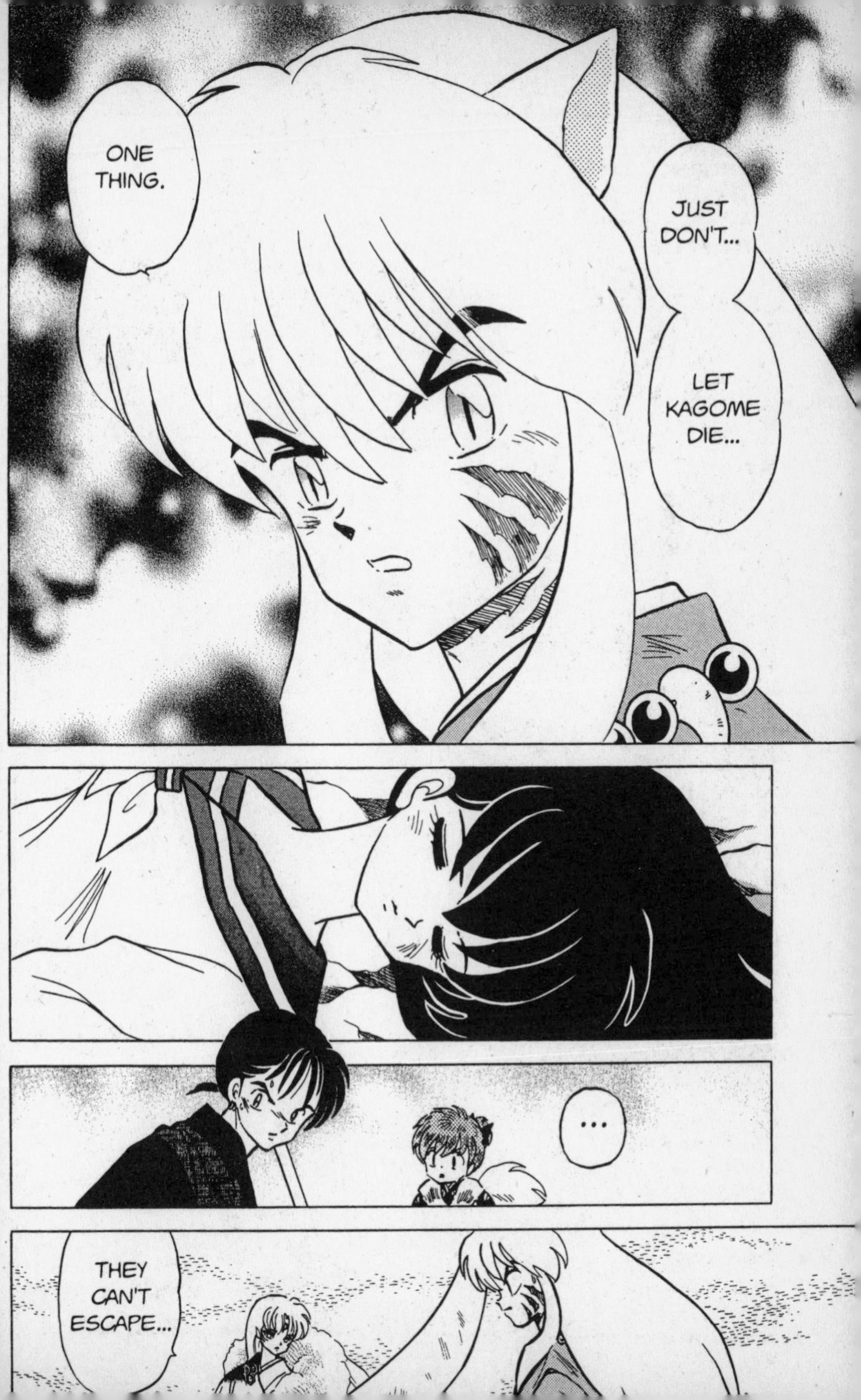
ONE THING.
JUST DON'T...
LET KAGOME DIE...
...
THEY CAN'T ESCAPE...

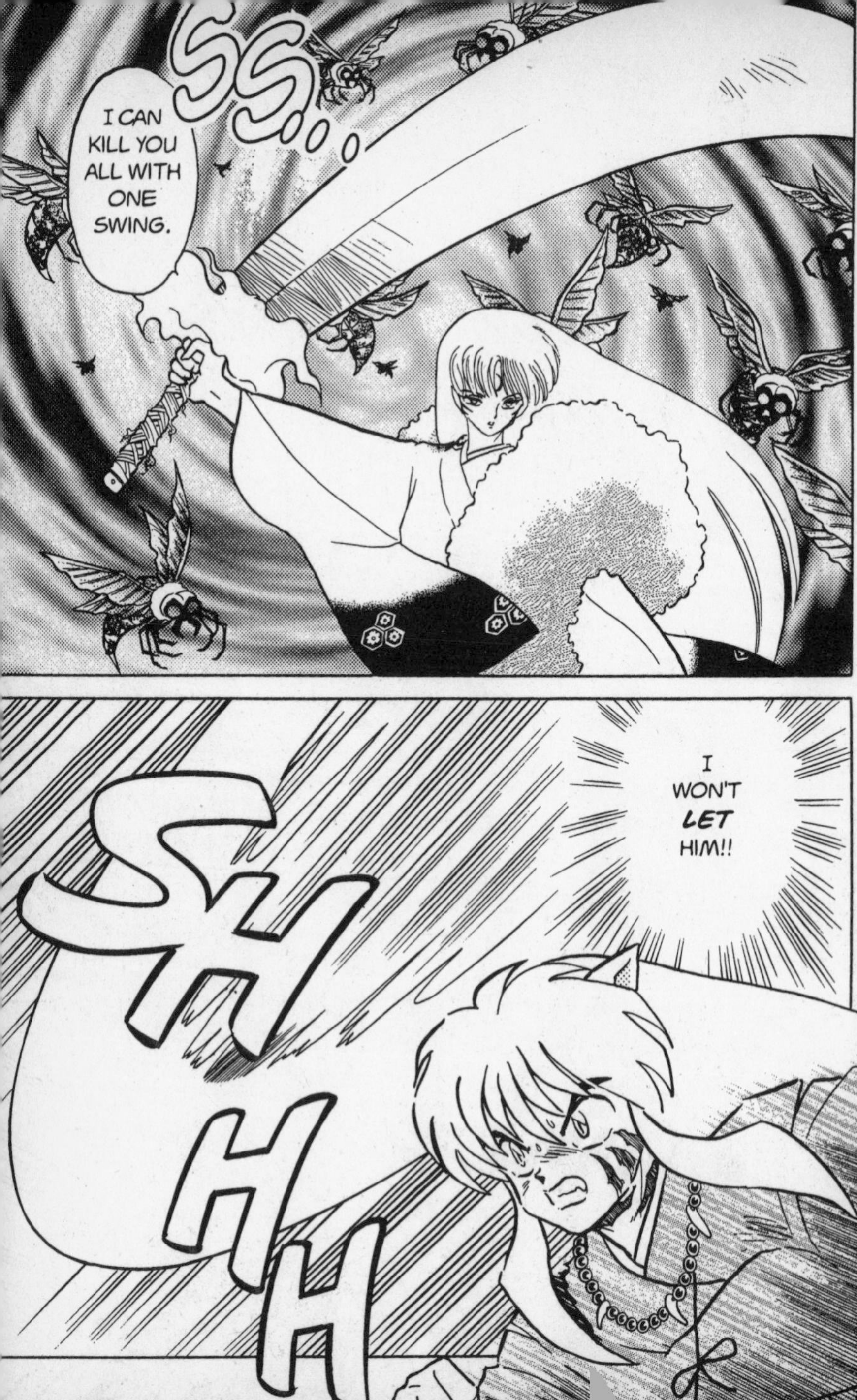
I CAN KILL YOU ALL WITH ONE SWING.
SS...
I WON'T LET HIM!!
SHHH

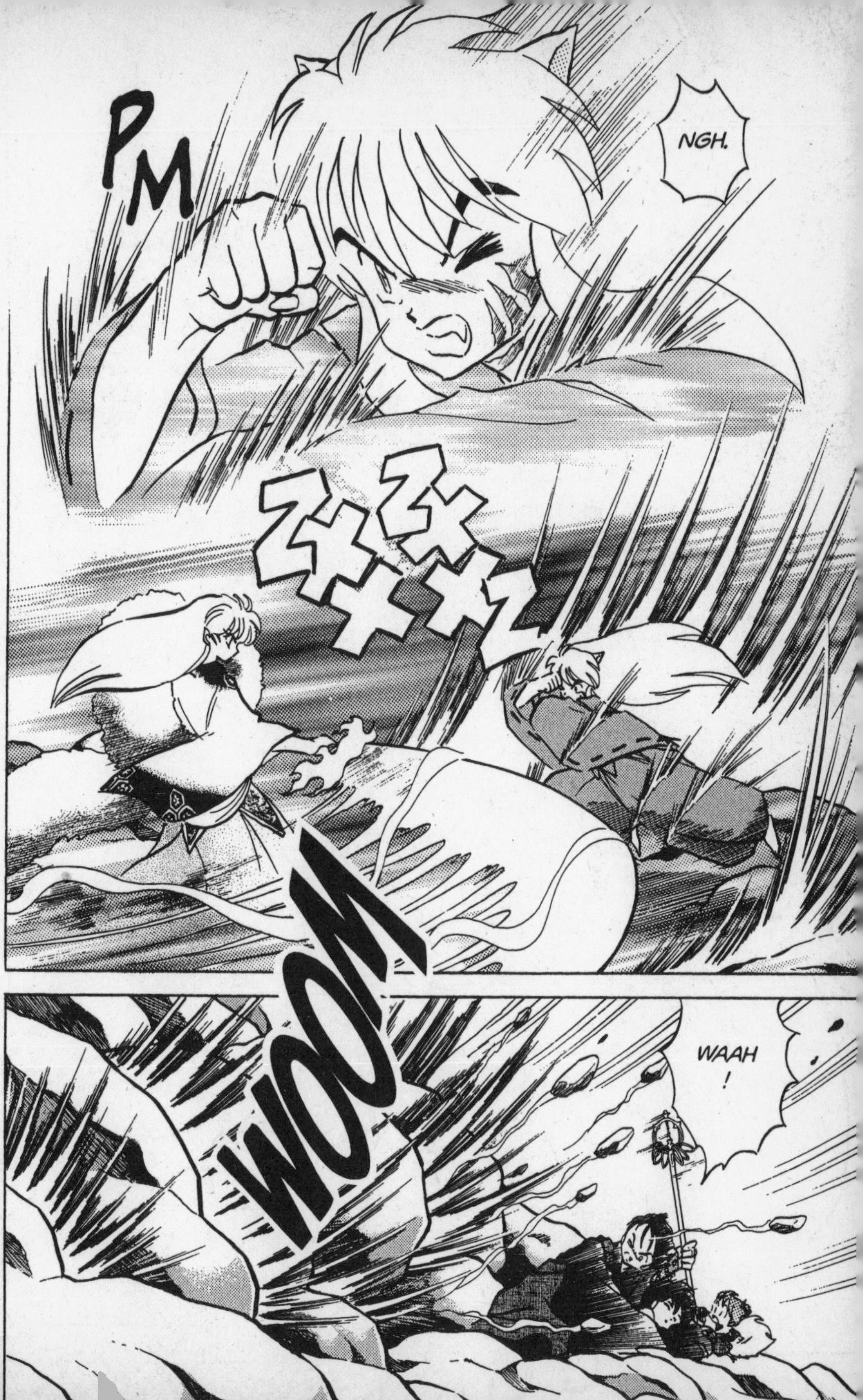
PM
NGH.
WOOM
WAAH!

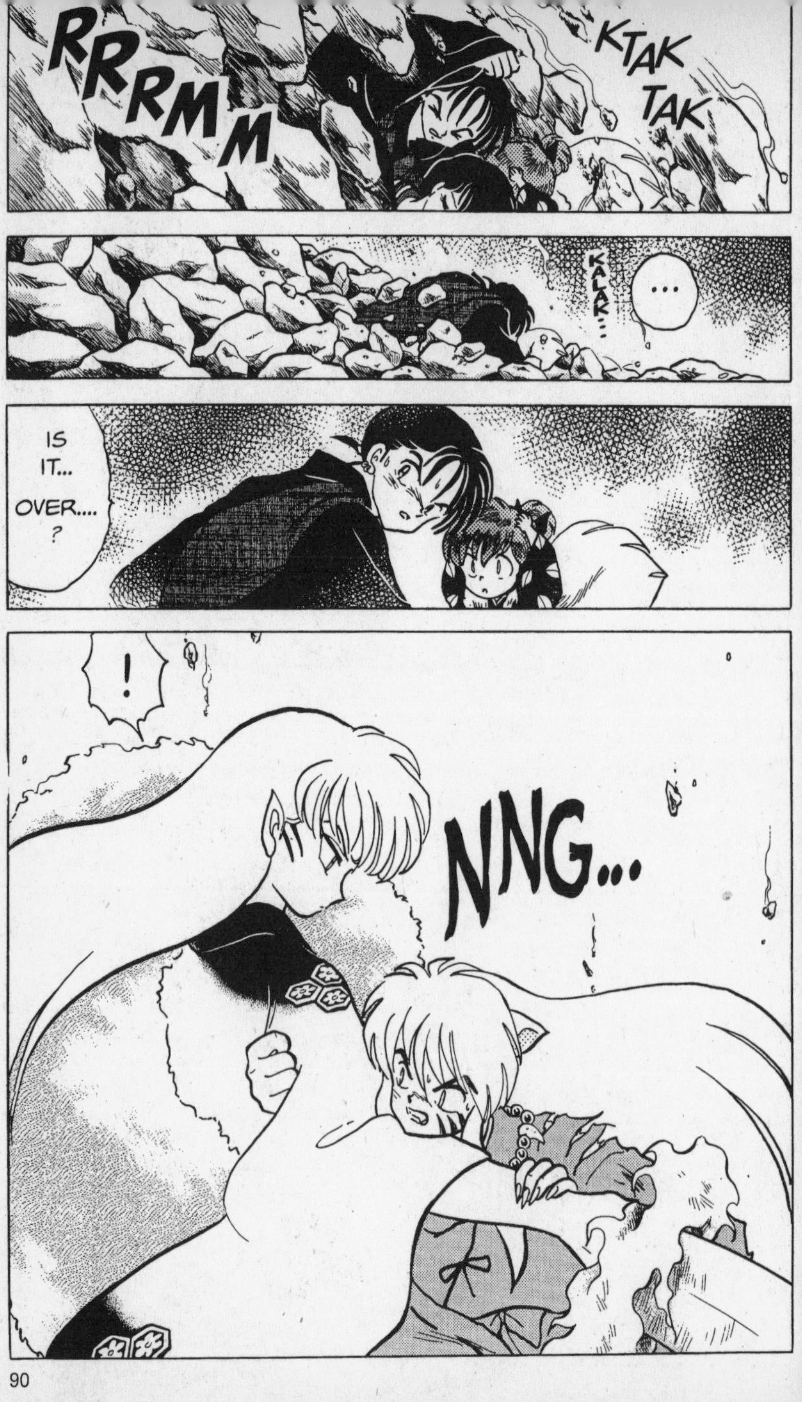
RRRMM
KTAK TAK
KALAK...
...
IS IT... OVER.... ?
!
NNG...

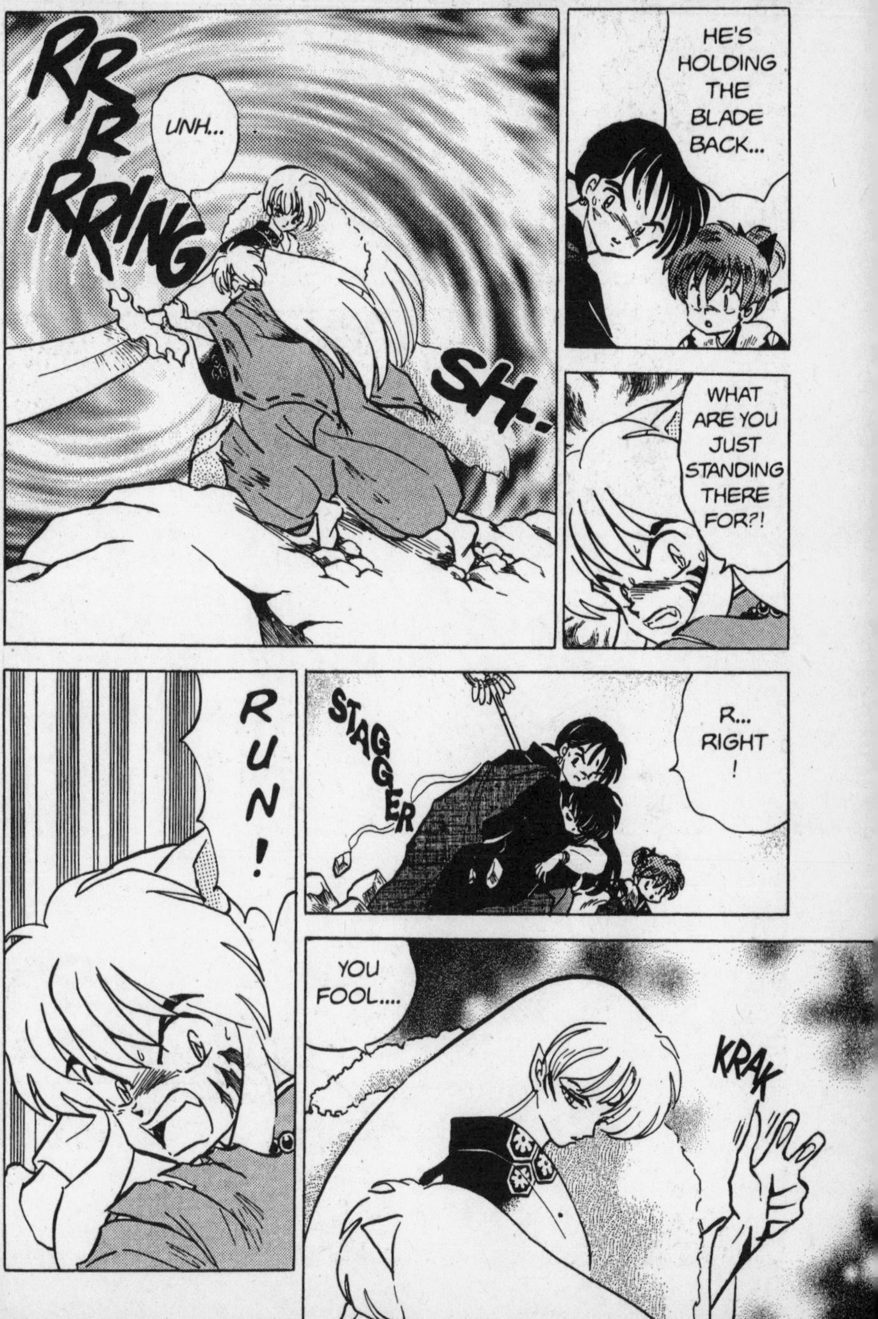
RRRRRRING
UNH...
SH--
HE'S HOLDING THE BLADE BACK...
WHAT ARE YOU JUST STANDING THERE FOR?!
RUN!
STAGGER
R... RIGHT!
YOU FOOL....
KRAK

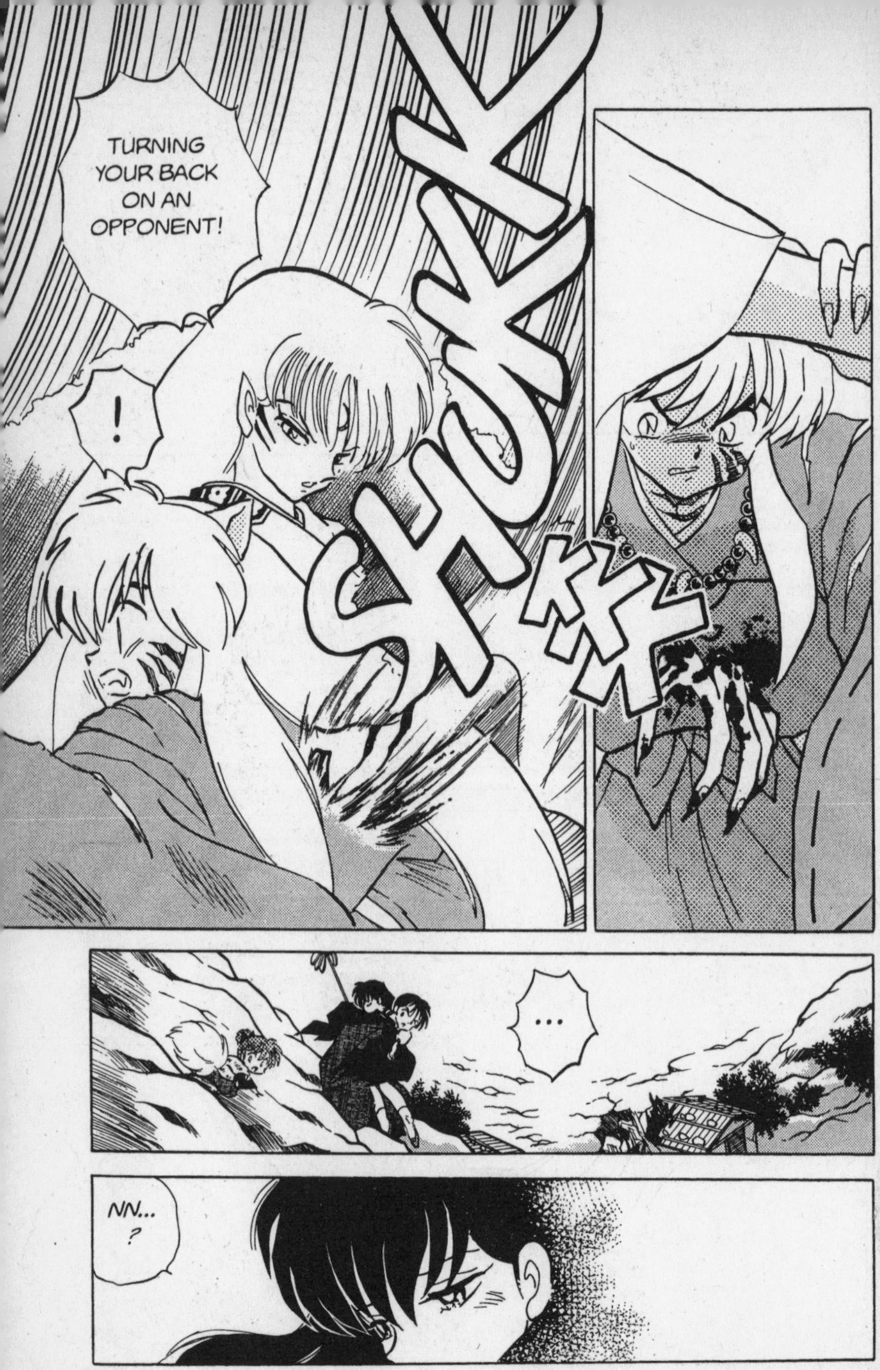
TURNING YOUR BACK ON AN OPPONENT!
!
SHUKK
...
NN... ?

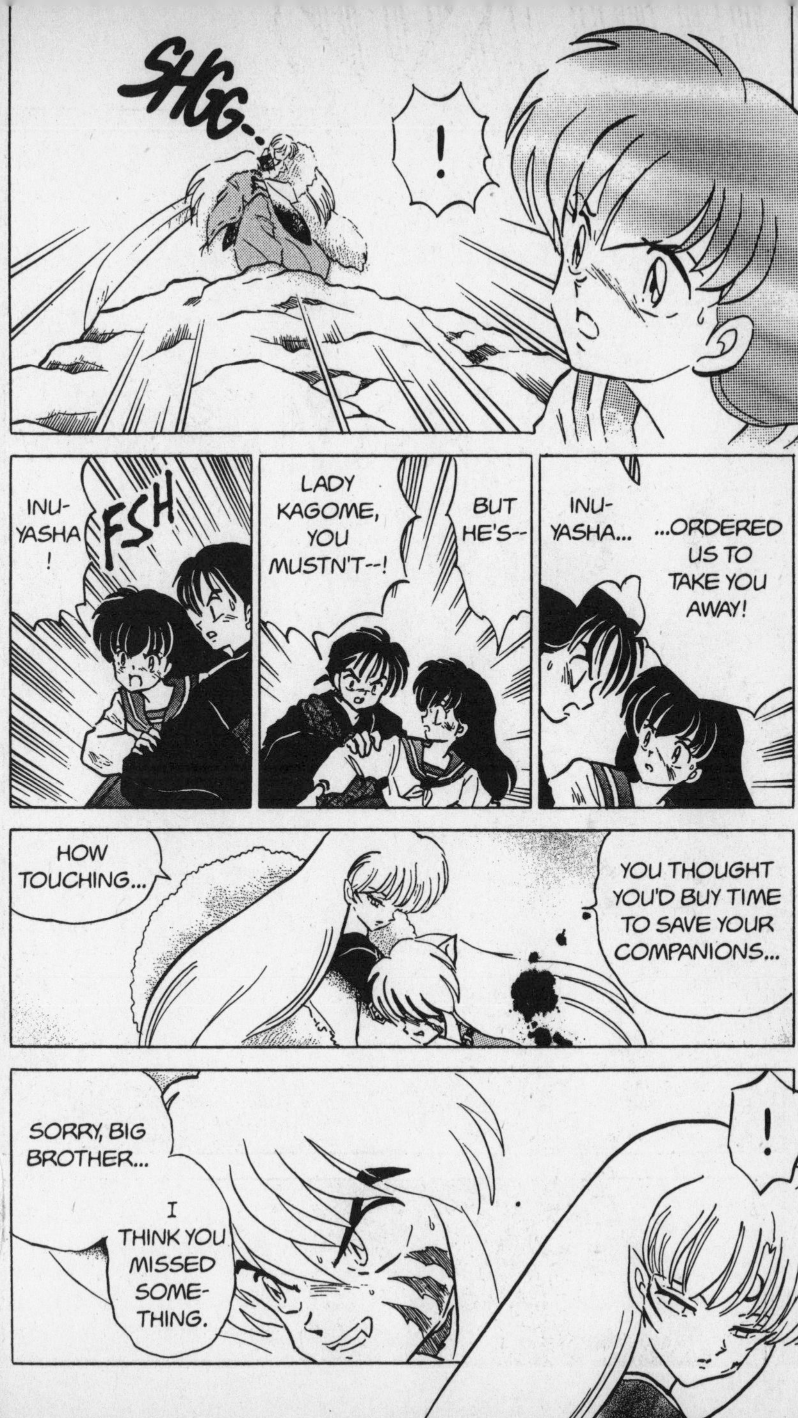
SHGG...
!
INU-YASHA!
FSH
LADY KAGOME, YOU MUSTN'T--!
BUT HE'S--
INU-YASHA...
...ORDERED US TO TAKE YOU AWAY!
HOW TOUCHING...
YOU THOUGHT YOU'D BUY TIME TO SAVE YOUR COMPANIONS...
SORRY, BIG BROTHER...
I THINK YOU MISSED SOME-THING.
!

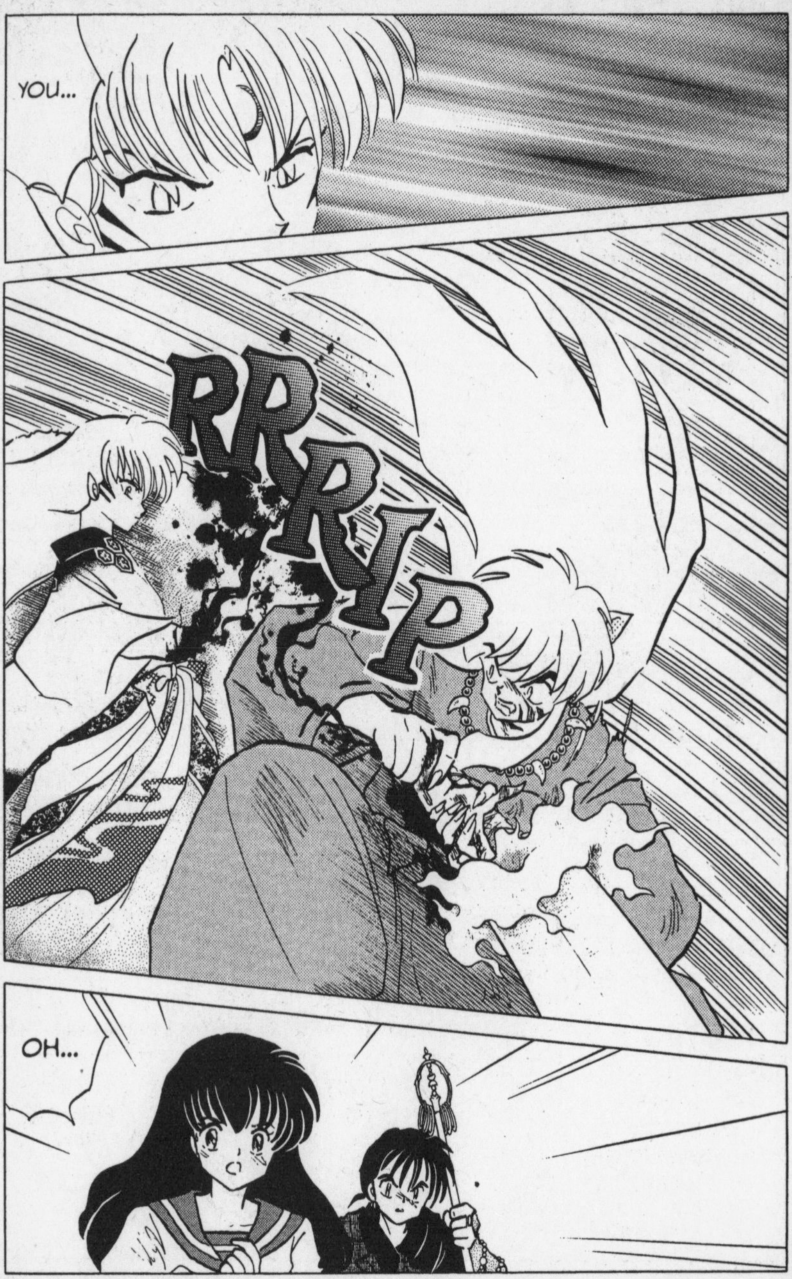
YOU...
RRRIP
OH...

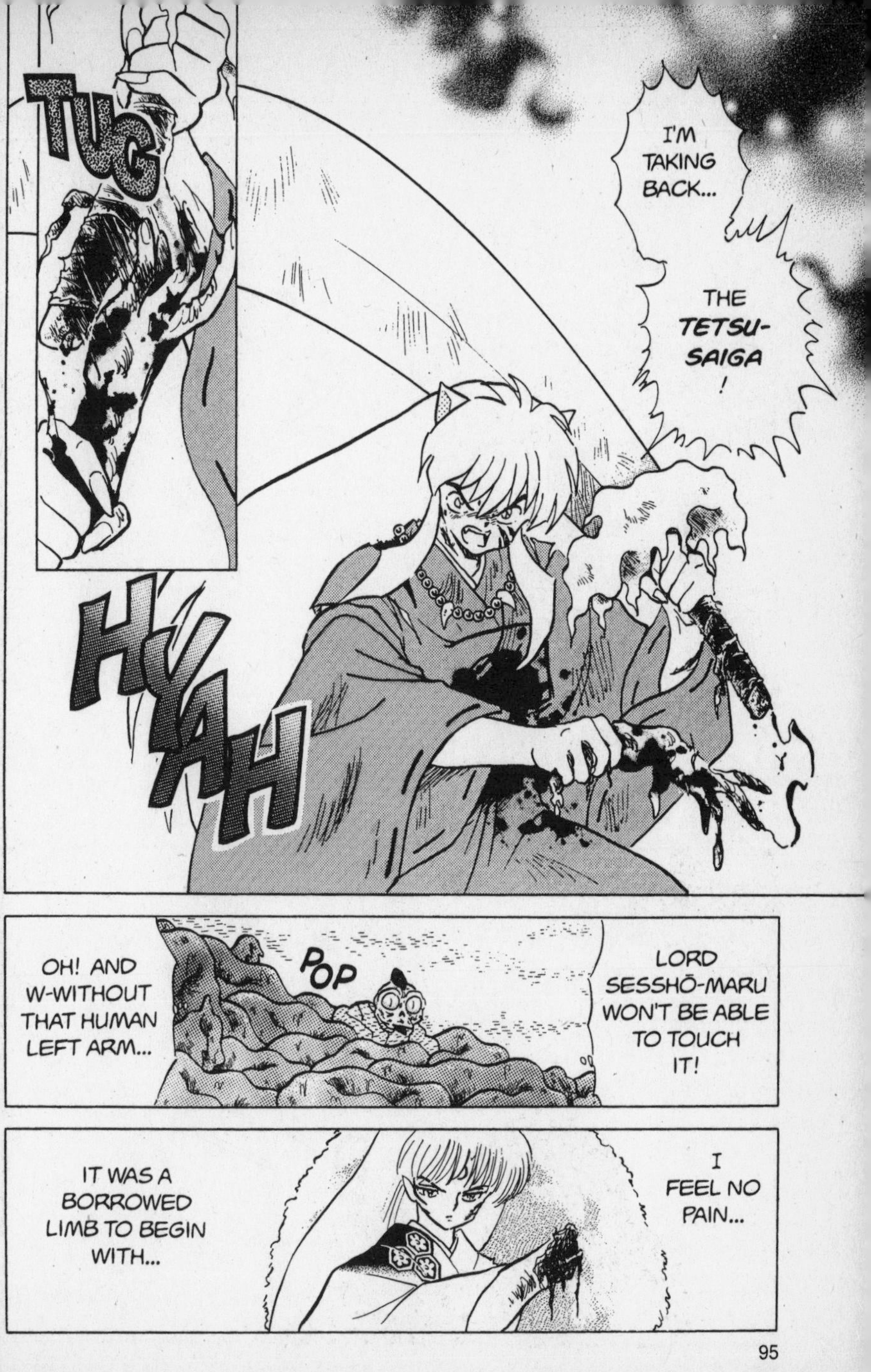
TUG
I'M TAKING BACK...
THE *TETSU-SAIGA* !
HYAH
OH! AND W-WITHOUT THAT HUMAN LEFT ARM...
POP
LORD SESSHŌ-MARU WON'T BE ABLE TO TOUCH IT!
IT WAS A BORROWED LIMB TO BEGIN WITH...
I FEEL NO PAIN...

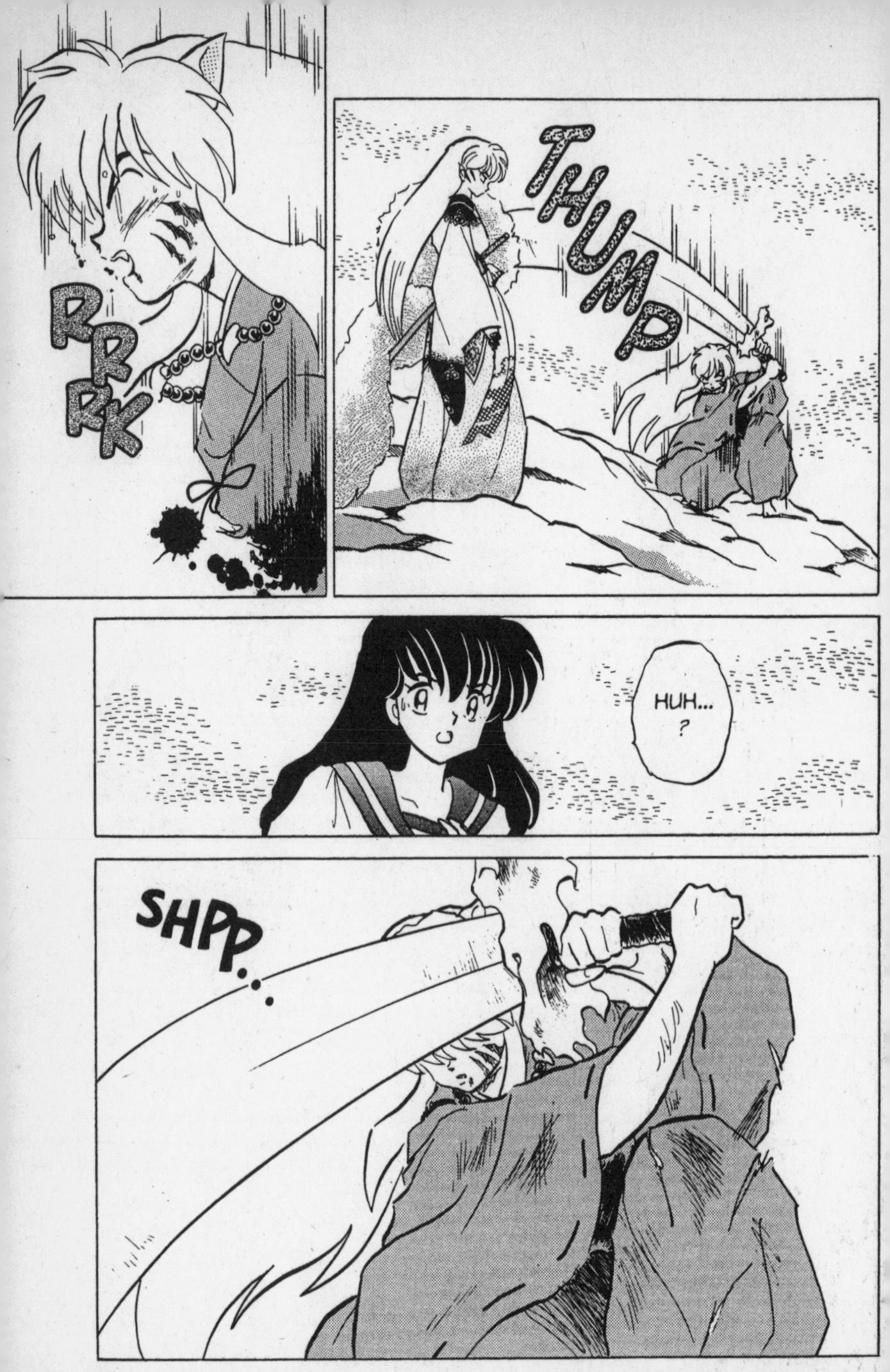
THUMP
RRRK
HUH... ?
SHPP...

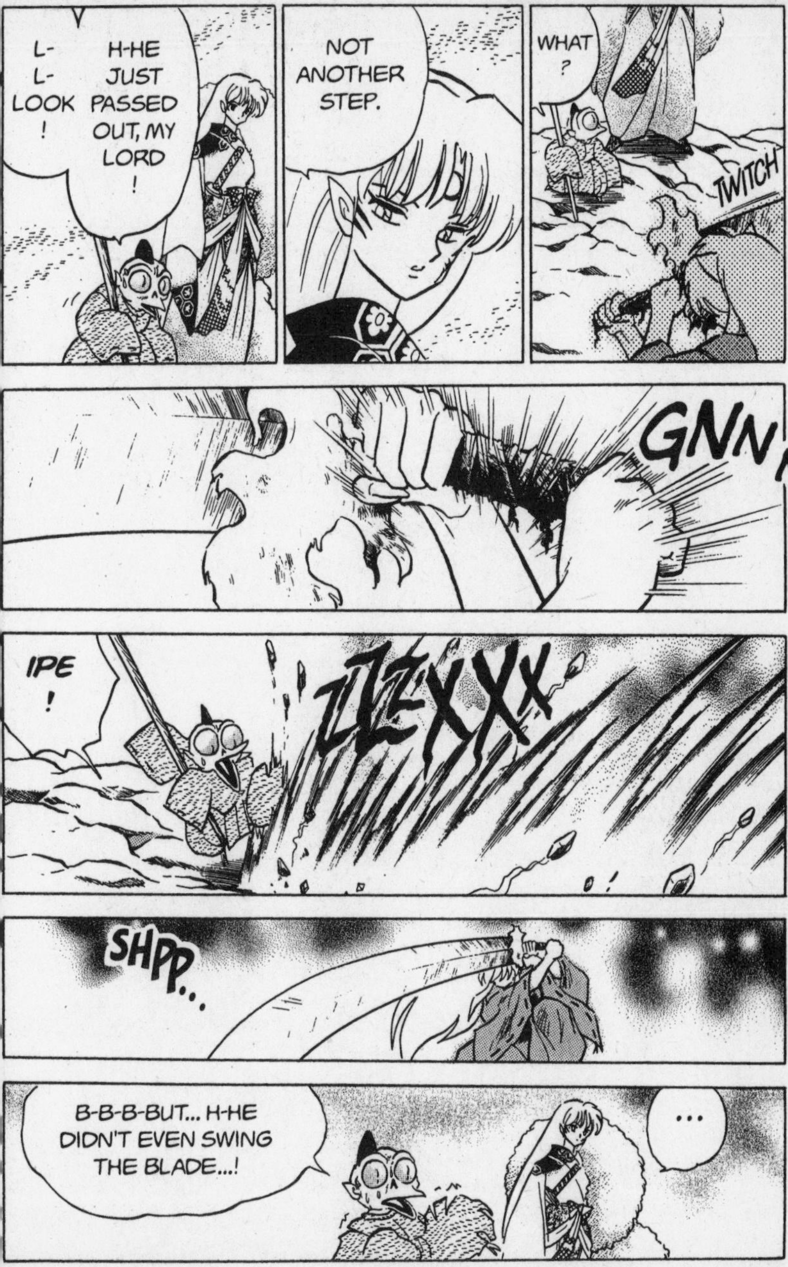
L-
L-
LOOK
!
H-HE
JUST
PASSED
OUT, MY
LORD
!
NOT
ANOTHER
STEP.
WHAT
?
TWITCH
GNNN
IPE
!
ZZZXXX
SHPP...
B-B-B-BUT... H-HE
DIDN'T EVEN SWING
THE BLADE...!
...

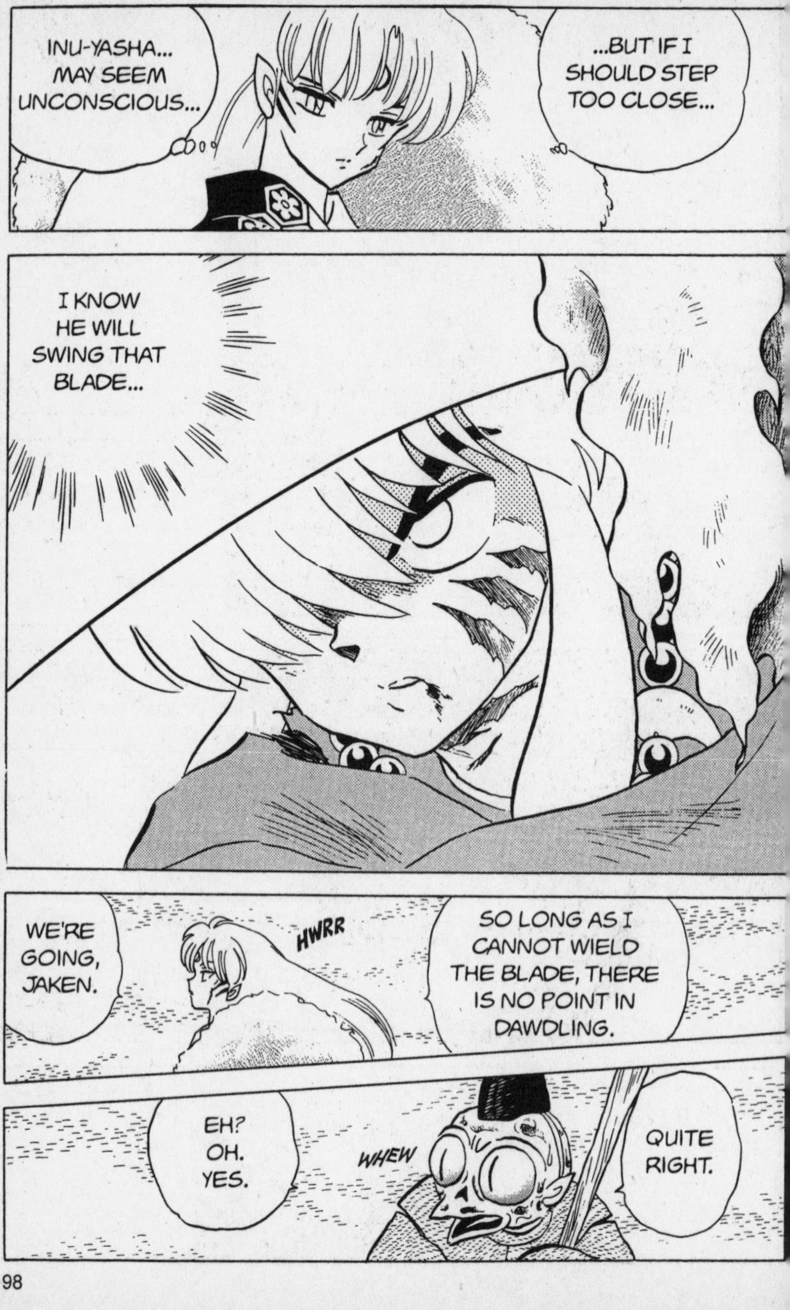
INU-YASHA... MAY SEEM UNCONSCIOUS...
...BUT IF I SHOULD STEP TOO CLOSE...
I KNOW HE WILL SWING THAT BLADE...
WE'RE GOING, JAKEN.
HWRR
SO LONG AS I CANNOT WIELD THE BLADE, THERE IS NO POINT IN DAWDLING.
EH? OH. YES.
WHEW
QUITE RIGHT.

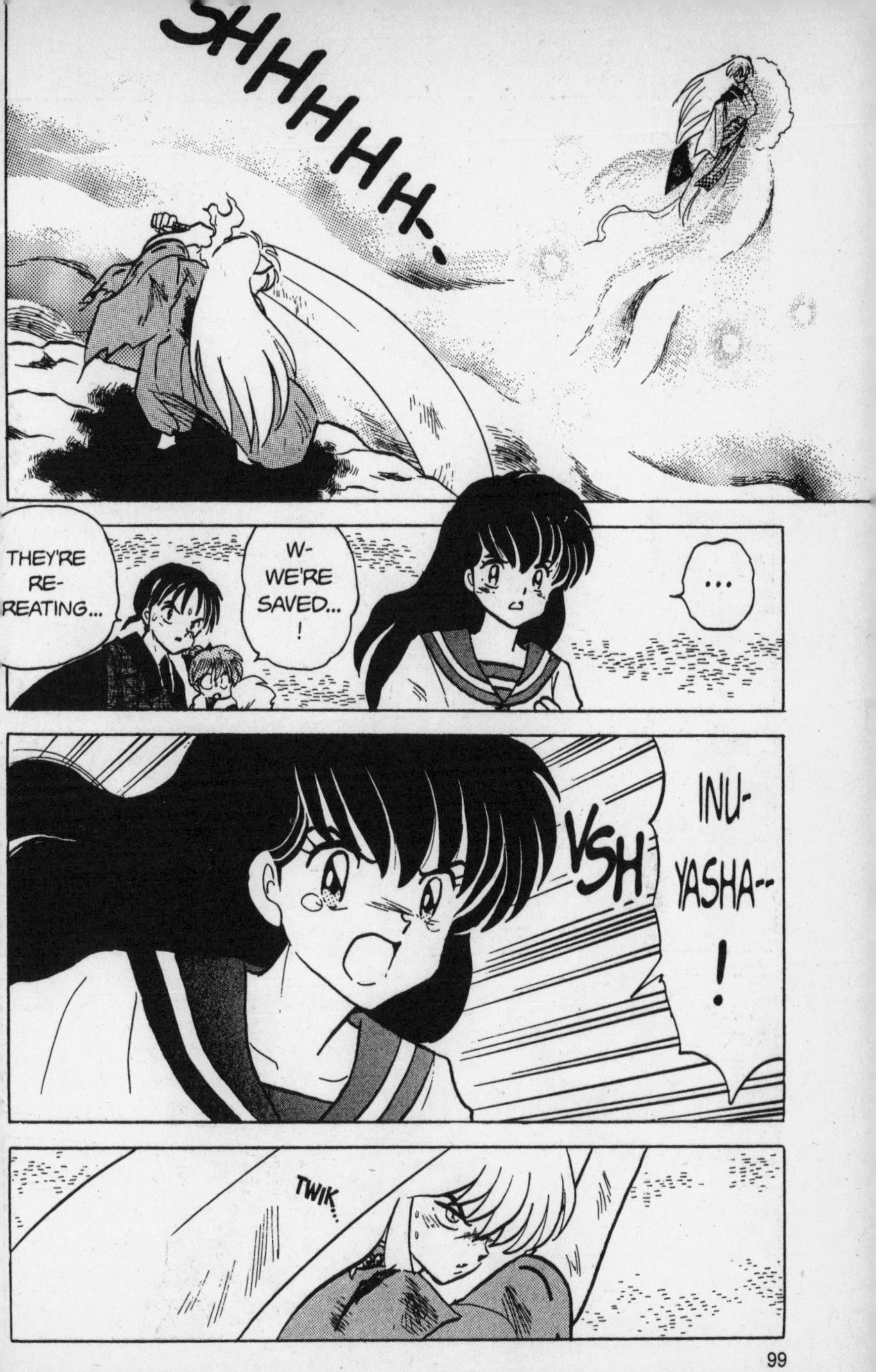
SHHHHH...
THEY'RE RE-REATING...
W-WE'RE SAVED...!
...
VSH
INU-YASHA--!
TWIK...

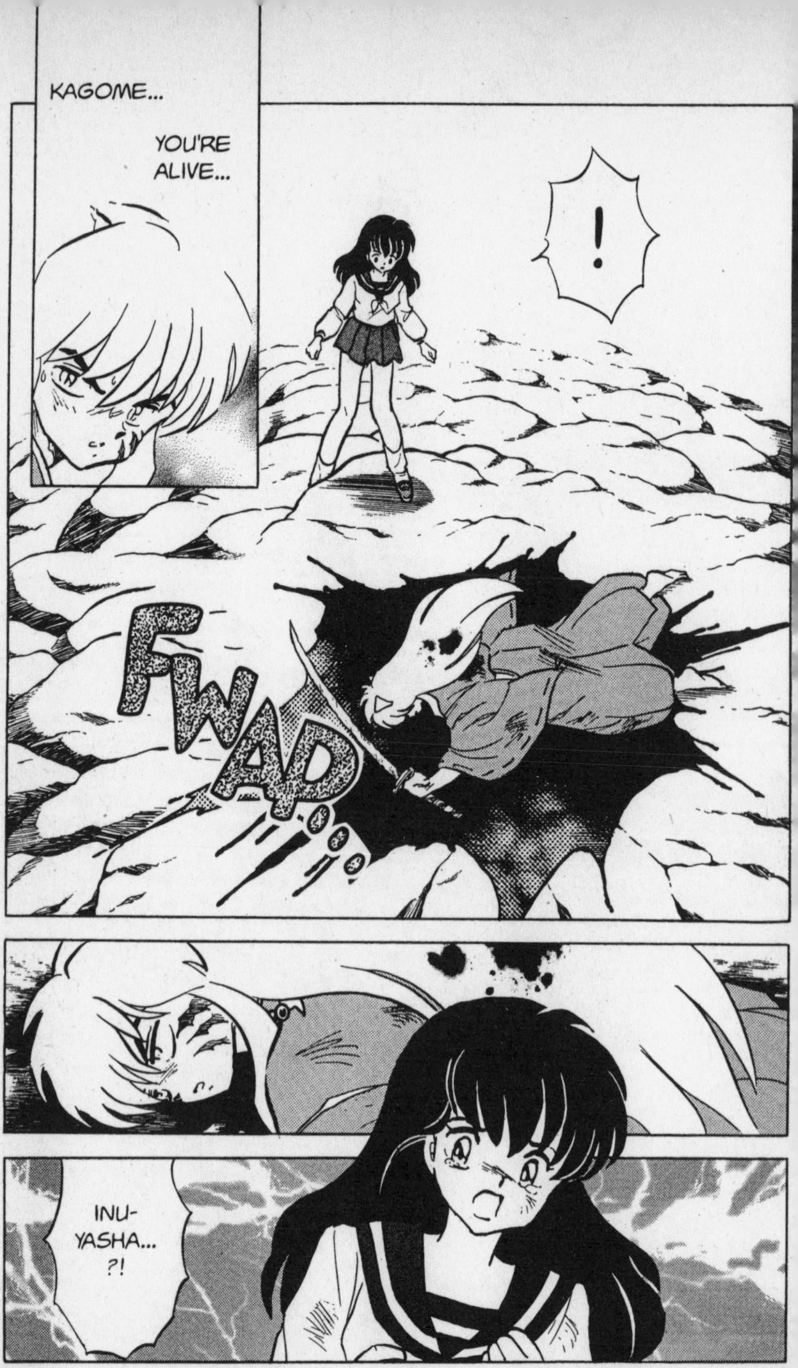
KAGOME...
YOU'RE ALIVE...
!
FWAP...
INU-YASHA...?!

SCROLL SIX

SEPARATE WAYS

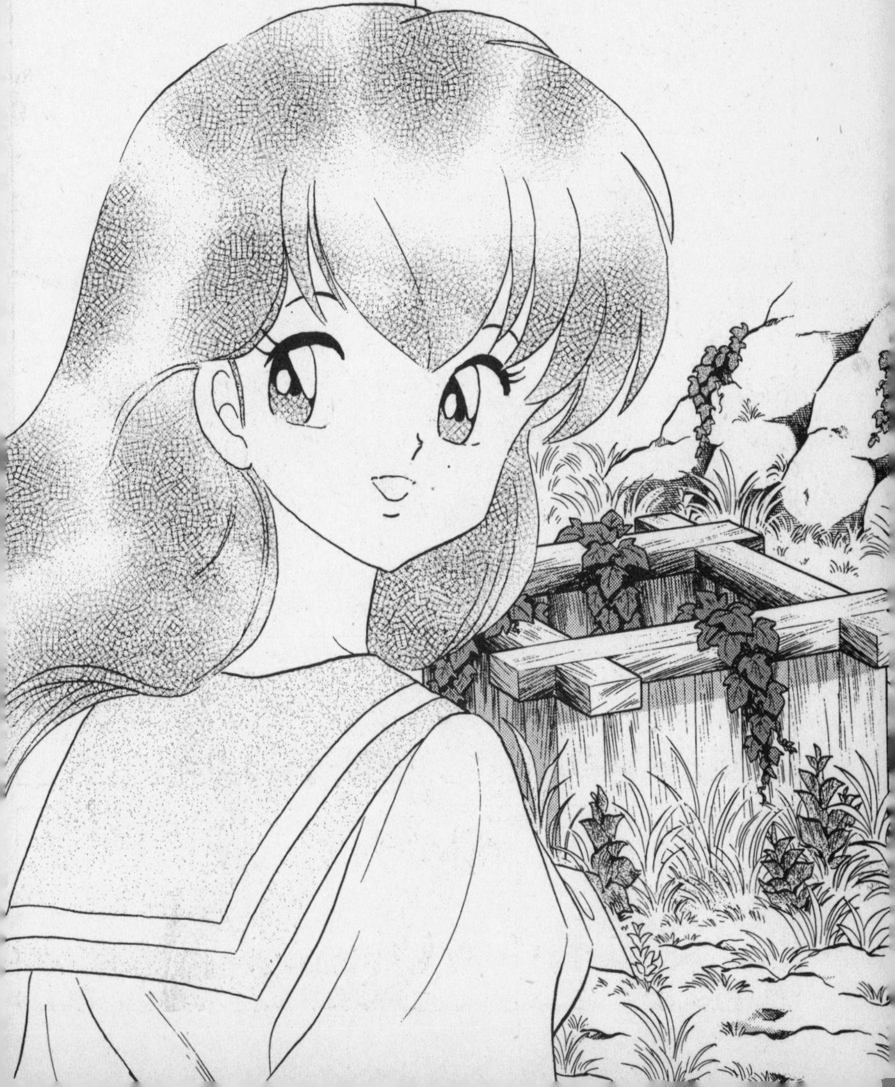

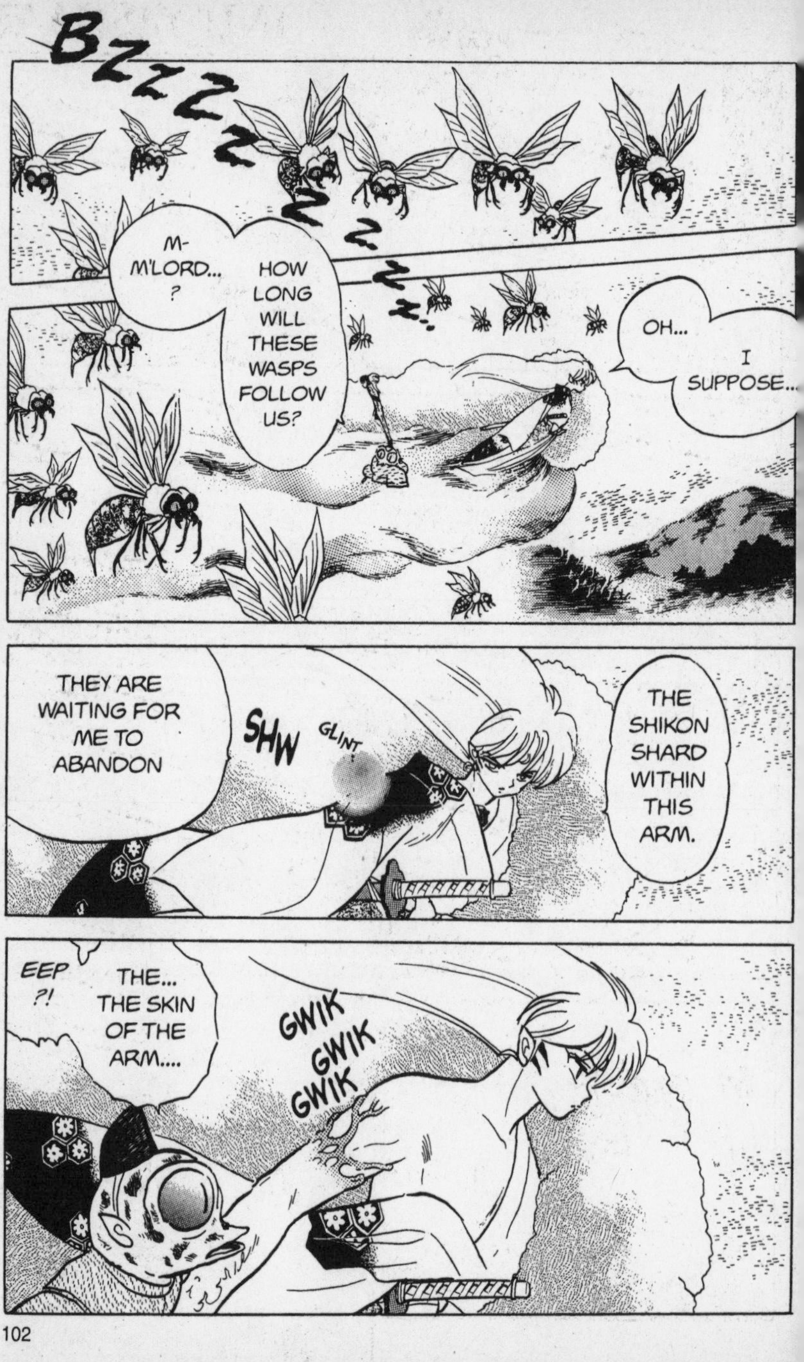
BZZZZZ
M-
M'LORD...
?
HOW
LONG
WILL
THESE
WASPS
FOLLOW
US?
ZZZZ...
OH...
I
SUPPOSE...
THEY ARE
WAITING FOR
ME TO
ABANDON
SHW
GLINT
THE
SHIKON
SHARD
WITHIN
THIS
ARM.
EEP
?!
THE...
THE SKIN
OF THE
ARM....
GWIK
GWIK
GWIK

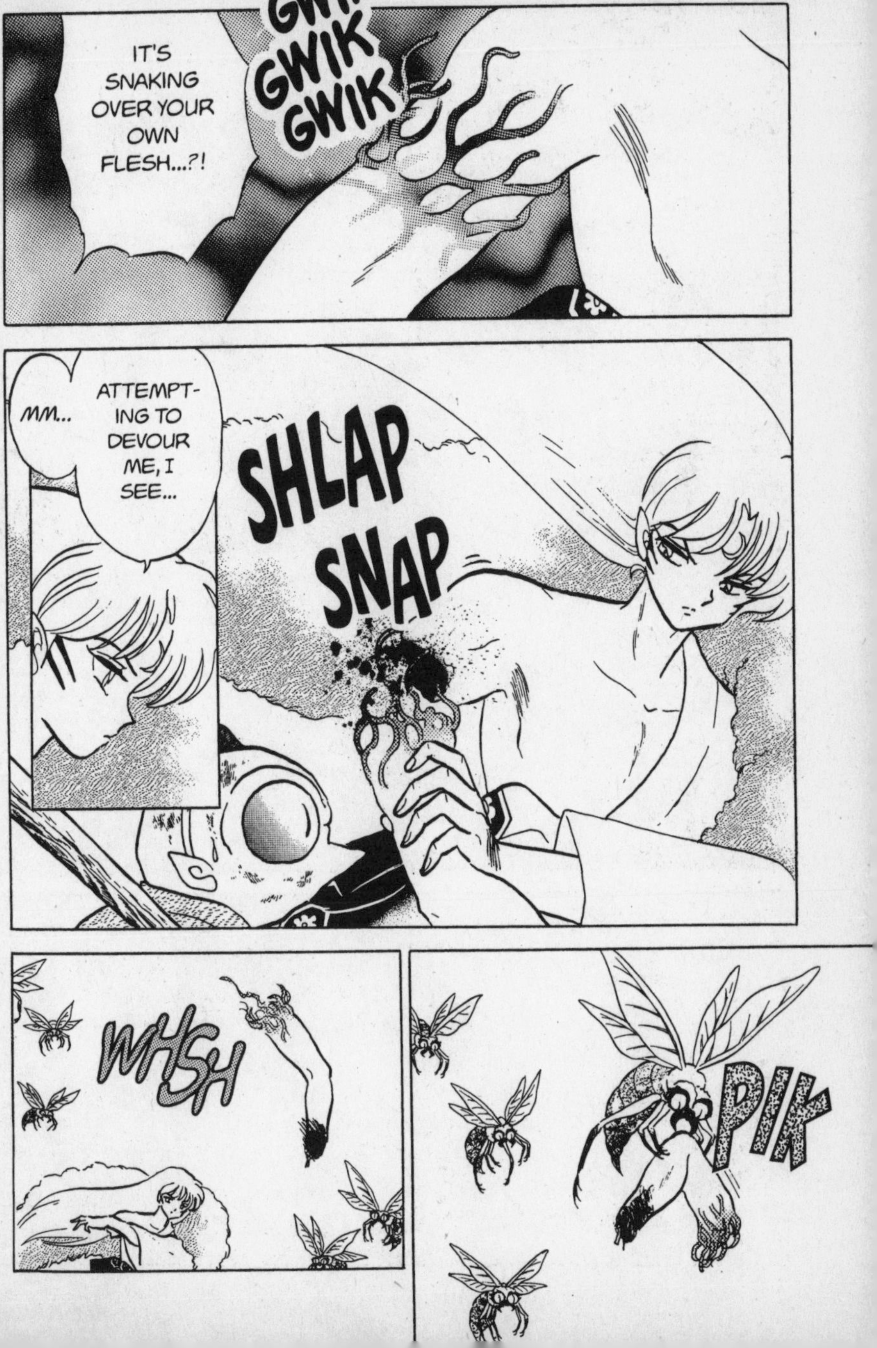
IT'S SNAKING OVER YOUR OWN FLESH...?!
GWIK GWIK GWIK
MM...
ATTEMPT-ING TO DEVOUR ME, I SEE...
SHLAP SNAP
WHSH
PIK

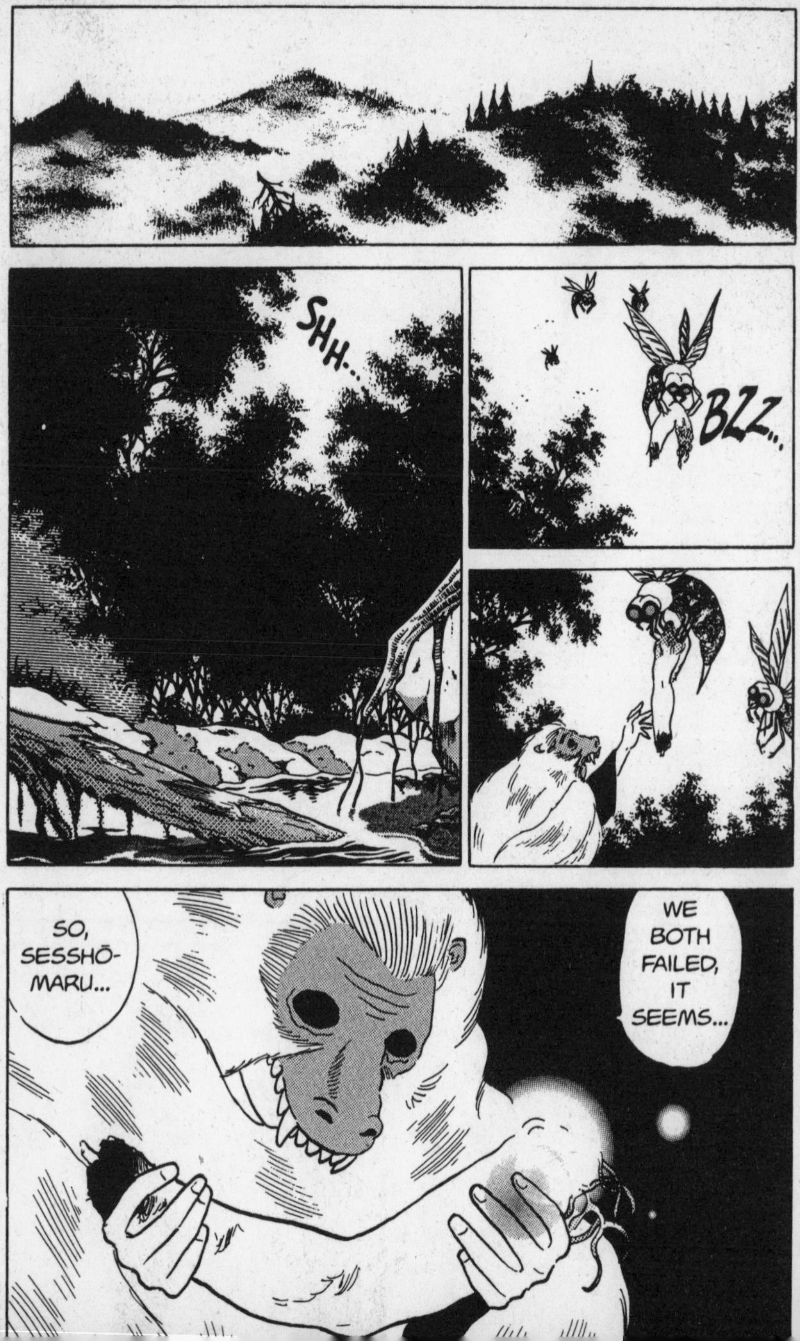
SHH...
BZZ...
SO, SESSHŌ-MARU...
WE BOTH FAILED, IT SEEMS...

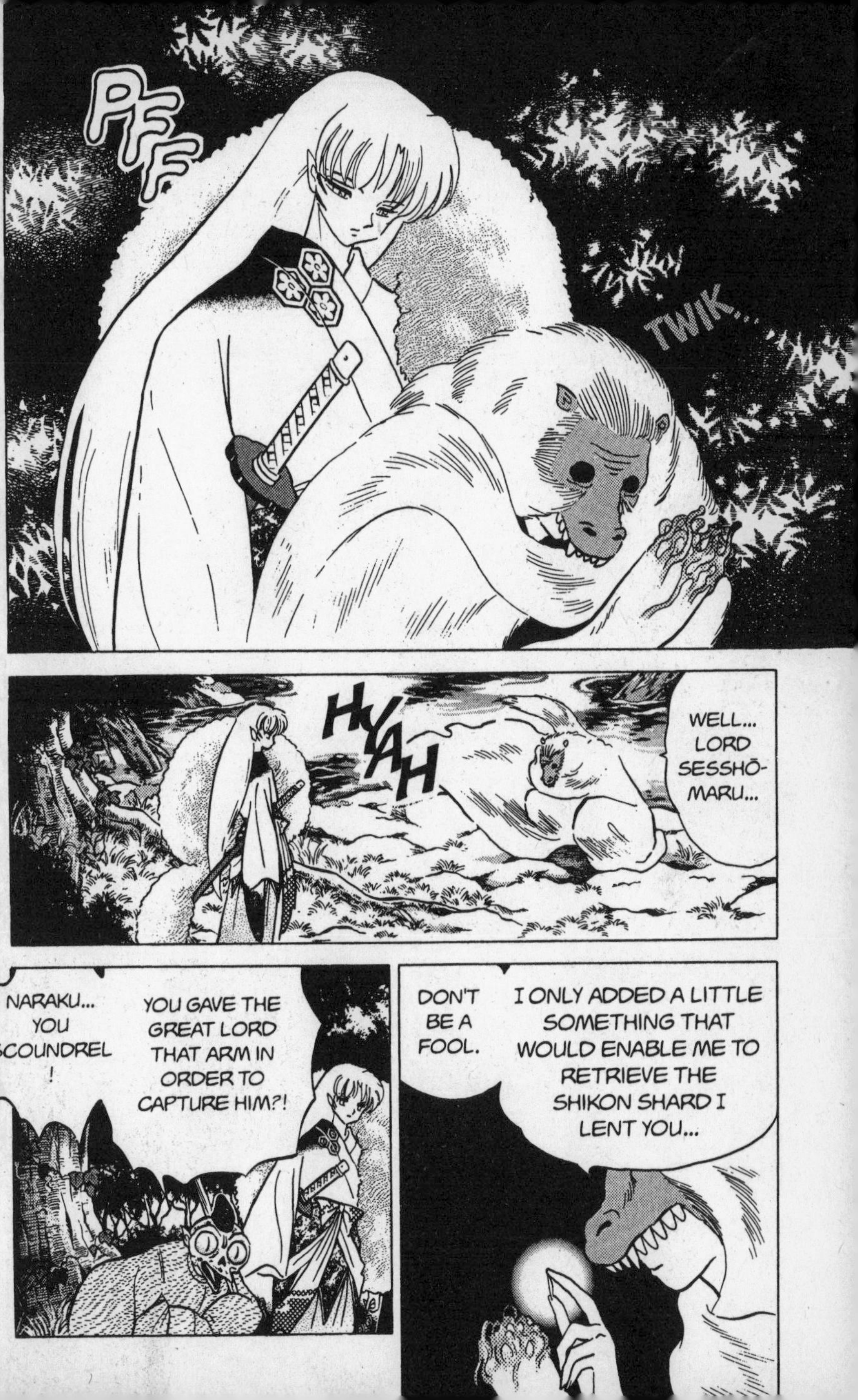
PFFF
TWIK...
HYAAH
WELL... LORD SESSHŌMARU...
NARAKU... YOU SCOUNDREL!
YOU GAVE THE GREAT LORD THAT ARM IN ORDER TO CAPTURE HIM?!
DON'T BE A FOOL.
I ONLY ADDED A LITTLE SOMETHING THAT WOULD ENABLE ME TO RETRIEVE THE SHIKON SHARD I LENT YOU...

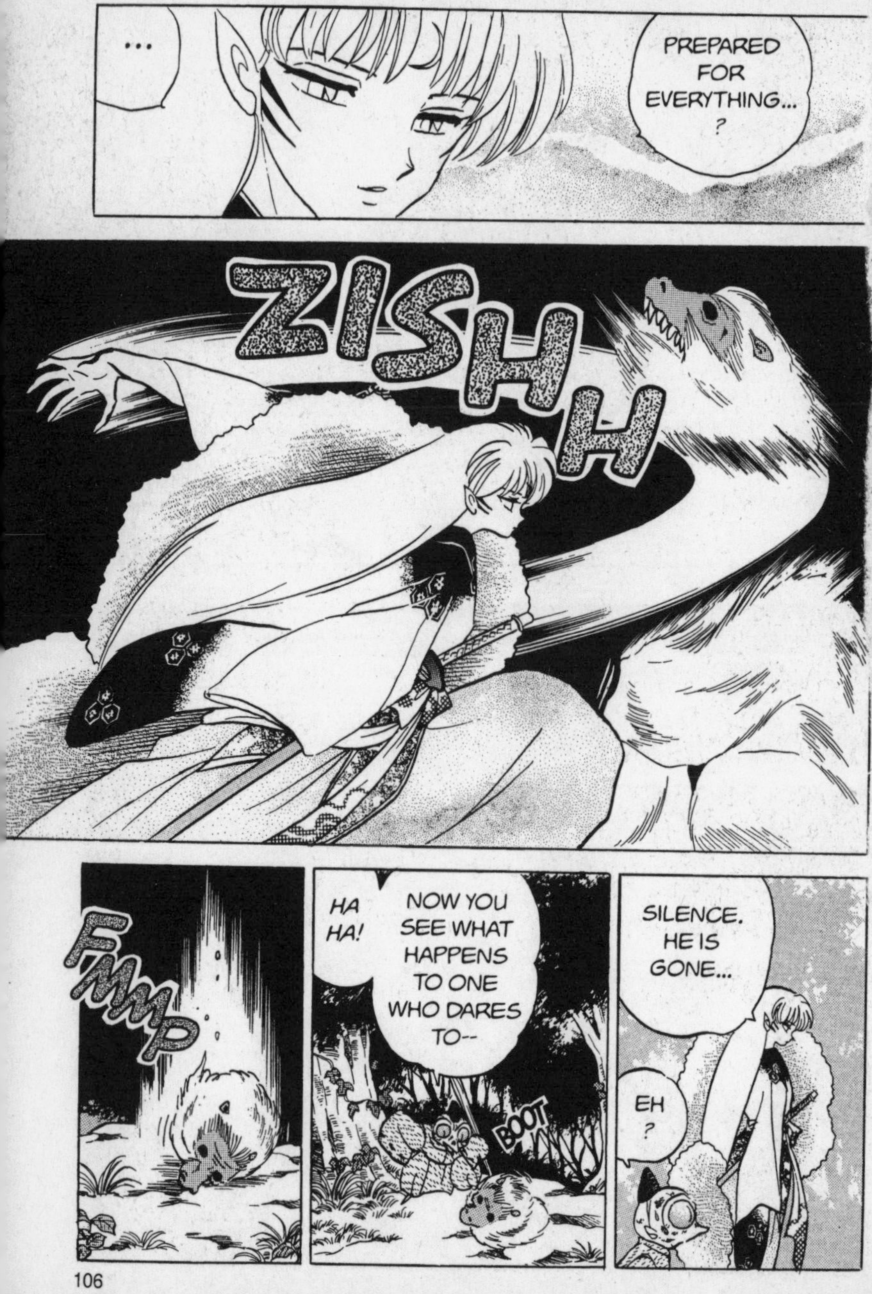
...
PREPARED FOR EVERYTHING... ?
ZISHHH
FMMP
HA HA!
NOW YOU SEE WHAT HAPPENS TO ONE WHO DARES TO--
BOOT
SILENCE. HE IS GONE...
EH ?

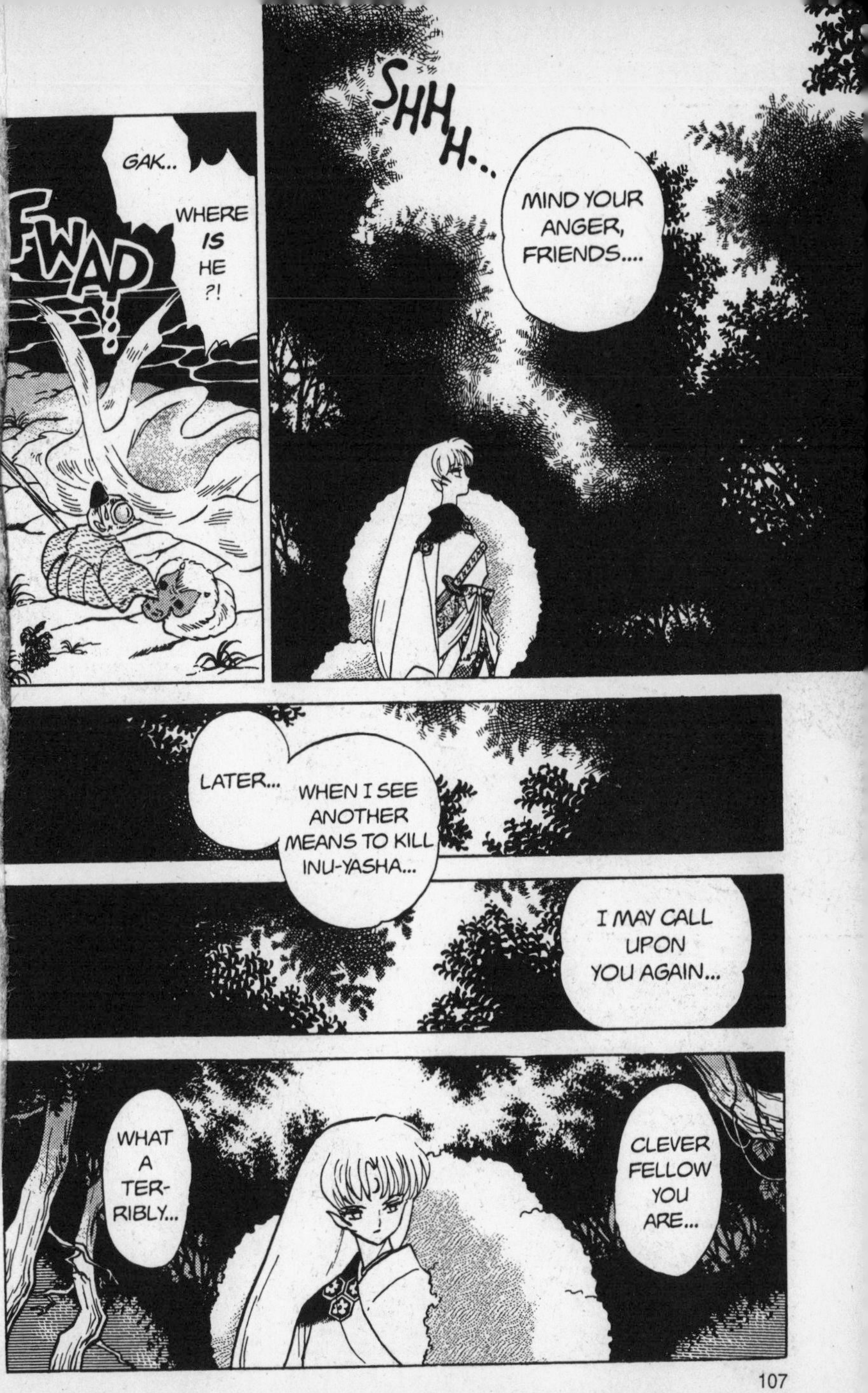

GAK...
FWAP
WHERE IS HE ?!
SHHH...
MIND YOUR ANGER, FRIENDS....
LATER...
WHEN I SEE ANOTHER MEANS TO KILL INU-YASHA...
I MAY CALL UPON YOU AGAIN...
WHAT A TER-RIBLY...
CLEVER FELLOW YOU ARE...

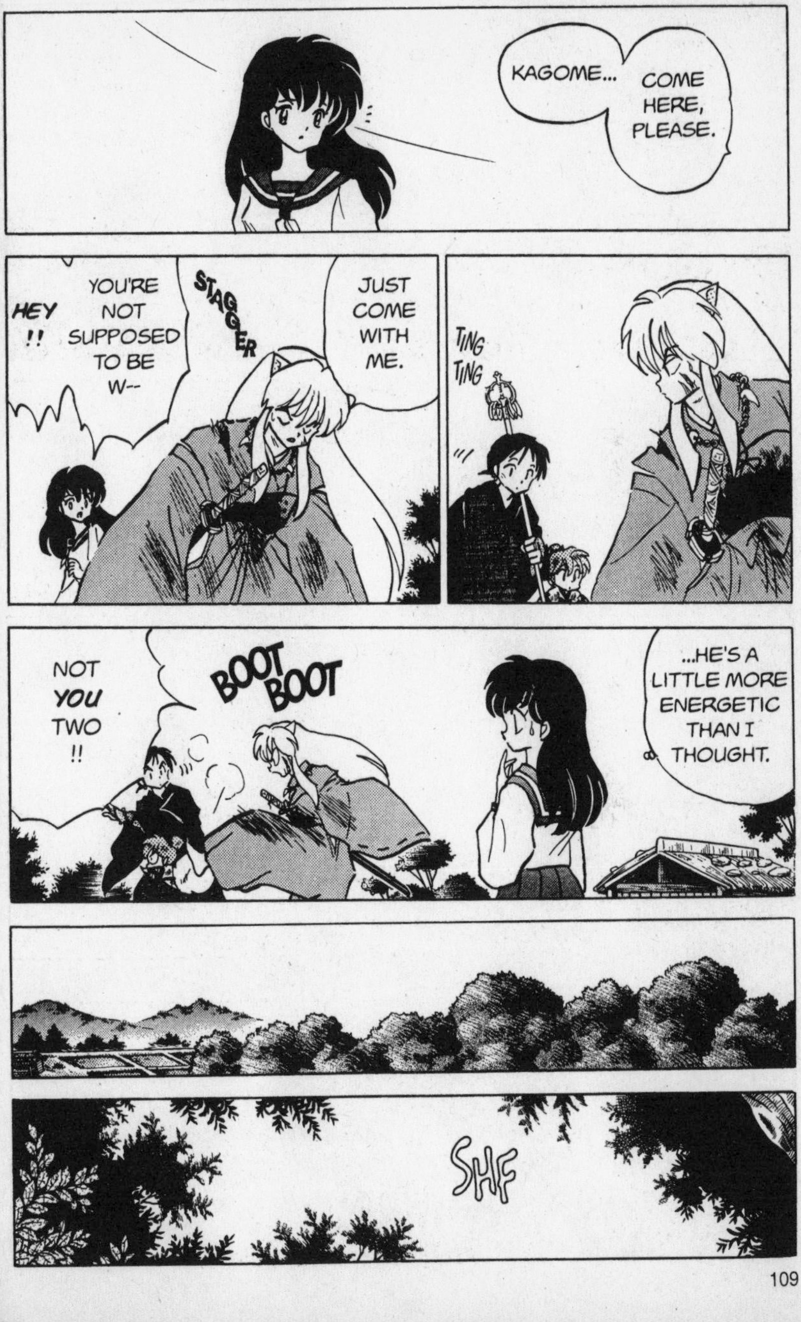
KAGOME...
COME HERE, PLEASE.
HEY !!
YOU'RE NOT SUPPOSED TO BE W--
STAGGER
JUST COME WITH ME.
TING TING
NOT YOU TWO !!
BOOT BOOT
...HE'S A LITTLE MORE ENERGETIC THAN I THOUGHT.
SHF

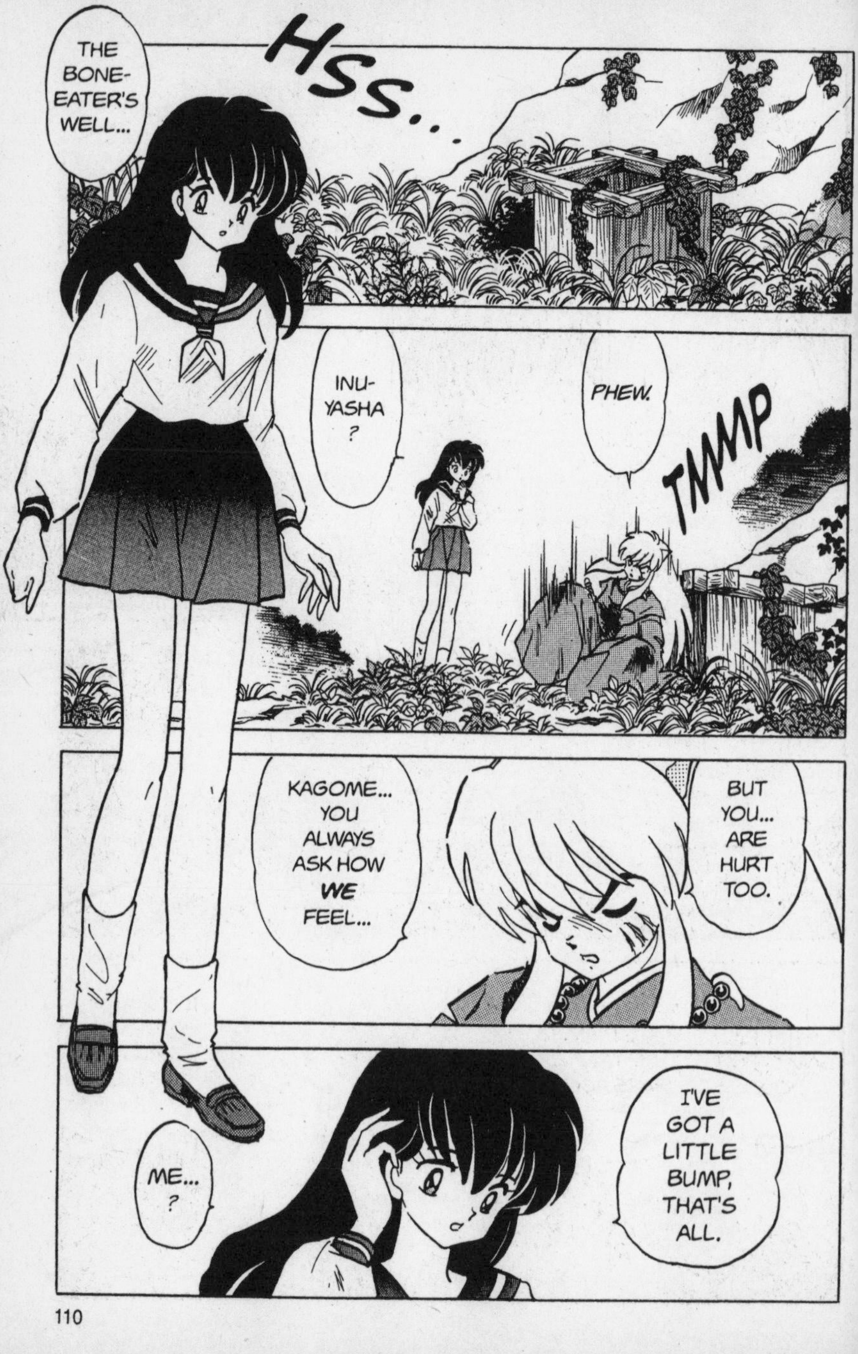
THE BONE-EATER'S WELL...
HSS...
INU-YASHA?
PHEW.
TMMP
KAGOME... YOU ALWAYS ASK HOW *WE* FEEL...
BUT YOU... ARE HURT TOO.
ME...?
I'VE GOT A LITTLE BUMP, THAT'S ALL.

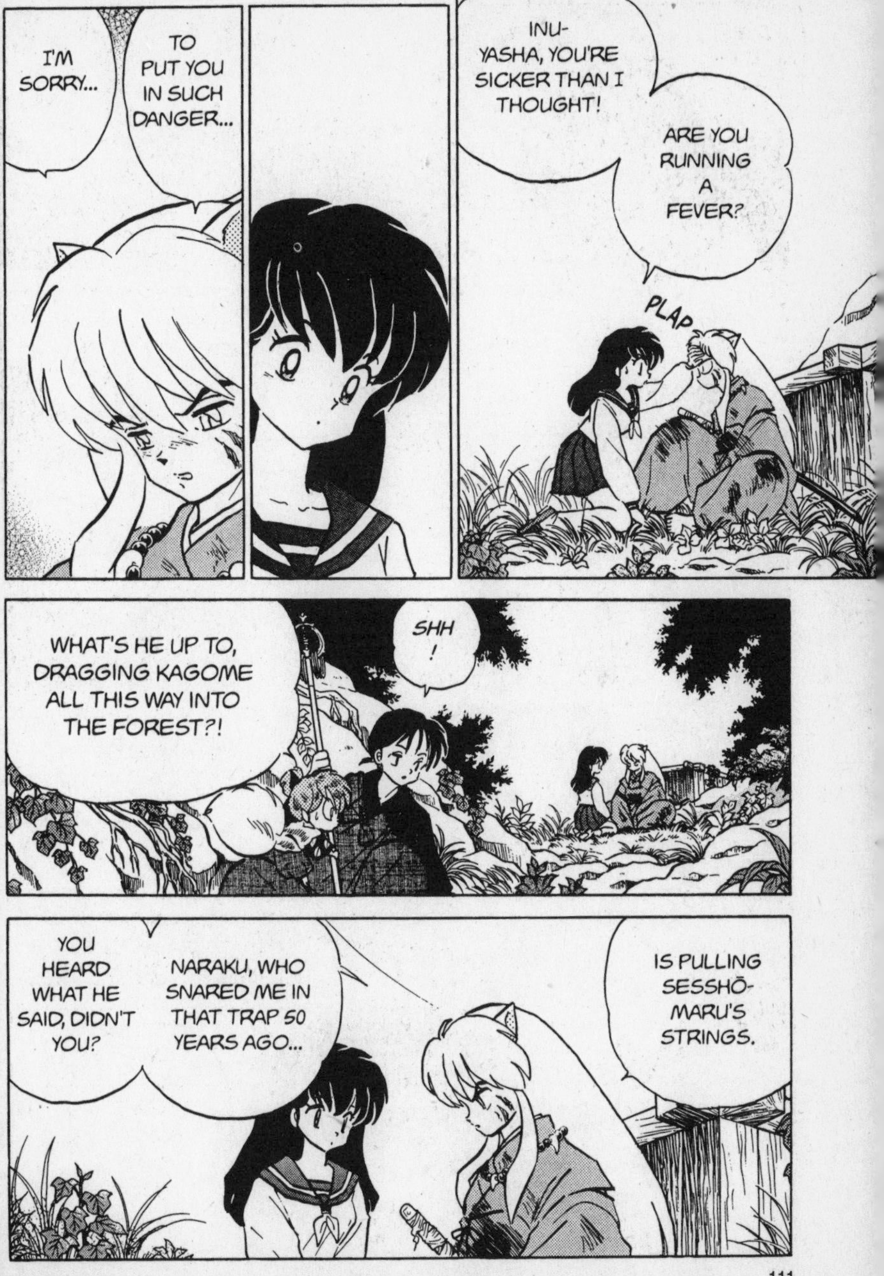
I'M SORRY...
TO PUT YOU IN SUCH DANGER...
INU-YASHA, YOU'RE SICKER THAN I THOUGHT!
ARE YOU RUNNING A FEVER?
PLAP
WHAT'S HE UP TO, DRAGGING KAGOME ALL THIS WAY INTO THE FOREST?!
SHH!
YOU HEARD WHAT HE SAID, DIDN'T YOU?
NARAKU, WHO SNARED ME IN THAT TRAP 50 YEARS AGO...
IS PULLING SESSHŌ-MARU'S STRINGS.

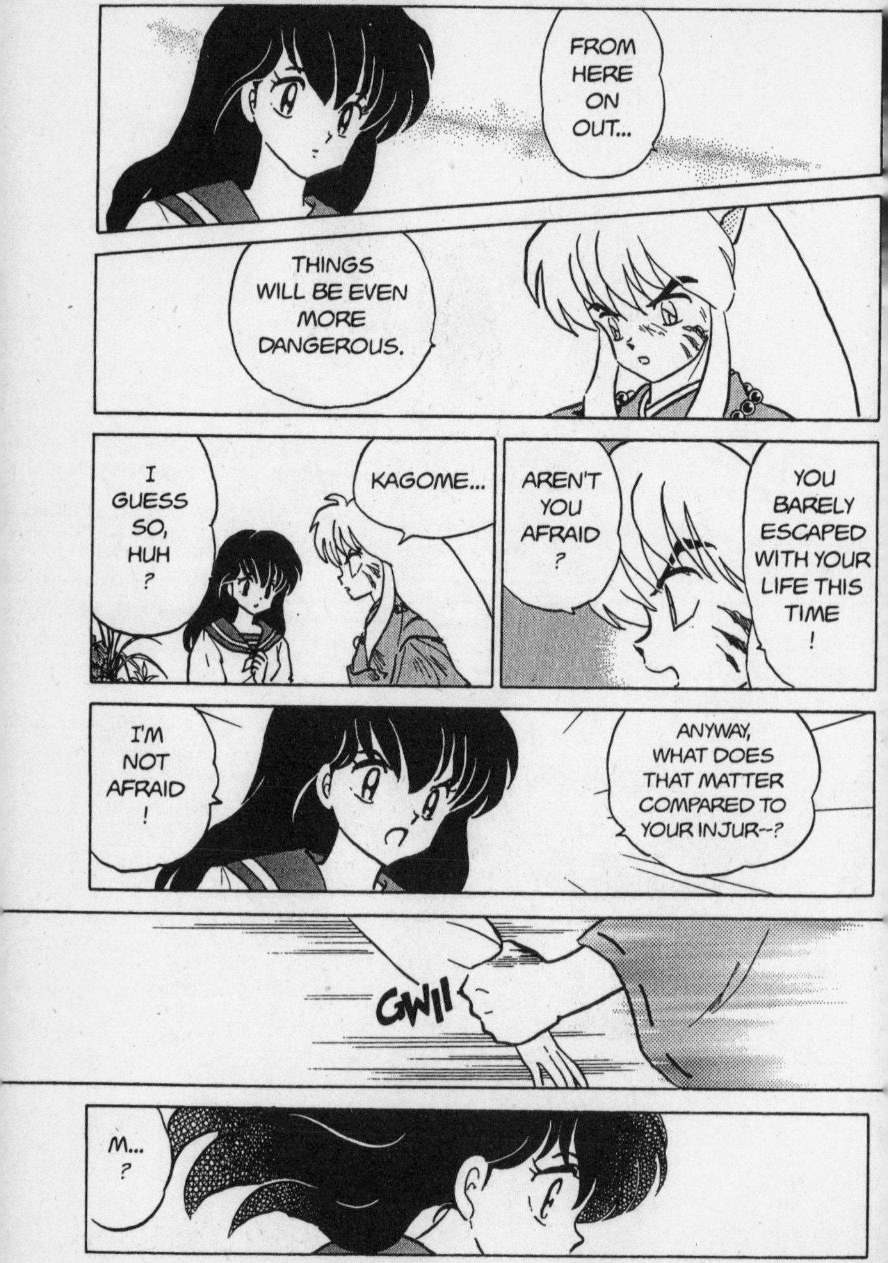
FROM HERE ON OUT...
THINGS WILL BE EVEN MORE DANGEROUS.
I GUESS SO, HUH?
KAGOME...
AREN'T YOU AFRAID?
YOU BARELY ESCAPED WITH YOUR LIFE THIS TIME!
I'M NOT AFRAID!
ANYWAY, WHAT DOES THAT MATTER COMPARED TO YOUR INJUR--?
GWII
M...?

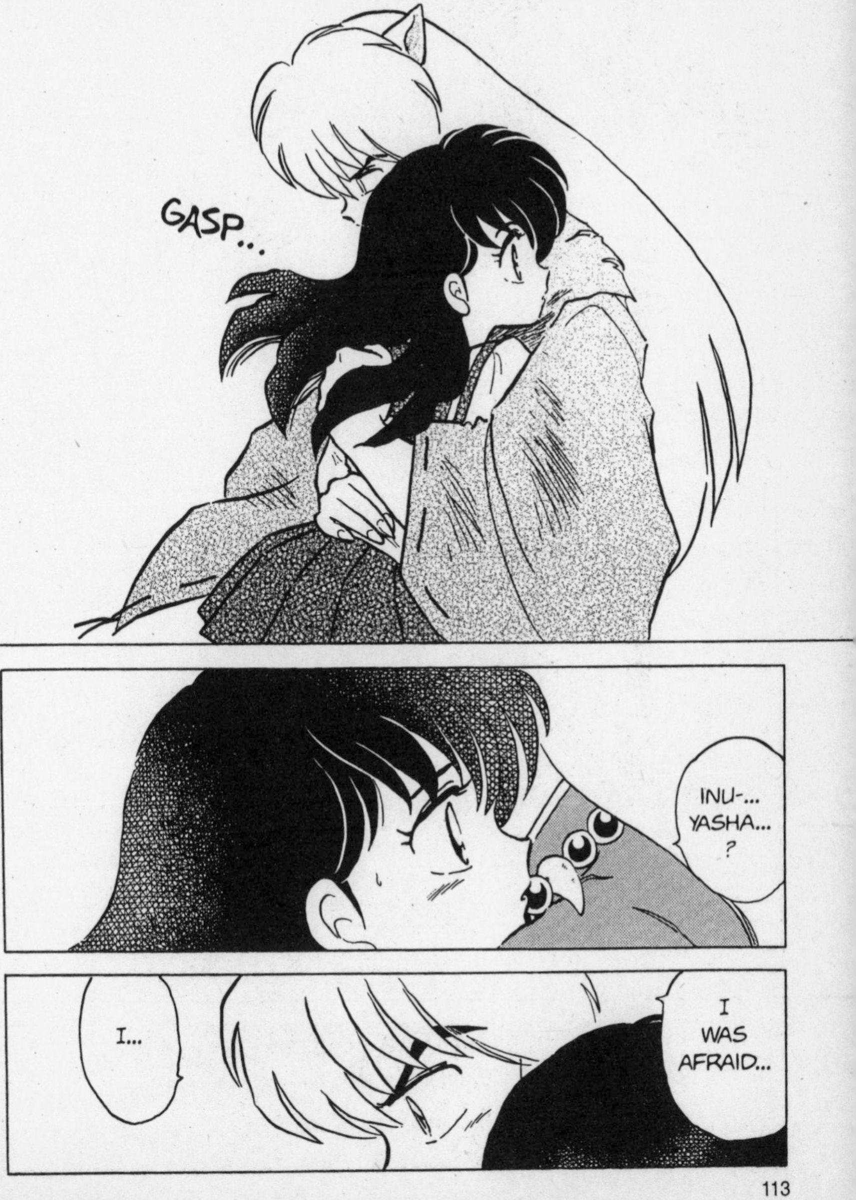
GASP...
INU-... YASHA... ?
I...
I WAS AFRAID...

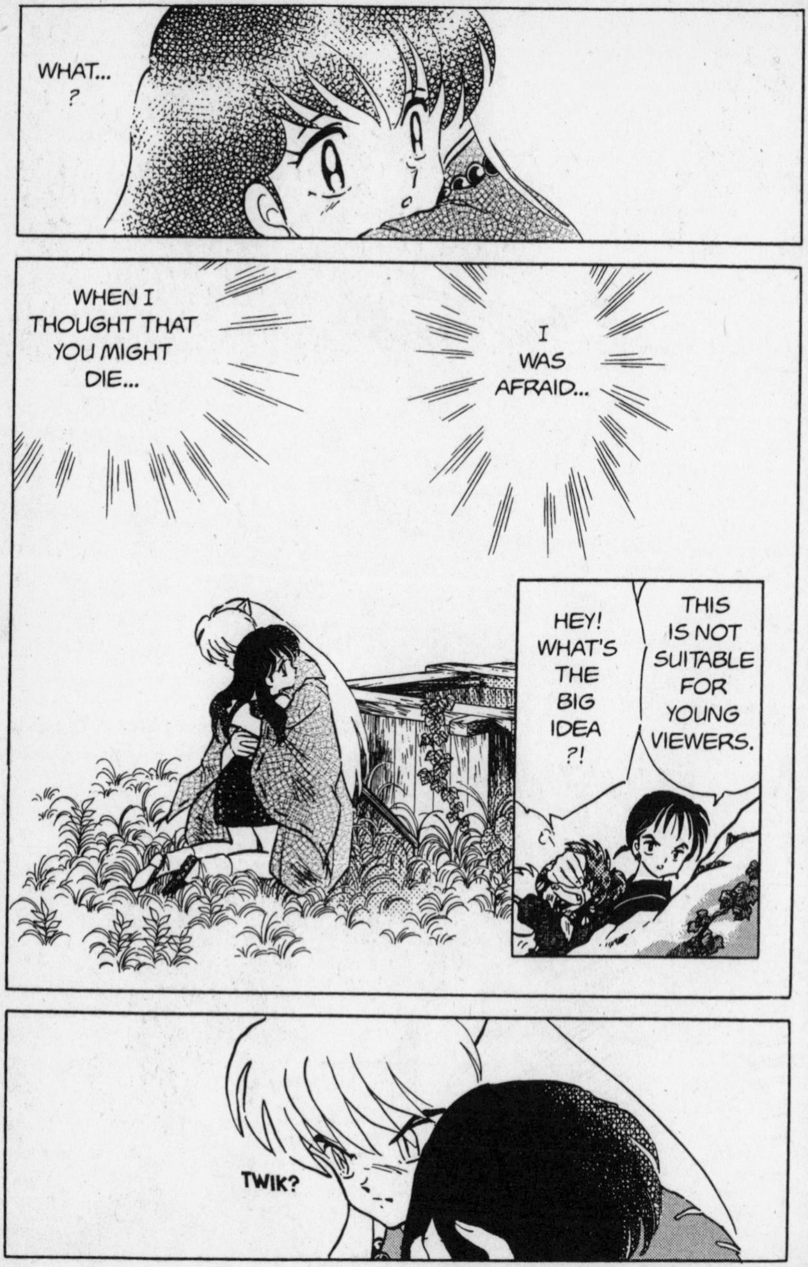
WHAT... ?
WHEN I THOUGHT THAT YOU MIGHT DIE...
I WAS AFRAID...
HEY! WHAT'S THE BIG IDEA ?!
THIS IS NOT SUITABLE FOR YOUNG VIEWERS.
TWIK?

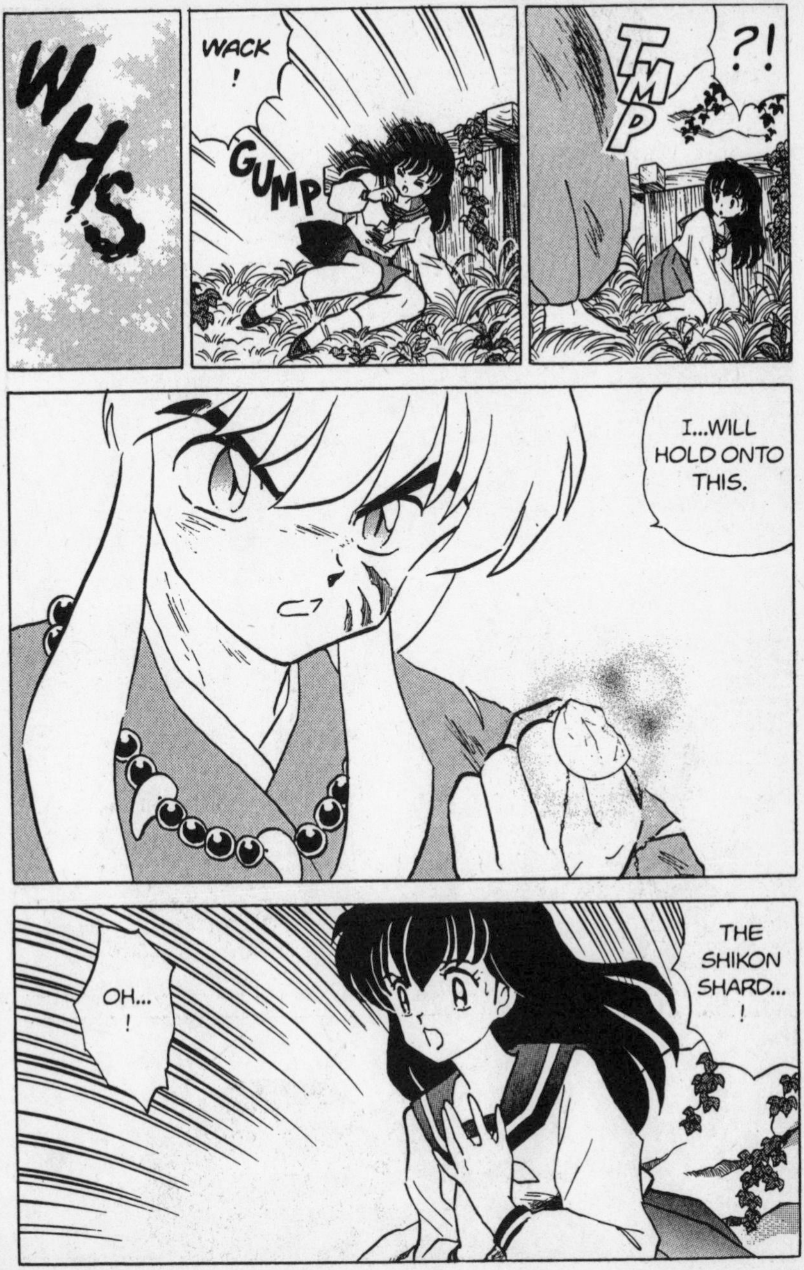
WHS
WACK !
GUMP
TMP
?!
I...WILL HOLD ONTO THIS.
OH... !
THE SHIKON SHARD... !

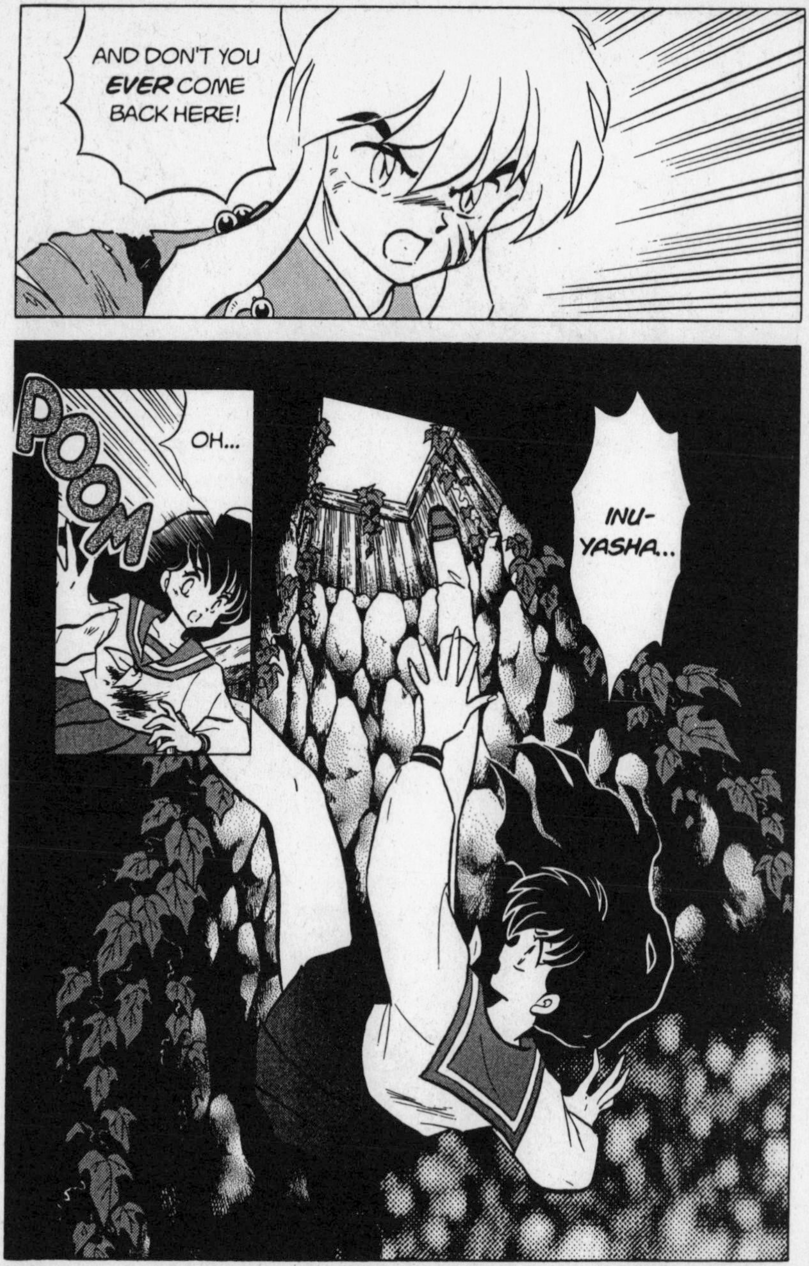
AND DON'T YOU EVER COME BACK HERE!
POOM
OH...
INU-YASHA...

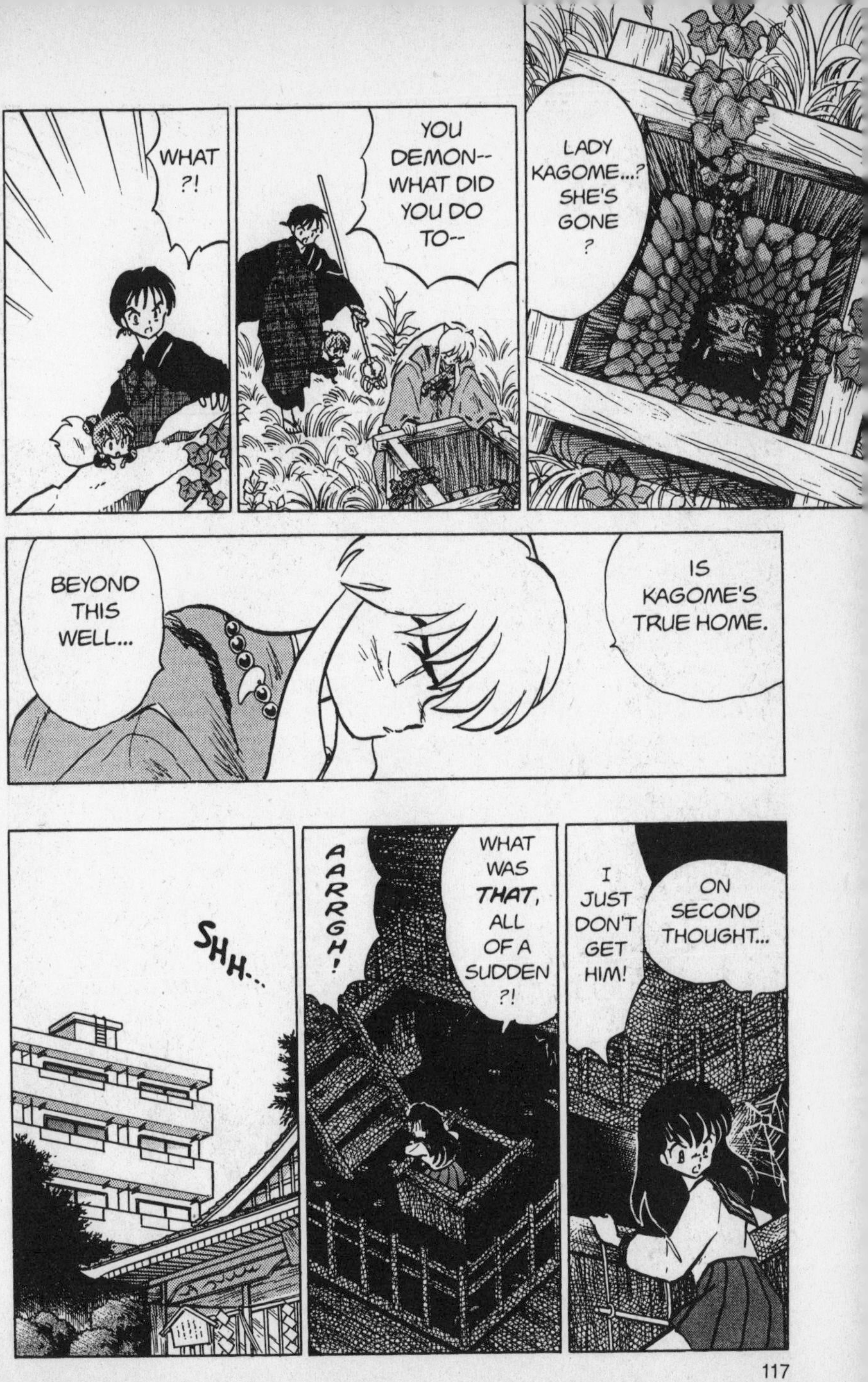
WHAT ?!
YOU DEMON-- WHAT DID YOU DO TO--
LADY KAGOME...? SHE'S GONE ?
BEYOND THIS WELL...
IS KAGOME'S TRUE HOME.
SHH...
AARRGH!
WHAT WAS *THAT*, ALL OF A SUDDEN ?!
I JUST DON'T GET HIM!
ON SECOND THOUGHT...

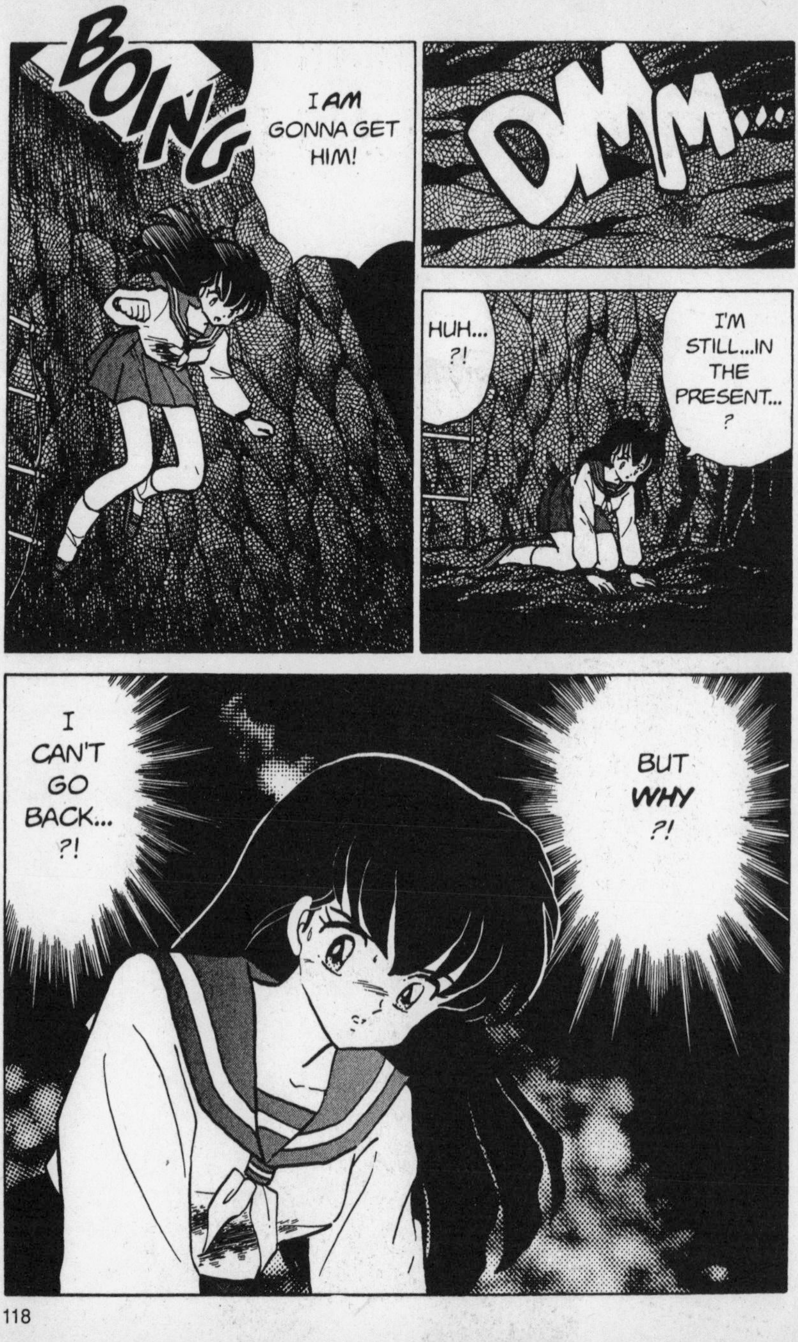
BOING
I AM GONNA GET HIM!
DMM...
HUH... ?!
I'M STILL...IN THE PRESENT... ?
I CAN'T GO BACK... ?!
BUT WHY ?!

SCROLL SEVEN

THE SPIDER'S LAIR

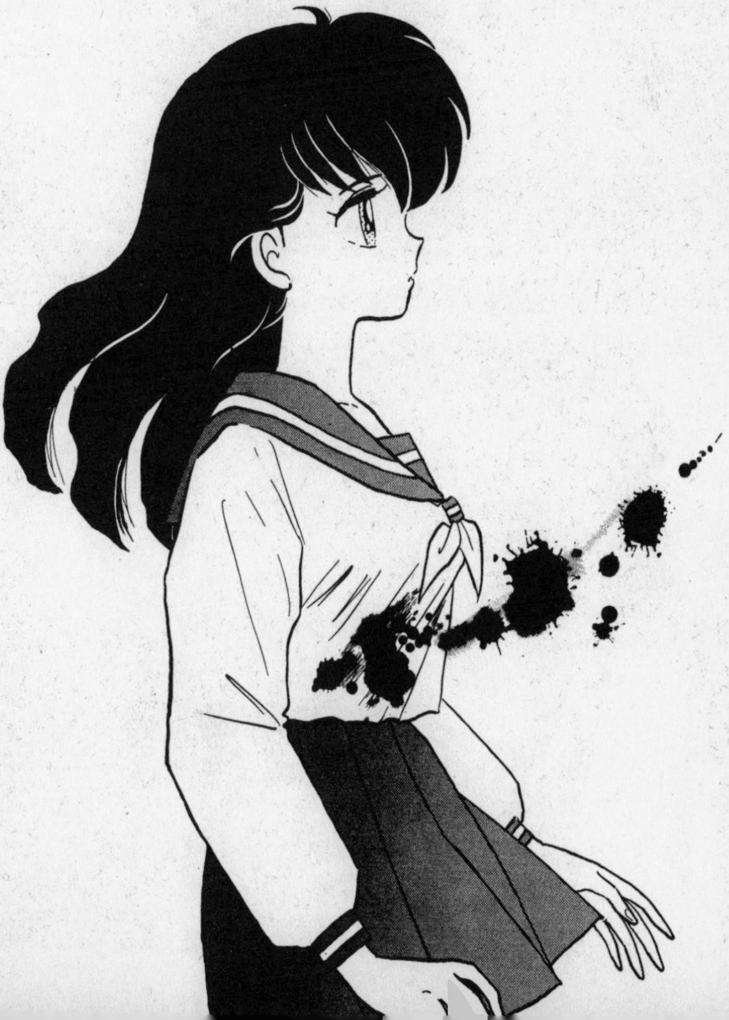

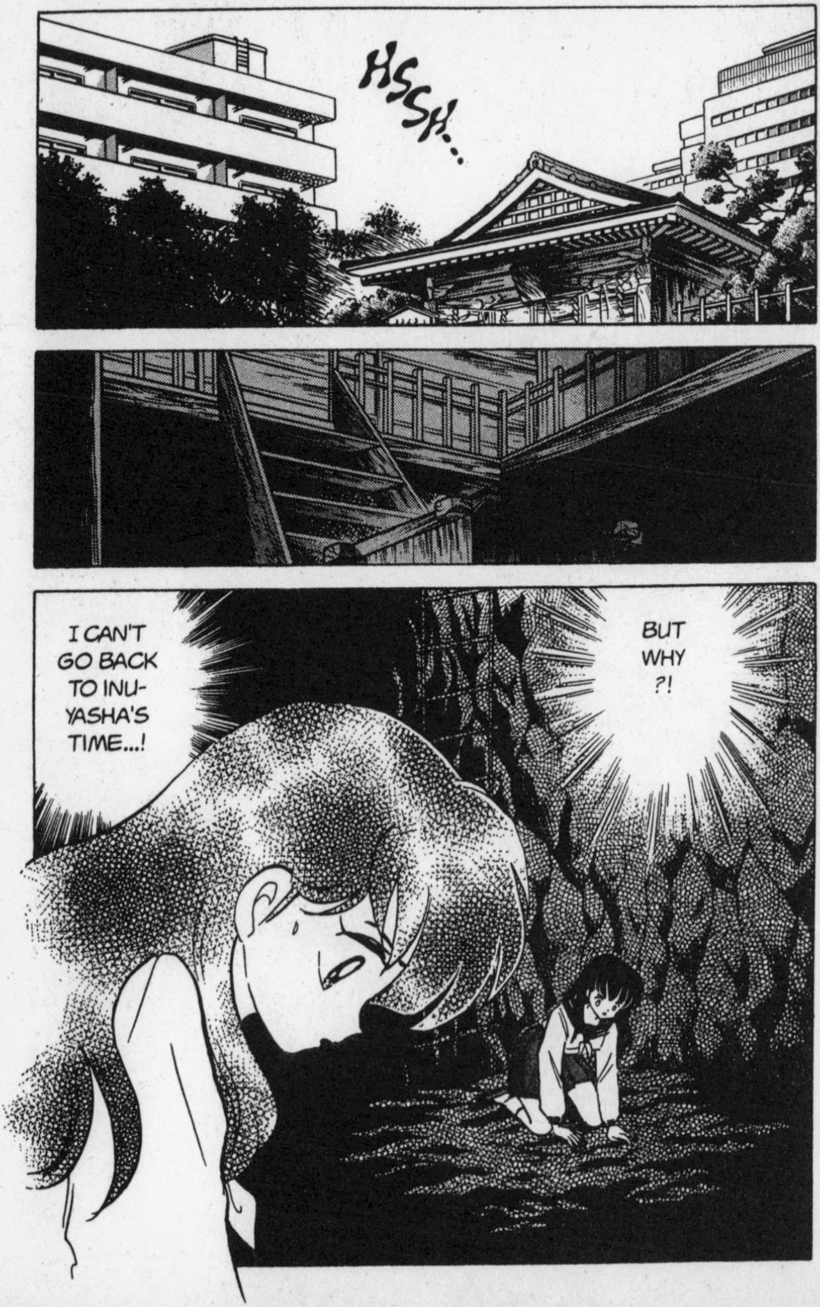
HSSH...
I CAN'T GO BACK TO INU-YASHA'S TIME...!
BUT WHY ?!

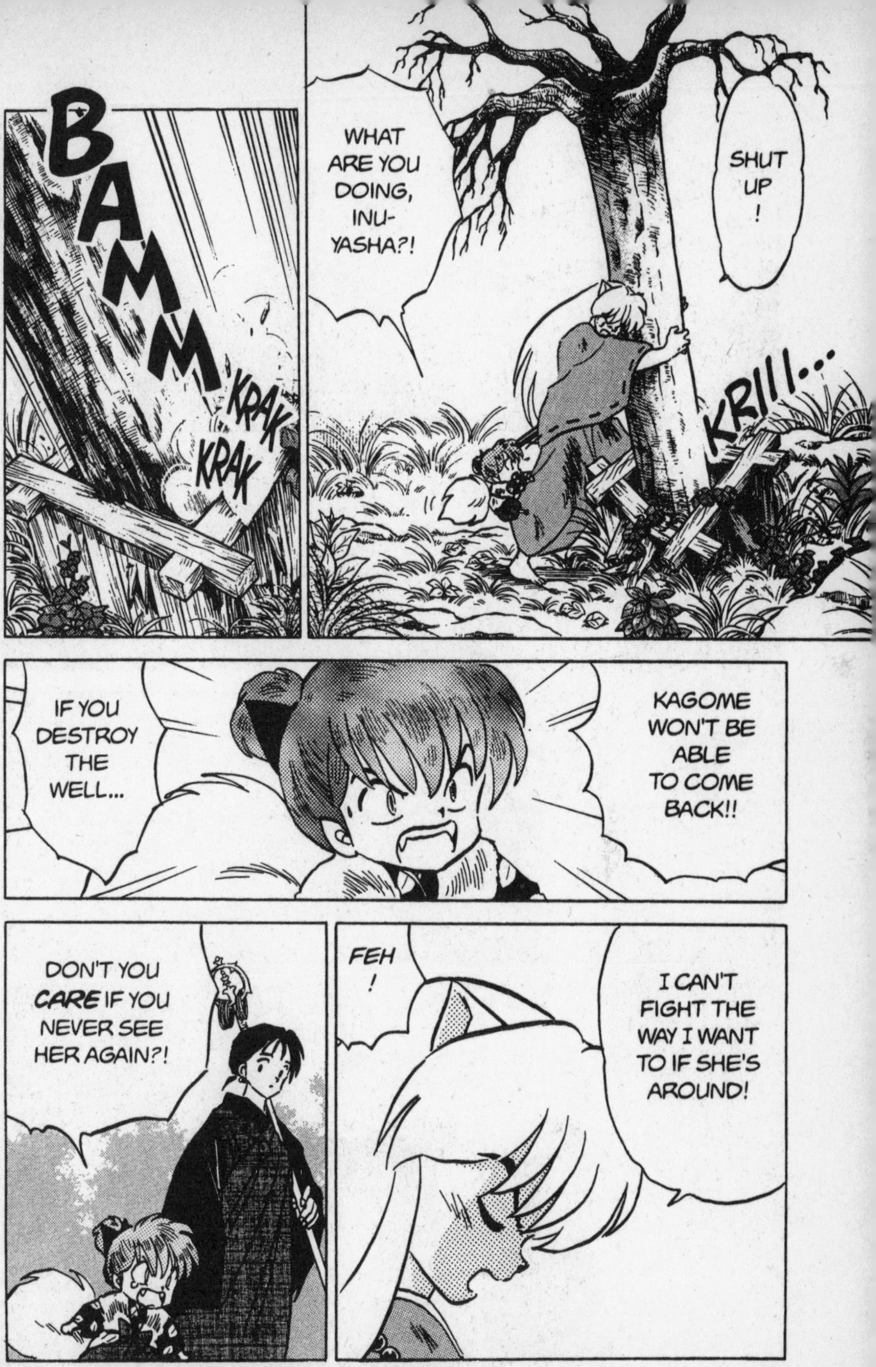
BAMM
KRAK
KRAK
WHAT ARE YOU DOING, INU-YASHA?!
SHUT UP!
KRIII...
IF YOU DESTROY THE WELL...
KAGOME WON'T BE ABLE TO COME BACK!!
DON'T YOU *CARE* IF YOU NEVER SEE HER AGAIN?!
FEH!
I CAN'T FIGHT THE WAY I WANT TO IF SHE'S AROUND!

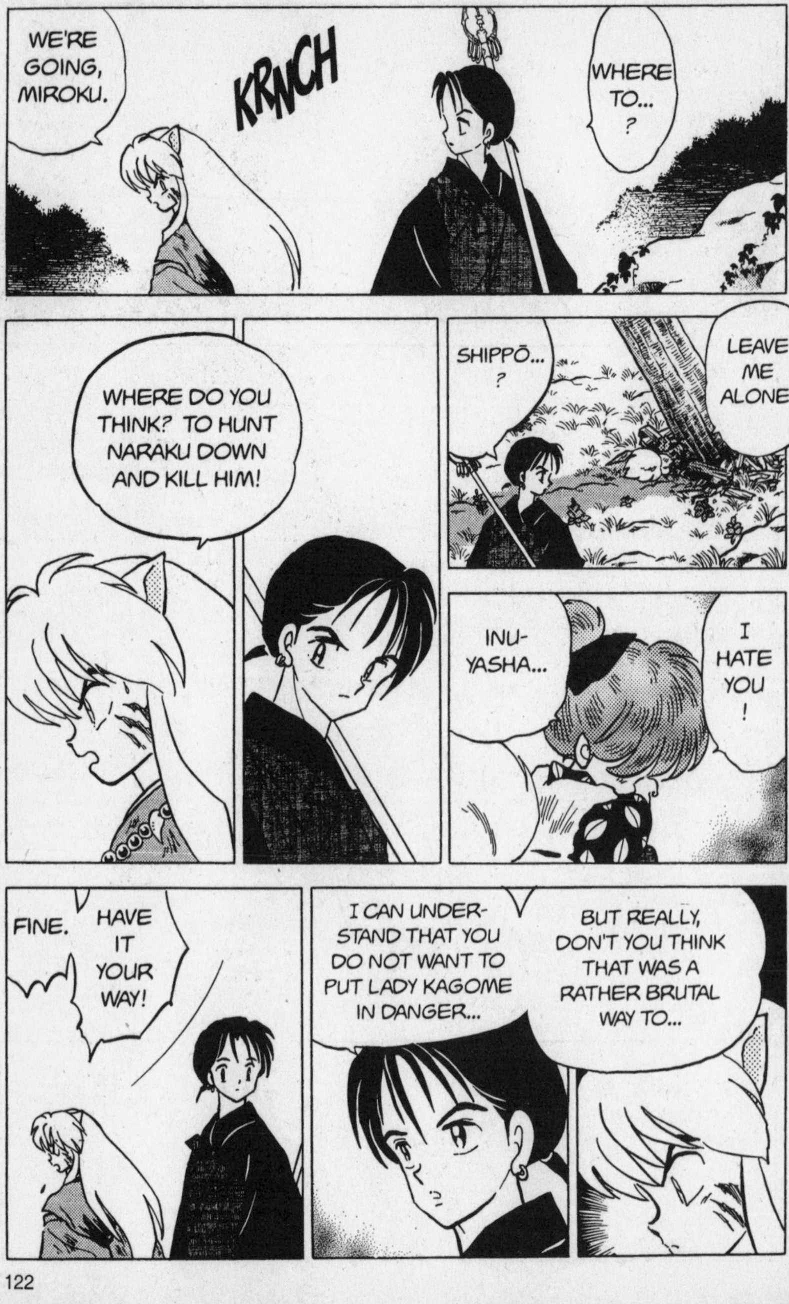
WE'RE GOING, MIROKU.
KRNCH
WHERE TO... ?
WHERE DO YOU THINK? TO HUNT NARAKU DOWN AND KILL HIM!
SHIPPŌ... ?
LEAVE ME ALONE.
INU-YASHA...
I HATE YOU !
FINE.
HAVE IT YOUR WAY!
I CAN UNDER-STAND THAT YOU DO NOT WANT TO PUT LADY KAGOME IN DANGER...
BUT REALLY, DON'T YOU THINK THAT WAS A RATHER BRUTAL WAY TO...

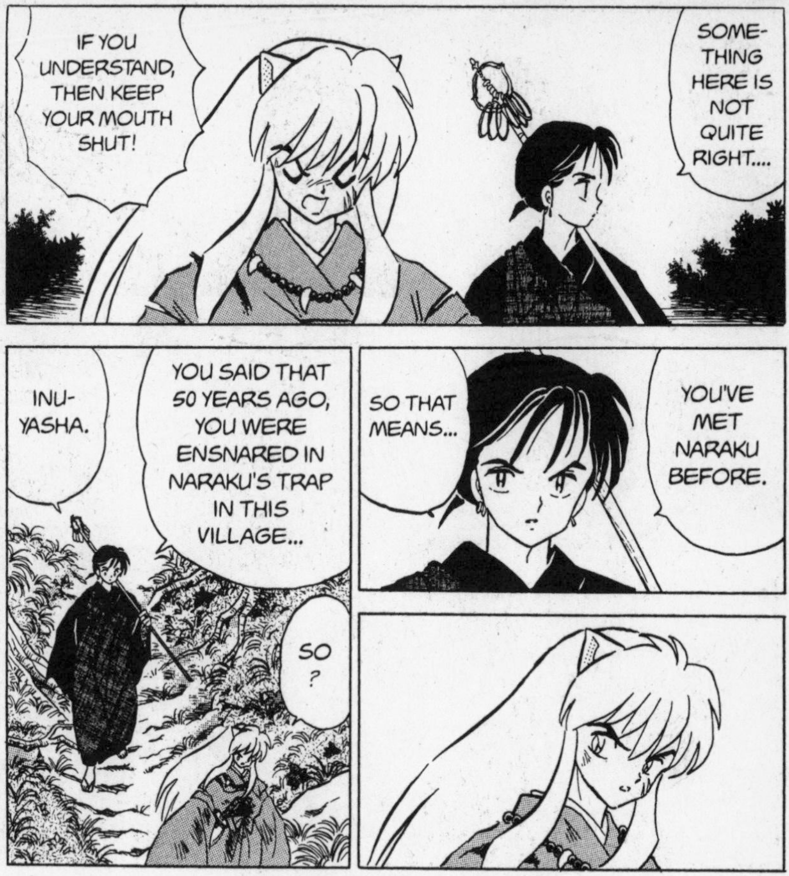
IF YOU UNDERSTAND, THEN KEEP YOUR MOUTH SHUT!
SOME-THING HERE IS NOT QUITE RIGHT....
INU-YASHA.
YOU SAID THAT 50 YEARS AGO, YOU WERE ENSNARED IN NARAKU'S TRAP IN THIS VILLAGE...
SO ?
SO THAT MEANS...
YOU'VE MET NARAKU BEFORE.
IF YOU WISH TO BE HUMAN, INU-YASHA...
USE THE SHIKON JEWEL.
TOMORROW, AT DAWN, TO THIS PLACE...
I WILL BRING THE SHIKON JEWEL.

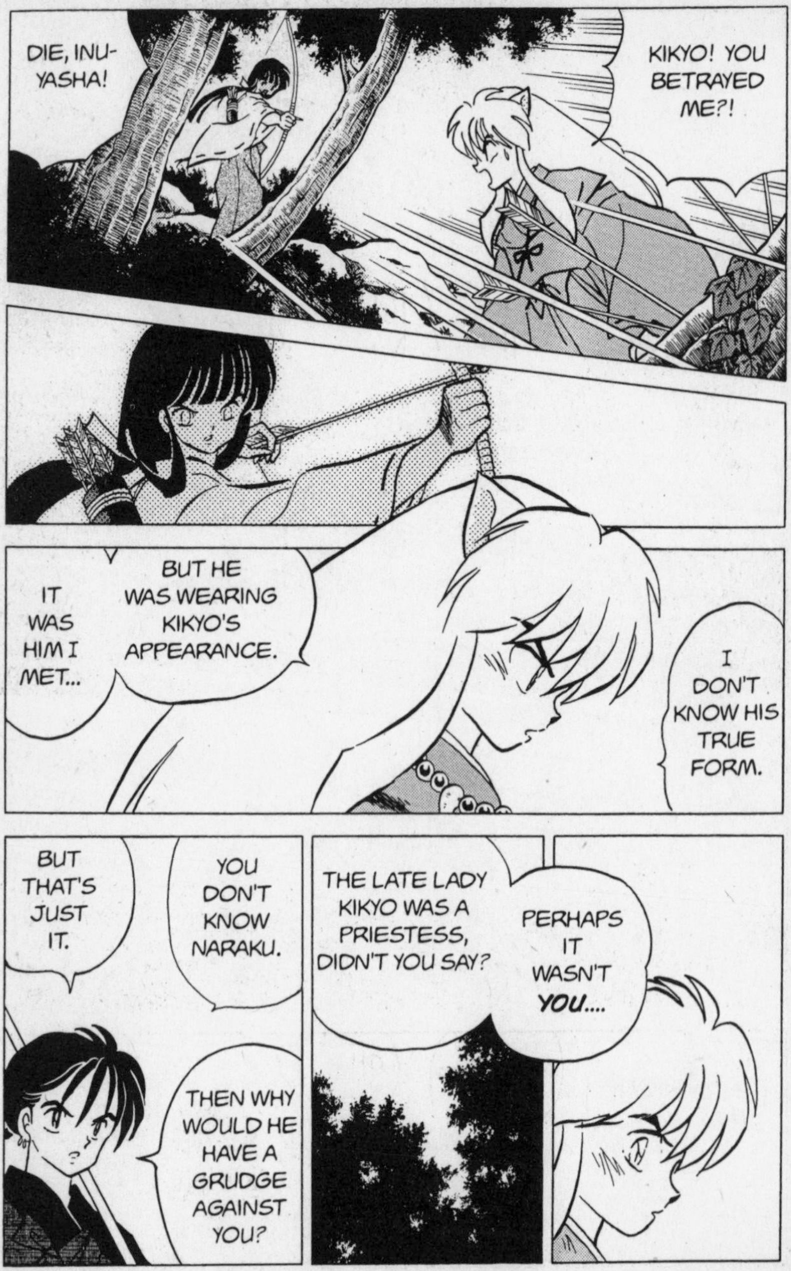
DIE, INU-YASHA!
KIKYO! YOU BETRAYED ME?!
IT WAS HIM I MET...
BUT HE WAS WEARING KIKYO'S APPEARANCE.
I DON'T KNOW HIS TRUE FORM.
BUT THAT'S JUST IT.
YOU DON'T KNOW NARAKU.
THEN WHY WOULD HE HAVE A GRUDGE AGAINST YOU?
THE LATE LADY KIKYO WAS A PRIESTESS, DIDN'T YOU SAY?
PERHAPS IT WASN'T ***YOU***....

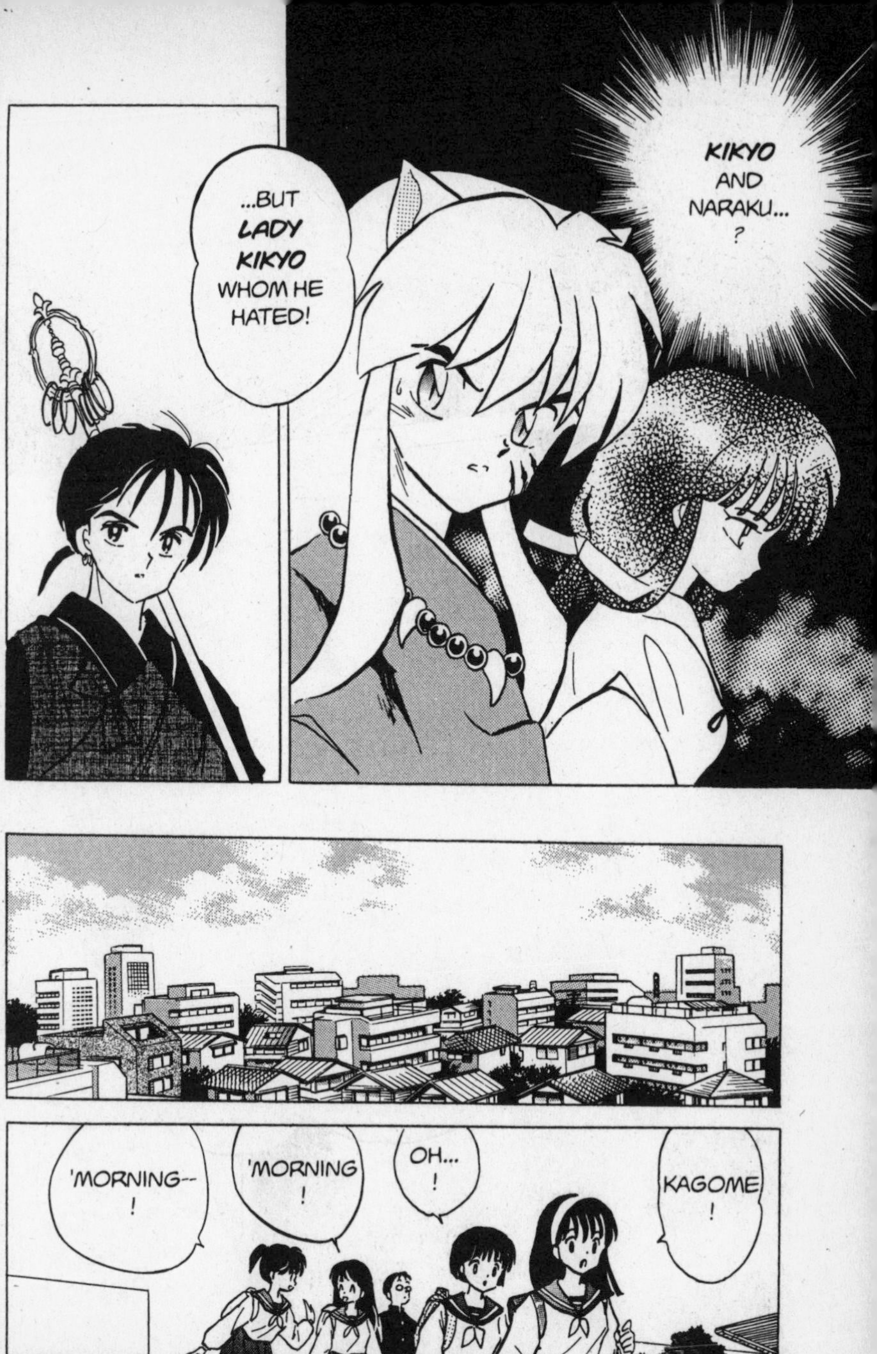
...BUT LADY KIKYO WHOM HE HATED!
KIKYO AND NARAKU...?
'MORNING--!
'MORNING!
OH...!
KAGOME!

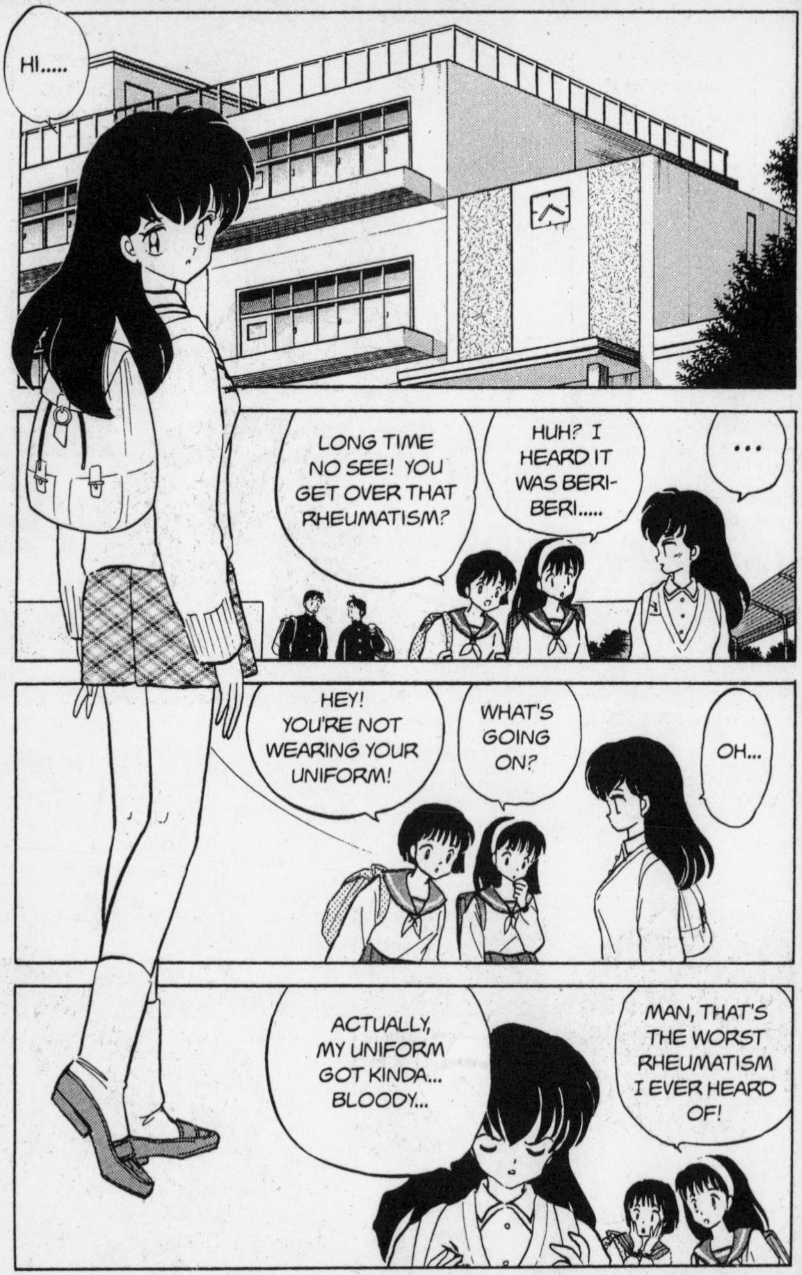
HI.....
LONG TIME NO SEE! YOU GET OVER THAT RHEUMATISM?
HUH? I HEARD IT WAS BERI-BERI.....
...
HEY! YOU'RE NOT WEARING YOUR UNIFORM!
WHAT'S GOING ON?
OH...
ACTUALLY, MY UNIFORM GOT KINDA... BLOODY...
MAN, THAT'S THE WORST RHEUMATISM I EVER HEARD OF!

INU-YASHA... HAD SOME PRETTY SERIOUS INJURIES.

HE... HADN'T STOPPED BLEEDING YET WHEN...

I WAS SO WORRIED ABOUT HIM...

BUT WHY....

WHY DID HE HOLD ME LIKE THAT...?

I...WILL HOLD ONTO THIS.

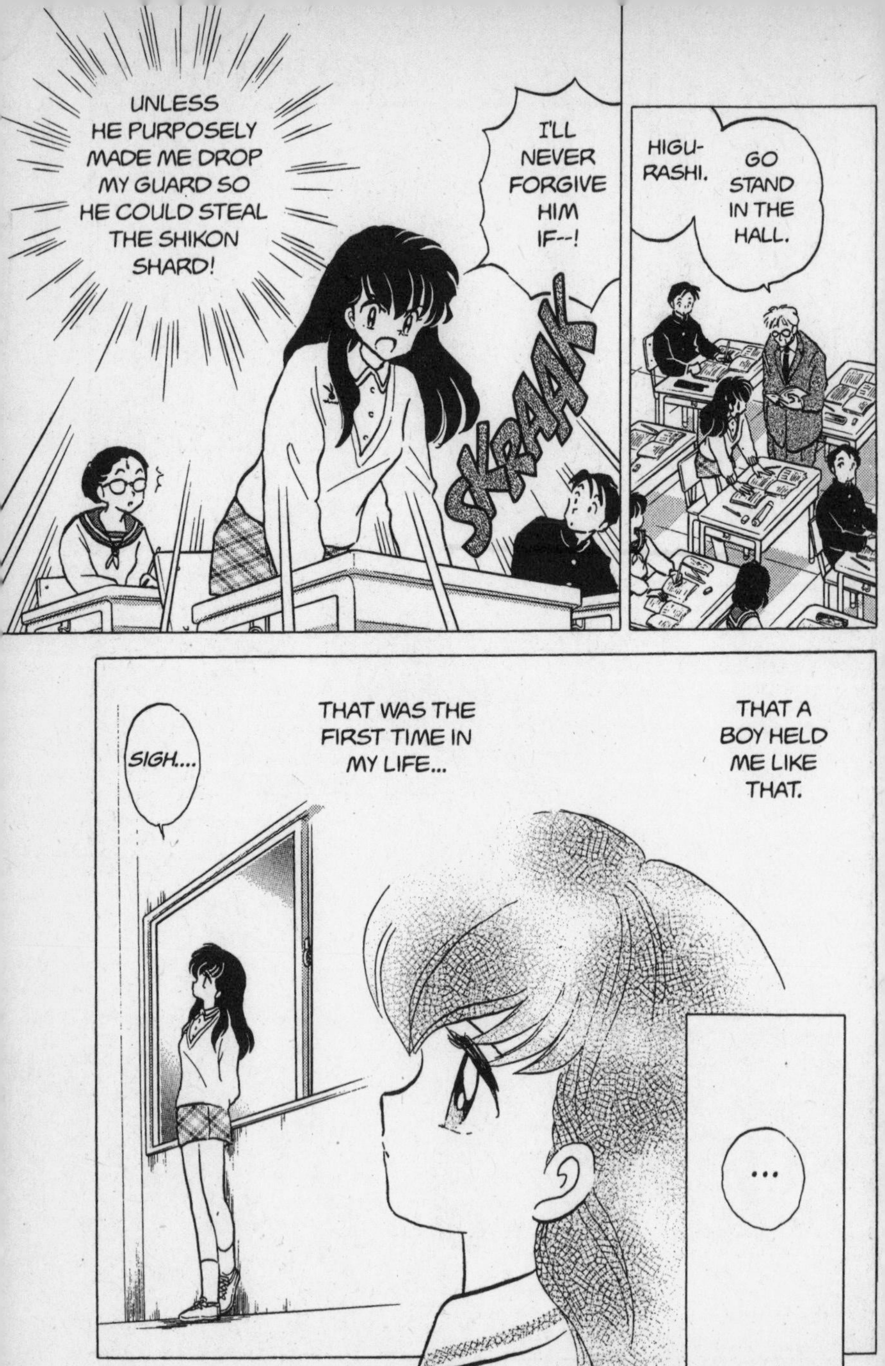
UNLESS HE PURPOSELY MADE ME DROP MY GUARD SO HE COULD STEAL THE SHIKON SHARD!
I'LL NEVER FORGIVE HIM IF--!
SKRAAK
HIGU-RASHI.
GO STAND IN THE HALL.
SIGH....
THAT WAS THE FIRST TIME IN MY LIFE...
THAT A BOY HELD ME LIKE THAT.
...

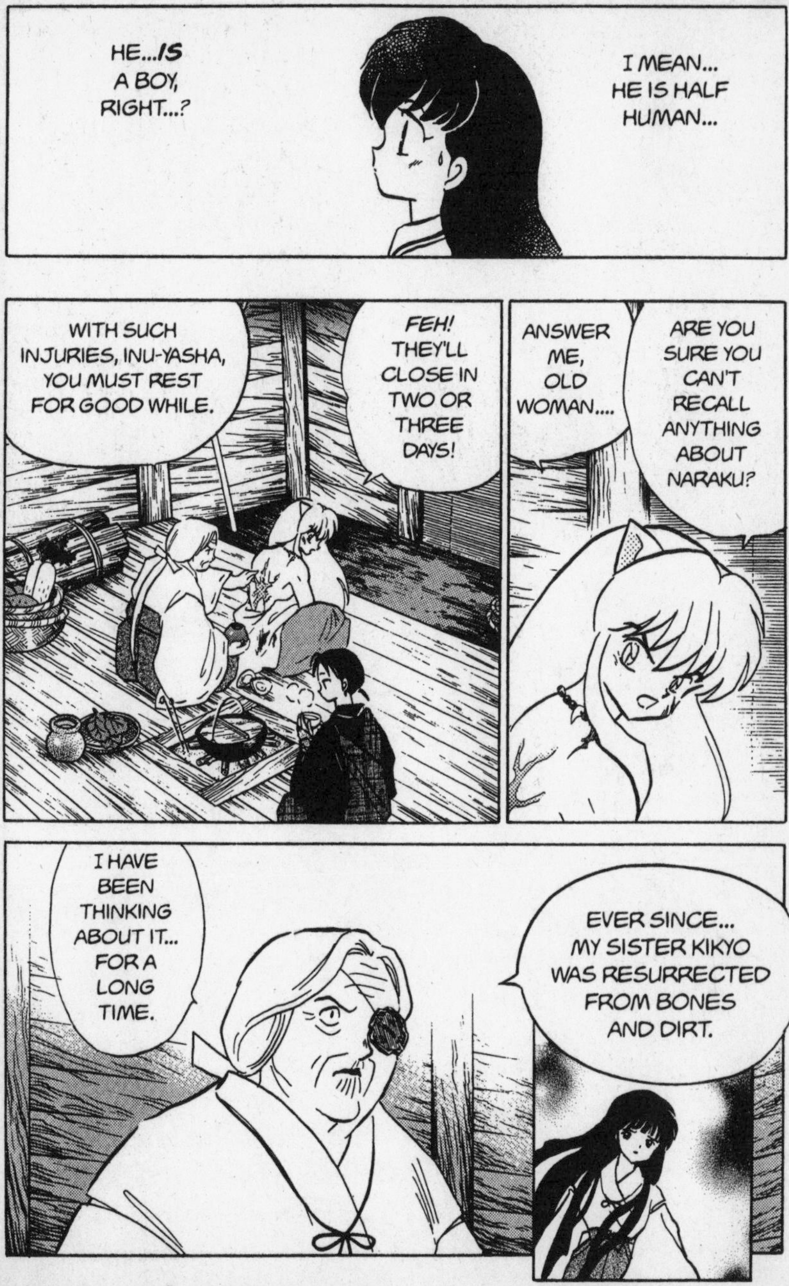
HE...*IS*
A BOY,
RIGHT...?
I MEAN...
HE IS HALF
HUMAN...
WITH SUCH
INJURIES, INU-YASHA,
YOU MUST REST
FOR GOOD WHILE.
FEH!
THEY'LL
CLOSE IN
TWO OR
THREE
DAYS!
ANSWER
ME,
OLD
WOMAN....
ARE YOU
SURE YOU
CAN'T
RECALL
ANYTHING
ABOUT
NARAKU?
I HAVE
BEEN
THINKING
ABOUT IT...
FOR A
LONG
TIME.
EVER SINCE...
MY SISTER KIKYO
WAS RESURRECTED
FROM BONES
AND DIRT.

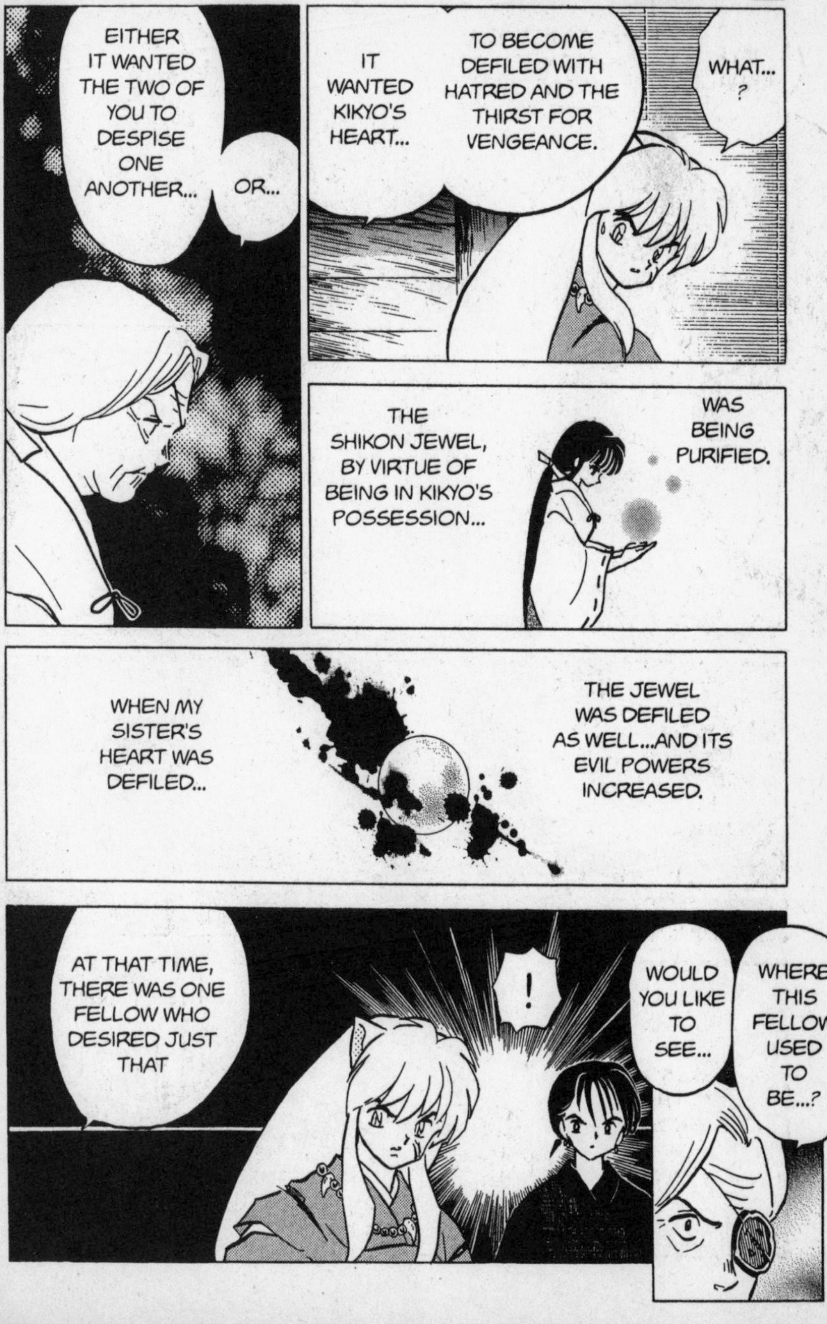
EITHER IT WANTED THE TWO OF YOU TO DESPISE ONE ANOTHER...
OR...
IT WANTED KIKYO'S HEART...
TO BECOME DEFILED WITH HATRED AND THE THIRST FOR VENGEANCE.
WHAT...?
THE SHIKON JEWEL, BY VIRTUE OF BEING IN KIKYO'S POSSESSION...
WAS BEING PURIFIED.
WHEN MY SISTER'S HEART WAS DEFILED...
THE JEWEL WAS DEFILED AS WELL...AND ITS EVIL POWERS INCREASED.
AT THAT TIME, THERE WAS ONE FELLOW WHO DESIRED JUST THAT
!
WOULD YOU LIKE TO SEE...
WHERE THIS FELLOW USED TO BE...?

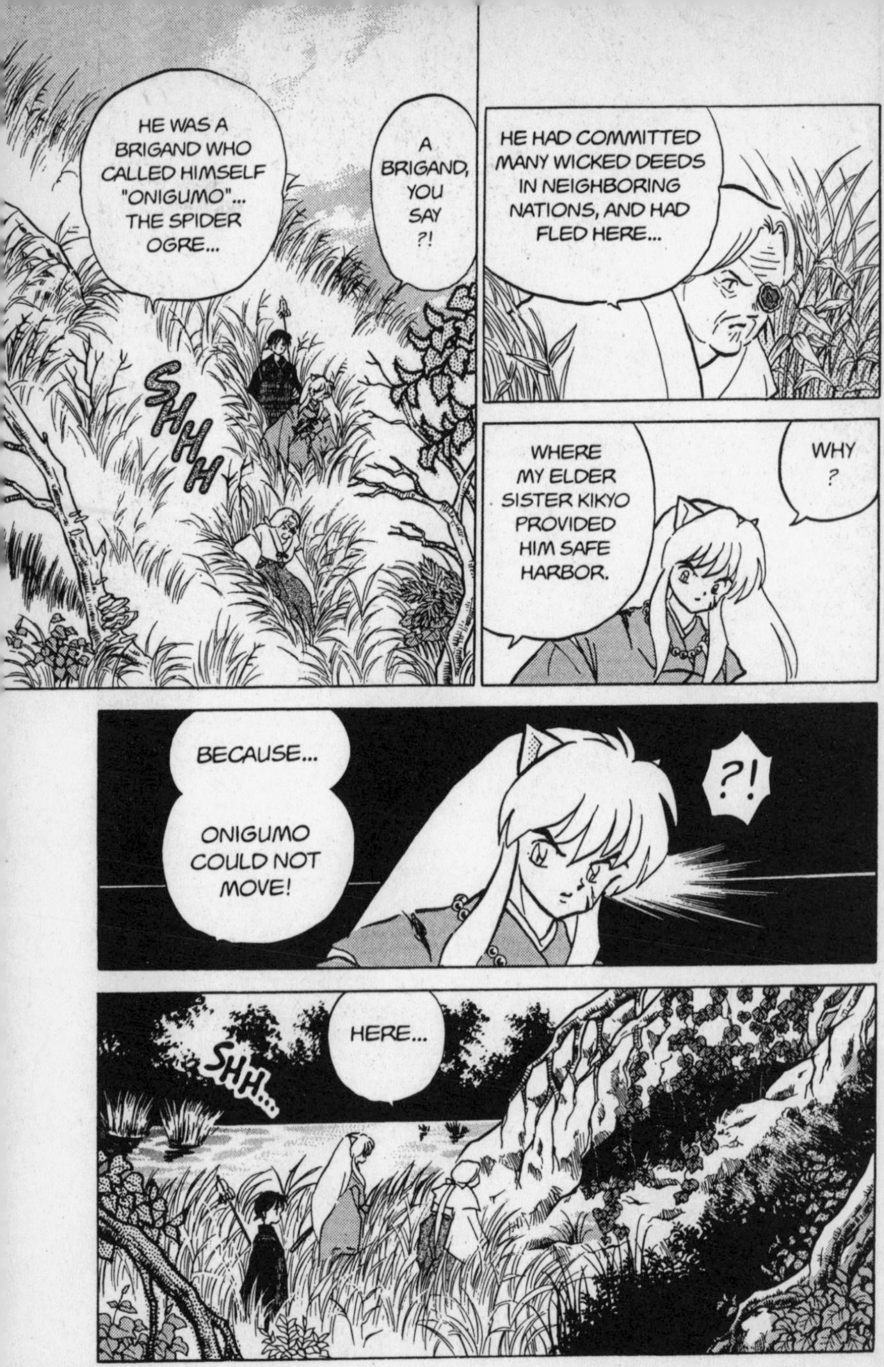
HE WAS A BRIGAND WHO CALLED HIMSELF "ONIGUMO"... THE SPIDER OGRE...
A BRIGAND, YOU SAY ?!
SHHH
HE HAD COMMITTED MANY WICKED DEEDS IN NEIGHBORING NATIONS, AND HAD FLED HERE...
WHERE MY ELDER SISTER KIKYO PROVIDED HIM SAFE HARBOR.
WHY ?
BECAUSE...
ONIGUMO COULD NOT MOVE!
?!
SHH...
HERE...

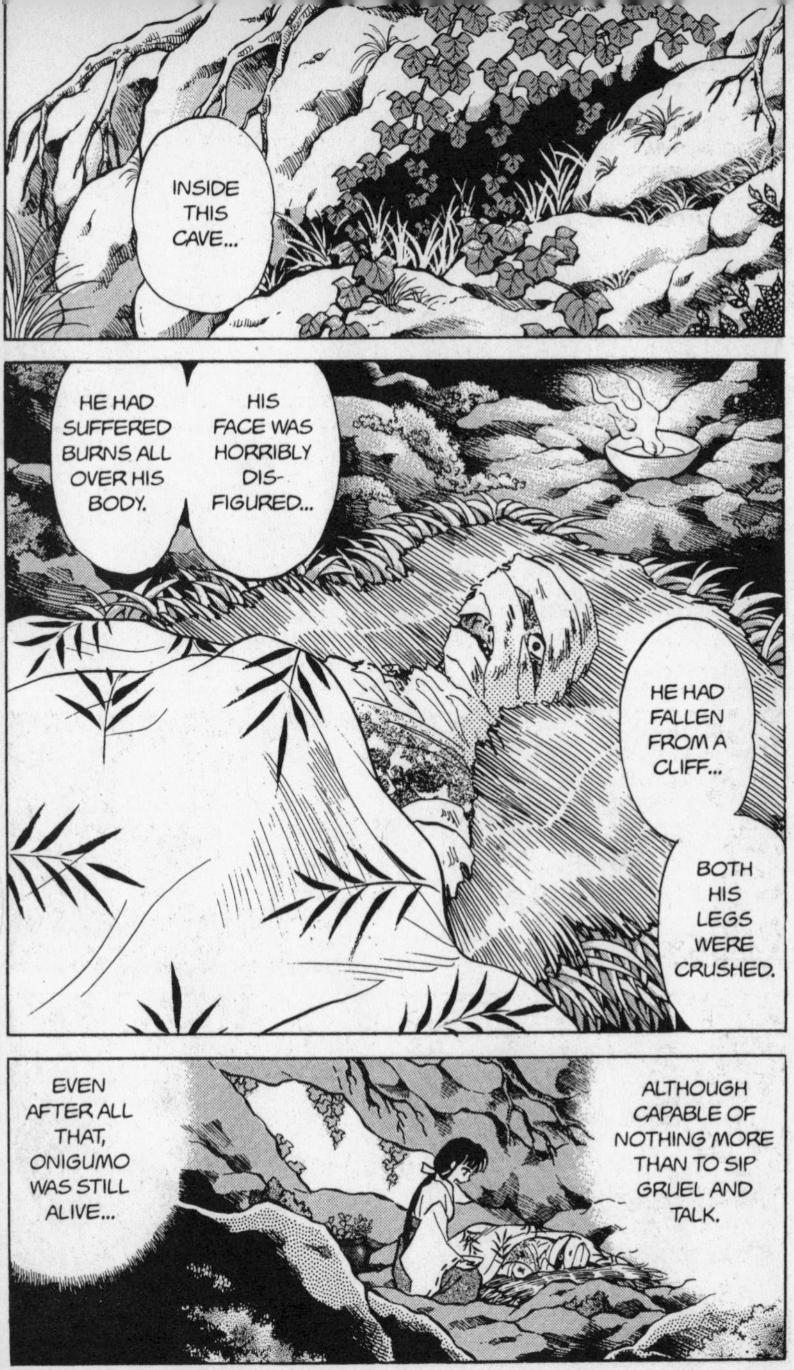
INSIDE THIS CAVE...
HE HAD SUFFERED BURNS ALL OVER HIS BODY.
HIS FACE WAS HORRIBLY DIS-FIGURED...
HE HAD FALLEN FROM A CLIFF...
BOTH HIS LEGS WERE CRUSHED.
EVEN AFTER ALL THAT, ONIGUMO WAS STILL ALIVE...
ALTHOUGH CAPABLE OF NOTHING MORE THAN TO SIP GRUEL AND TALK.

134

KIKYO, I DON'T LIKE THAT MAN.

SO... ONIGUMO SAID SUCH THINGS, DID HE...?

YOU MUST FORGIVE HIM.

THAT MAN WILL PROBABLY NEVER BE ABLE TO MOVE FROM THAT SPOT ON HIS OWN.

IT WAS ALMOST IMMEDIATELY AFTERWARD...

THAT MY SISTER SHOT YOU, INU-YASHA... AND DIED HERSELF.

DAYS LATER, WHEN I CAME HERE TO CHECK ON HIM,

THE CAVE HAD BURNED AND COLLAPSED.

I ASSUMED THAT HIS CAMPFIRE HAD FLARED UP AND BURNED OUT OF CONTROL...

AND THAT ONIGUMO, UNABLE TO ESCAPE...

HAD BURNED TO DEATH WITHOUT EVEN LEAVING A TRACE OF HIS BONES BEHIND.

WAIT, KAEDE, WAIT....

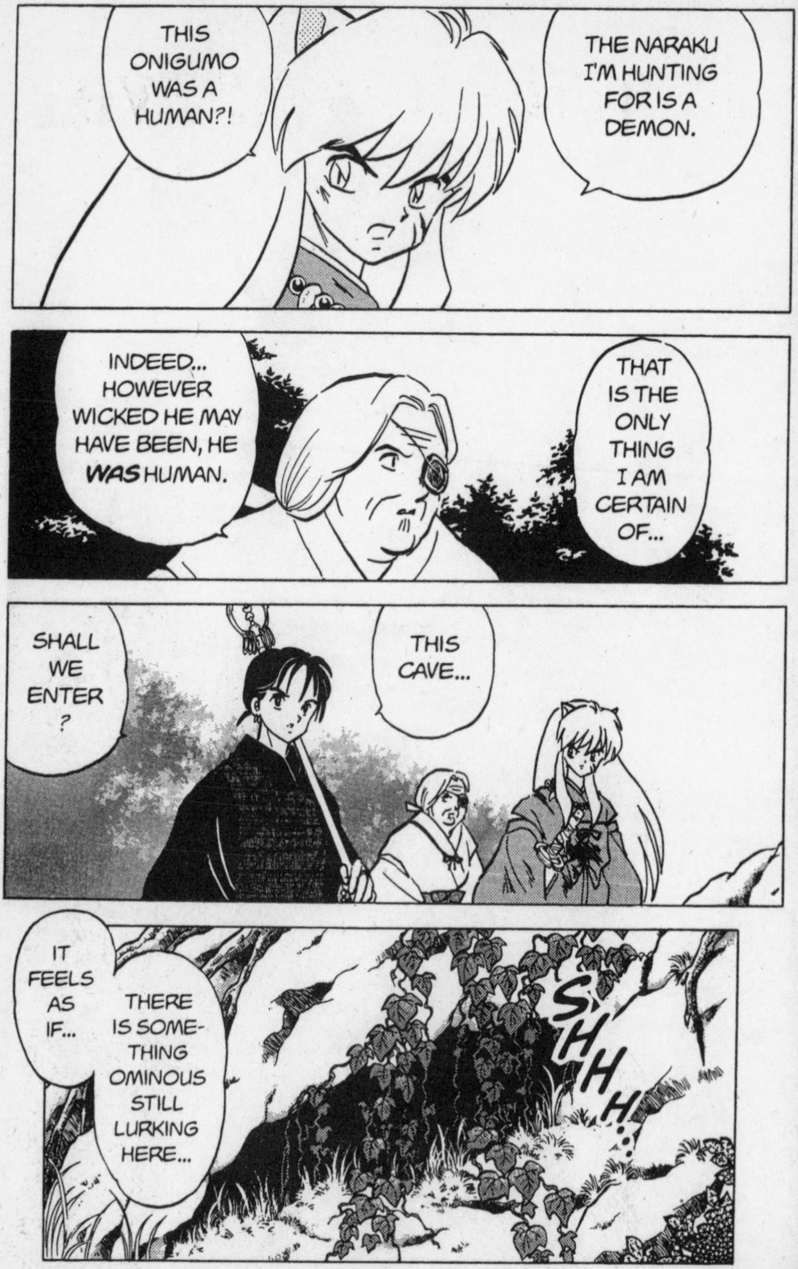
THIS ONIGUMO WAS A HUMAN?!
THE NARAKU I'M HUNTING FOR IS A DEMON.
INDEED... HOWEVER WICKED HE MAY HAVE BEEN, HE **WAS** HUMAN.
THAT IS THE ONLY THING I AM CERTAIN OF...
SHALL WE ENTER?
THIS CAVE...
IT FEELS AS IF...
THERE IS SOMETHING OMINOUS STILL LURKING HERE...
SHHH...

SCROLL EIGHT

THE SHADOW OF EVIL

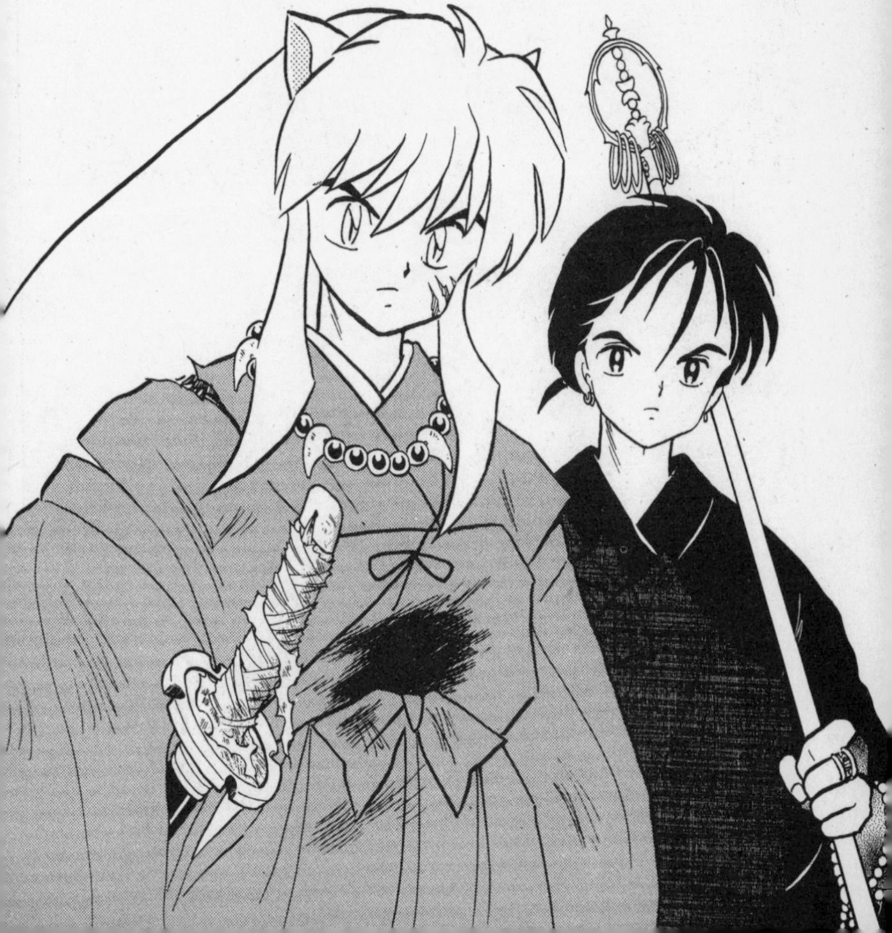

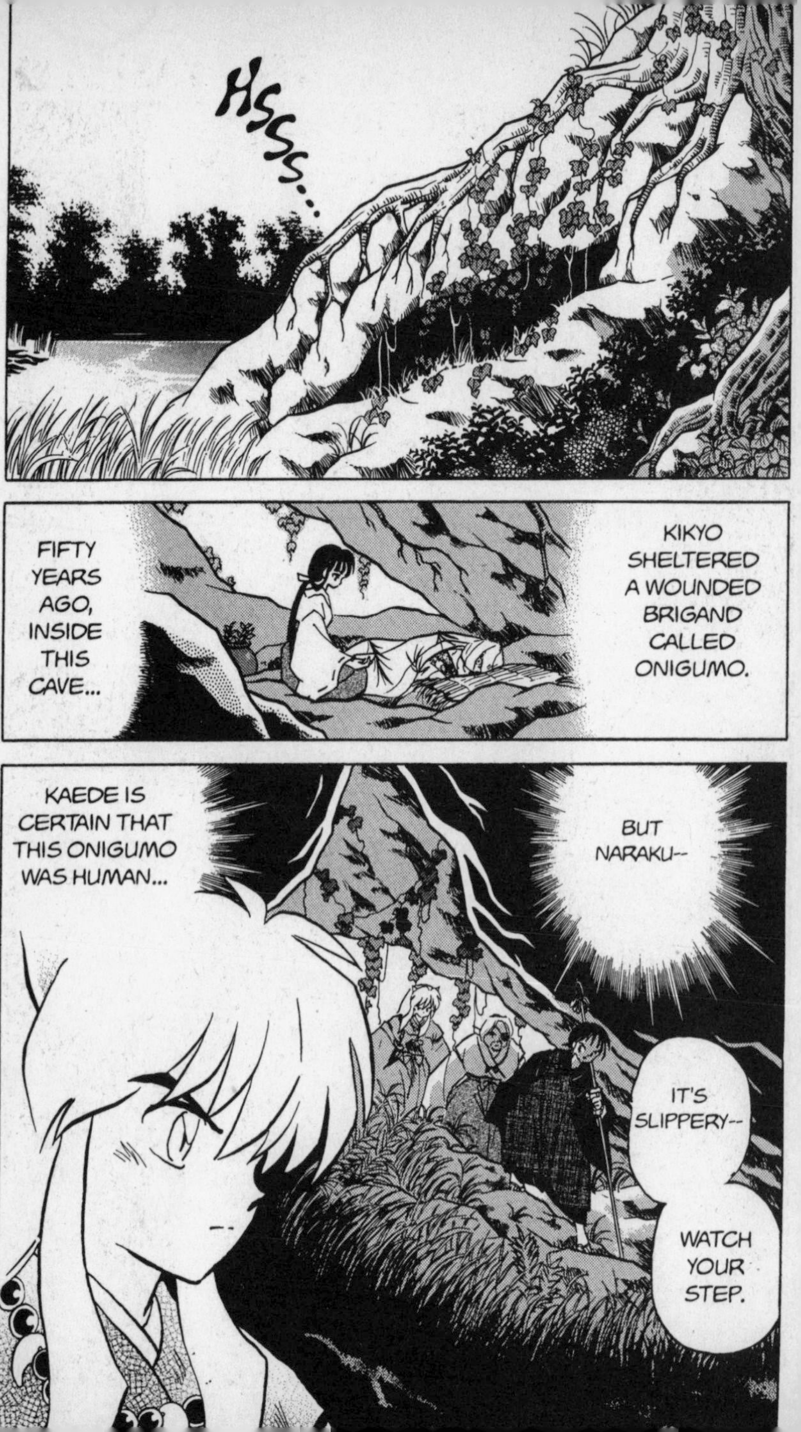
HSSS...
FIFTY YEARS AGO, INSIDE THIS CAVE...
KIKYO SHELTERED A WOUNDED BRIGAND CALLED ONIGUMO.
KAEDE IS CERTAIN THAT THIS ONIGUMO WAS HUMAN...
BUT NARAKU--
IT'S SLIPPERY--
WATCH YOUR STEP.

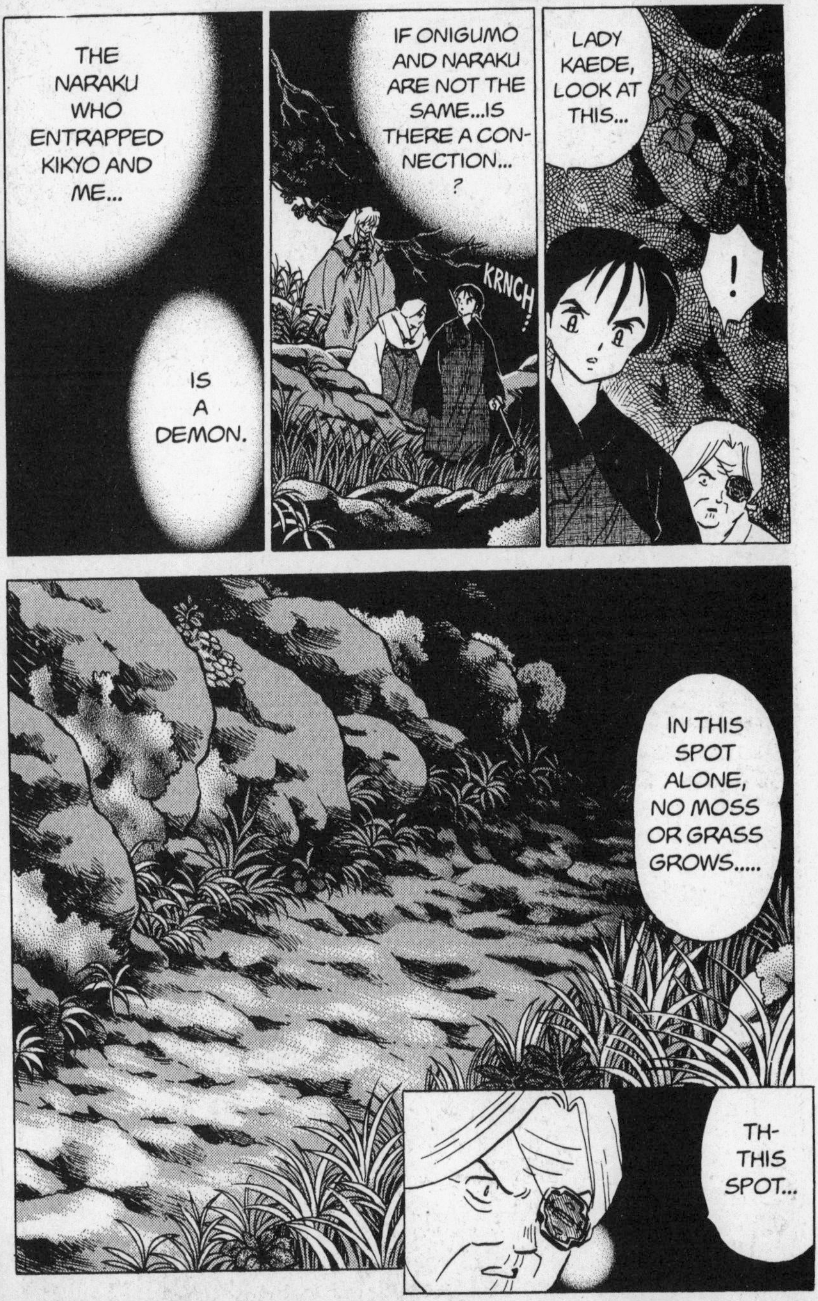
THE NARAKU WHO ENTRAPPED KIKYO AND ME...
IS A DEMON.
IF ONIGUMO AND NARAKU ARE NOT THE SAME...IS THERE A CONNECTION...?
KRNCH
LADY KAEDE, LOOK AT THIS...
!
IN THIS SPOT ALONE, NO MOSS OR GRASS GROWS.....
TH-THIS SPOT...

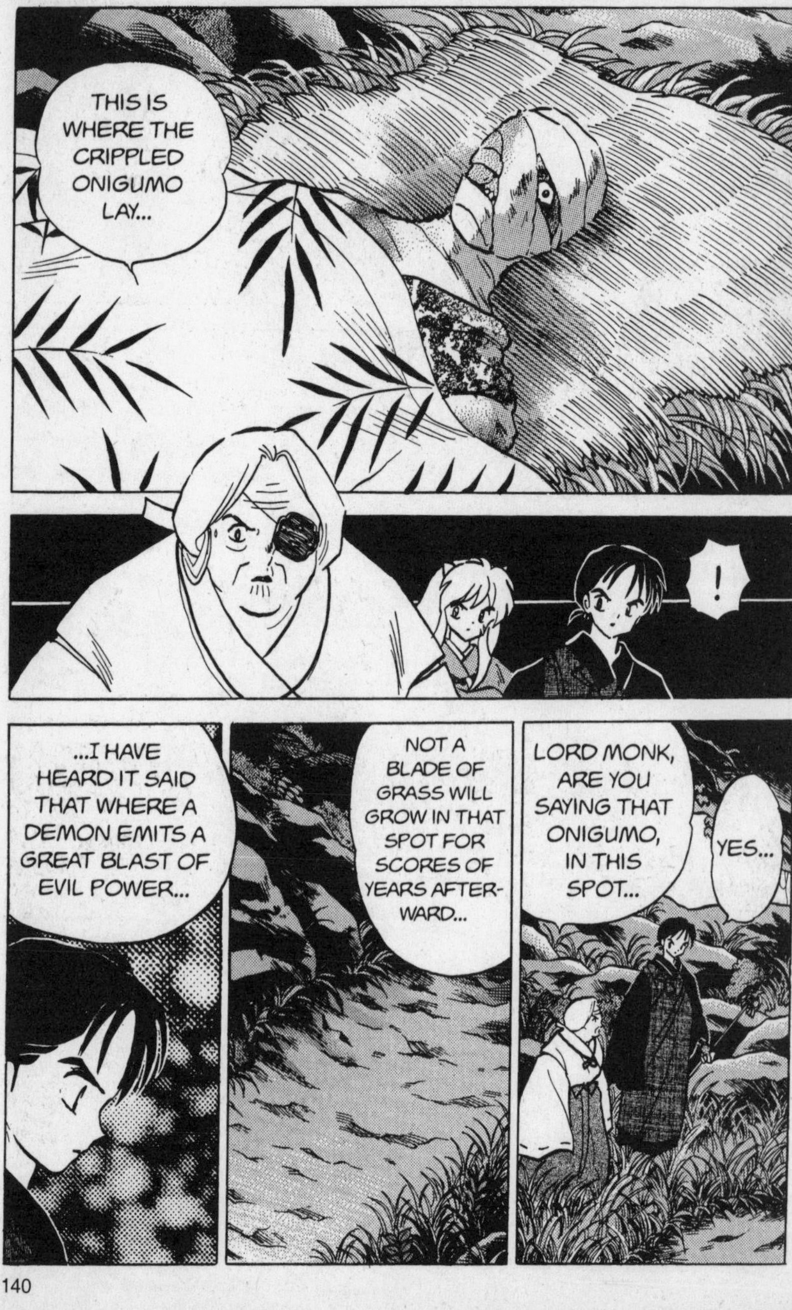
THIS IS WHERE THE CRIPPLED ONIGUMO LAY...
!
...I HAVE HEARD IT SAID THAT WHERE A DEMON EMITS A GREAT BLAST OF EVIL POWER...
NOT A BLADE OF GRASS WILL GROW IN THAT SPOT FOR SCORES OF YEARS AFTER-WARD...
LORD MONK, ARE YOU SAYING THAT ONIGUMO, IN THIS SPOT...
YES...

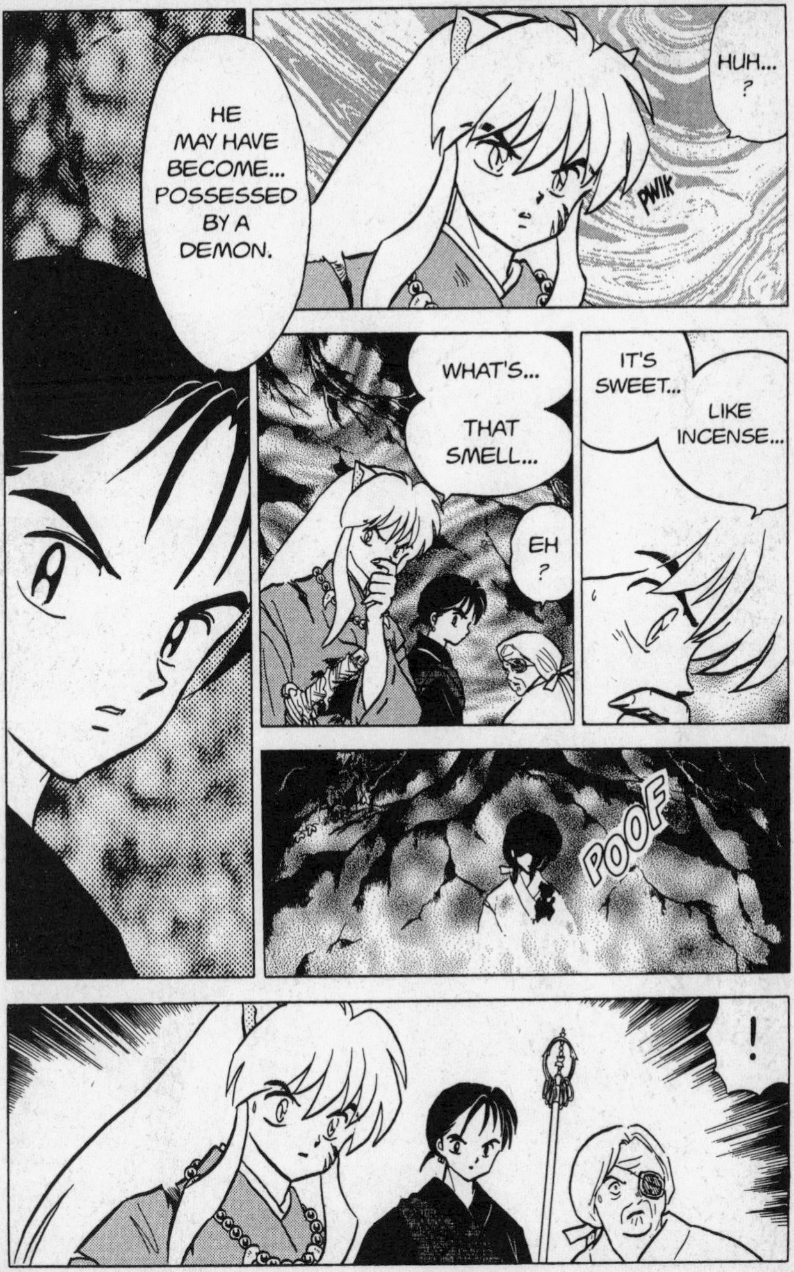
HE MAY HAVE BECOME... POSSESSED BY A DEMON.
HUH...?
PWIK
WHAT'S... THAT SMELL...
EH?
IT'S SWEET... LIKE INCENSE...
POOF
!

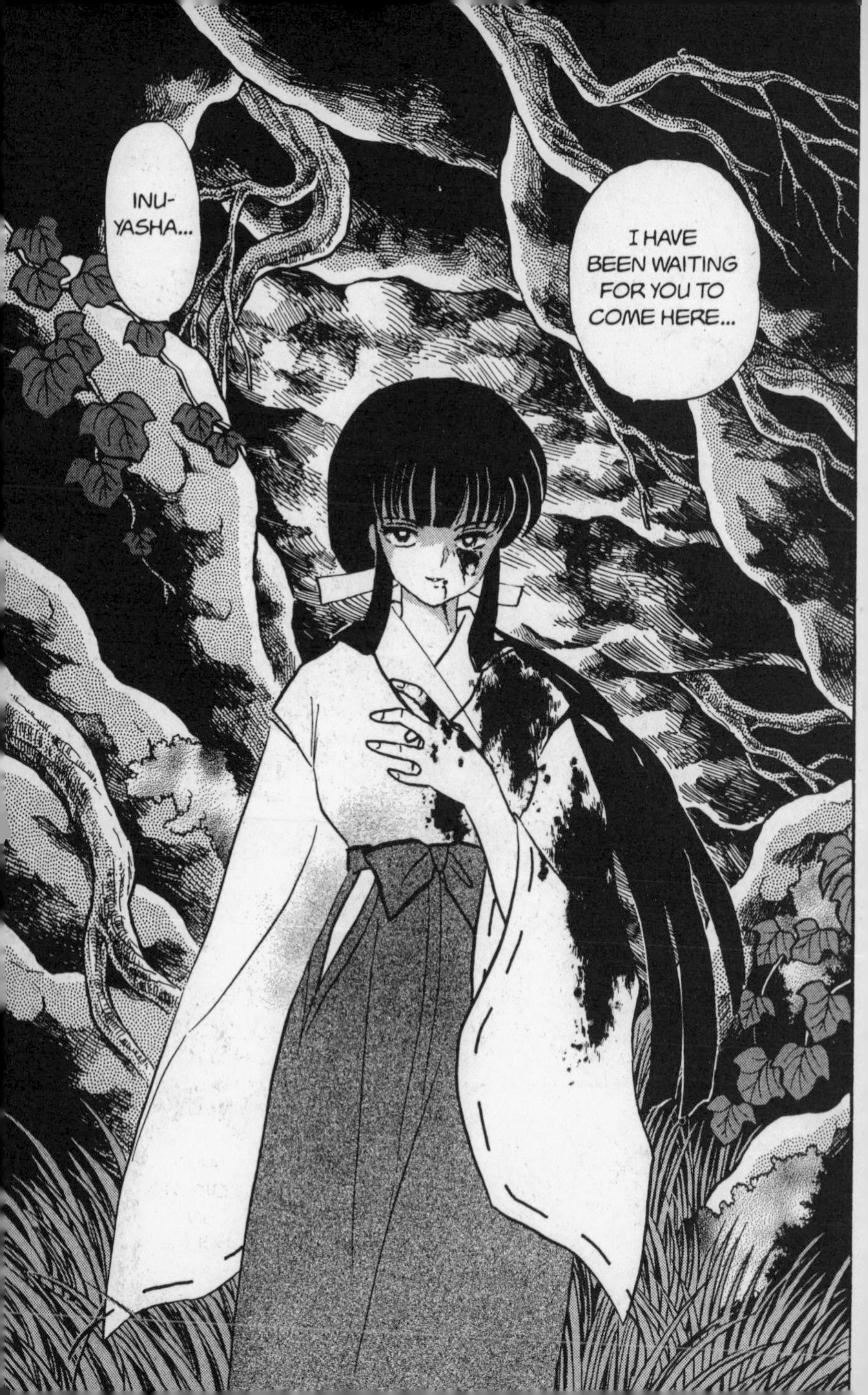
INU-
YASHA...
I HAVE
BEEN WAITING
FOR YOU TO
COME HERE...

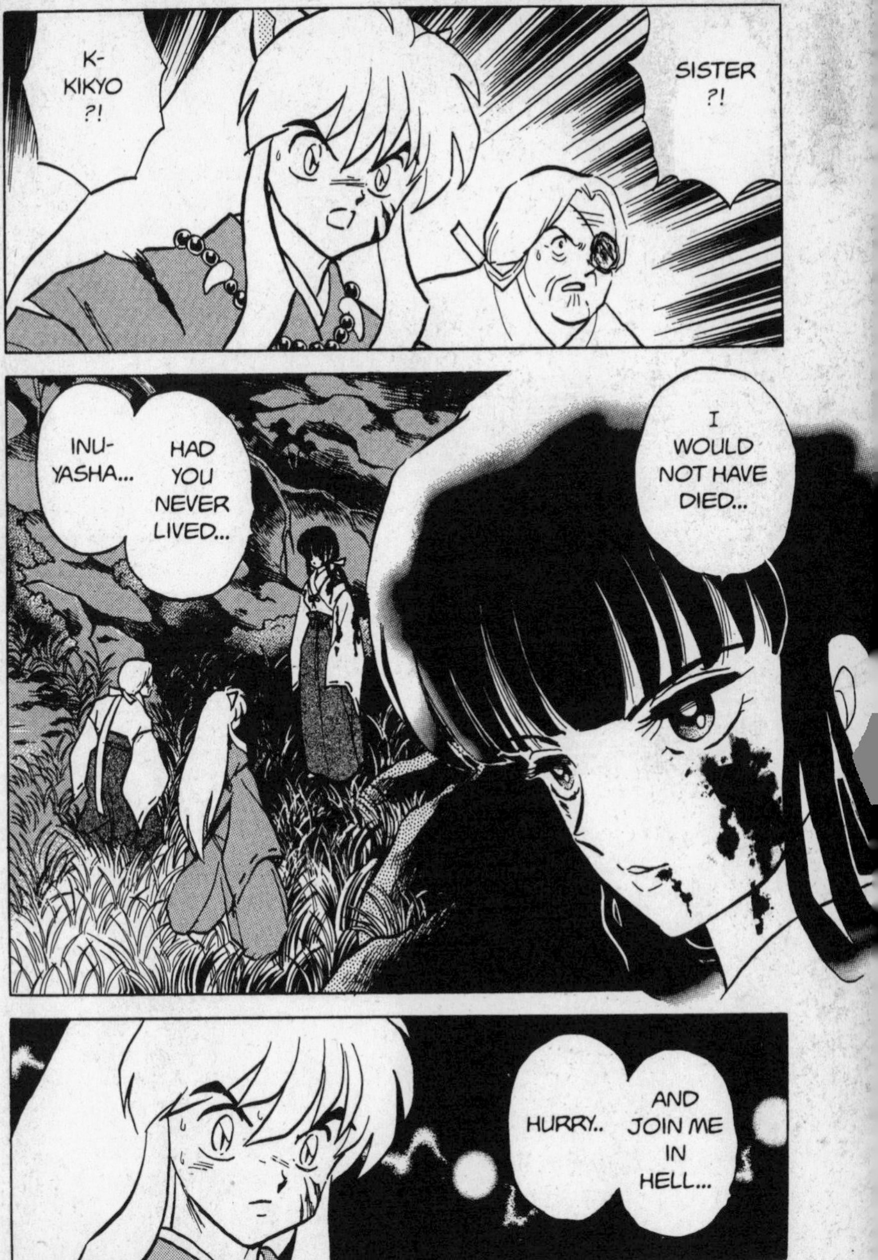
K-
KIKYO
?!
SISTER
?!
INU-
YASHA...
HAD
YOU
NEVER
LIVED...
I
WOULD
NOT HAVE
DIED...
HURRY..
AND
JOIN ME
IN
HELL...

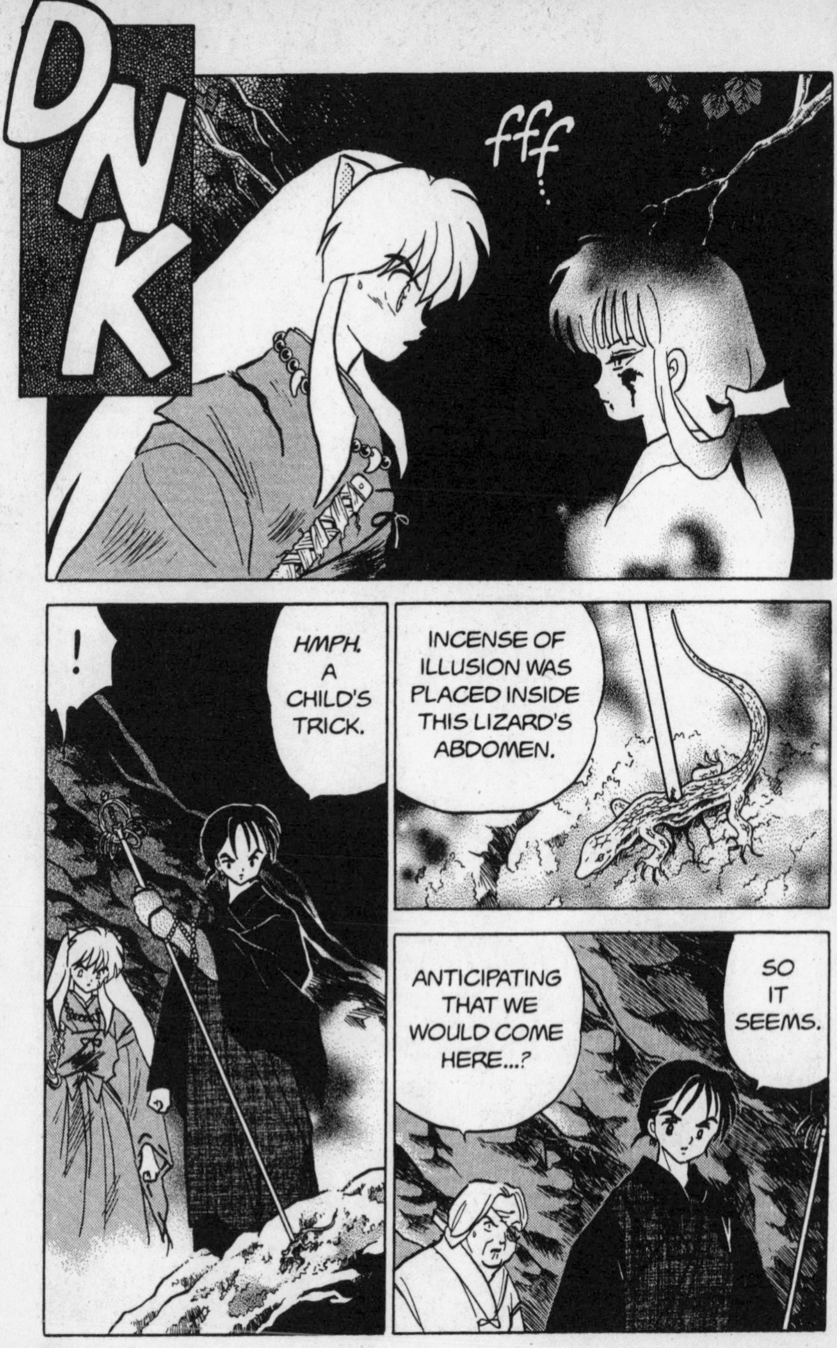
DNK
fff...
!
HMPH. A CHILD'S TRICK.
INCENSE OF ILLUSION WAS PLACED INSIDE THIS LIZARD'S ABDOMEN.
ANTICIPATING THAT WE WOULD COME HERE...?
SO IT SEEMS.

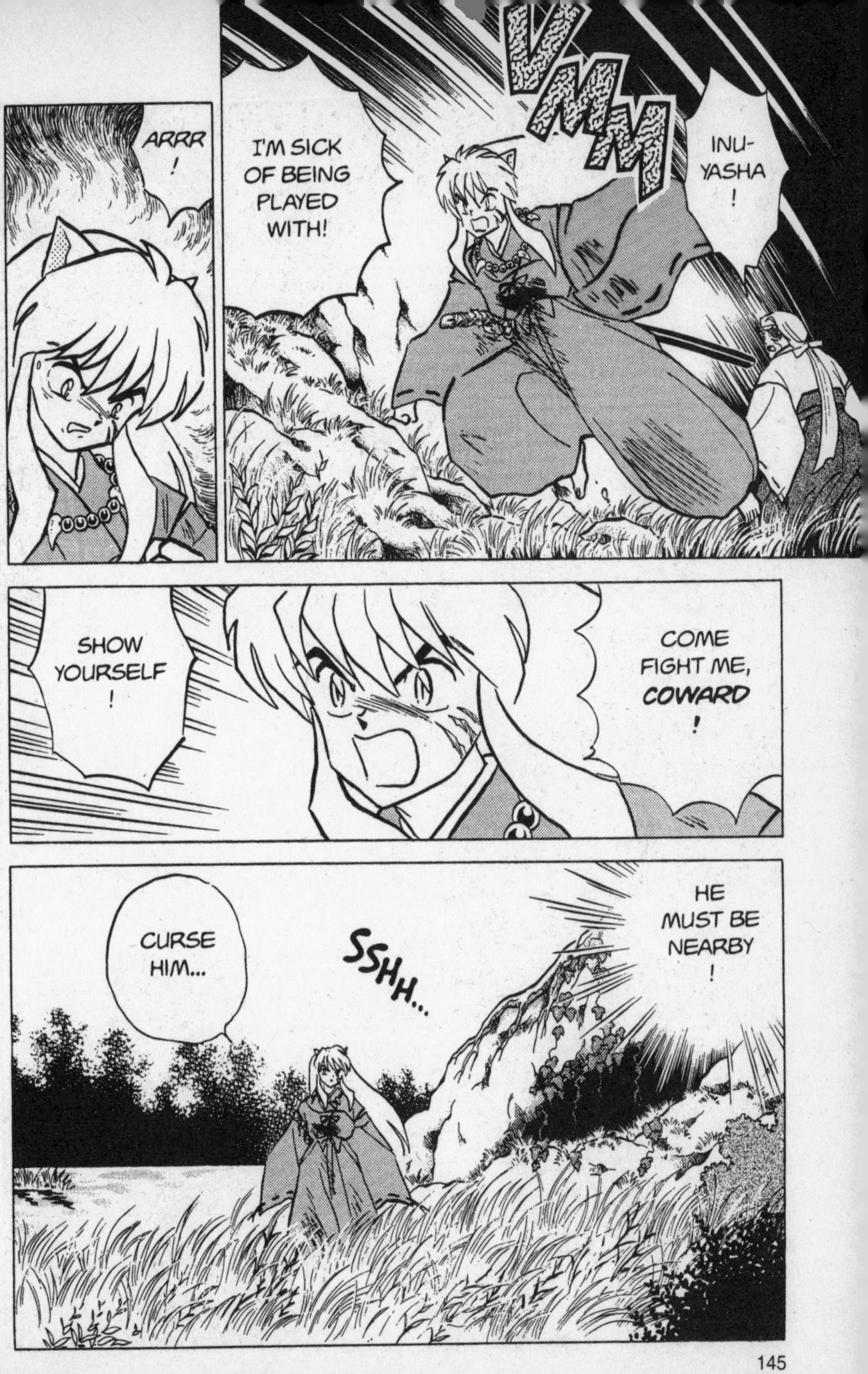
ARRR!
I'M SICK OF BEING PLAYED WITH!
VMM
INU-YASHA!
SHOW YOURSELF!
COME FIGHT ME, COWARD!
CURSE HIM...
SSHH...
HE MUST BE NEARBY!

SSSH...

HOOO...

CAN'T EVEN BUDGE IT...

BUT UNLESS THE WELL IS FIXED, KAGOME CAN'T COME BACK!

UGGH~!

N N N G

WILL WE REALLY NEVER...

...SEE HER AGAIN...?

I CAN'T FIGHT THE WAY I WANT TO IF SHE'S AROUND!

GRR GRR GRR

WHO DIED AND MADE HIM EMPEROR?!

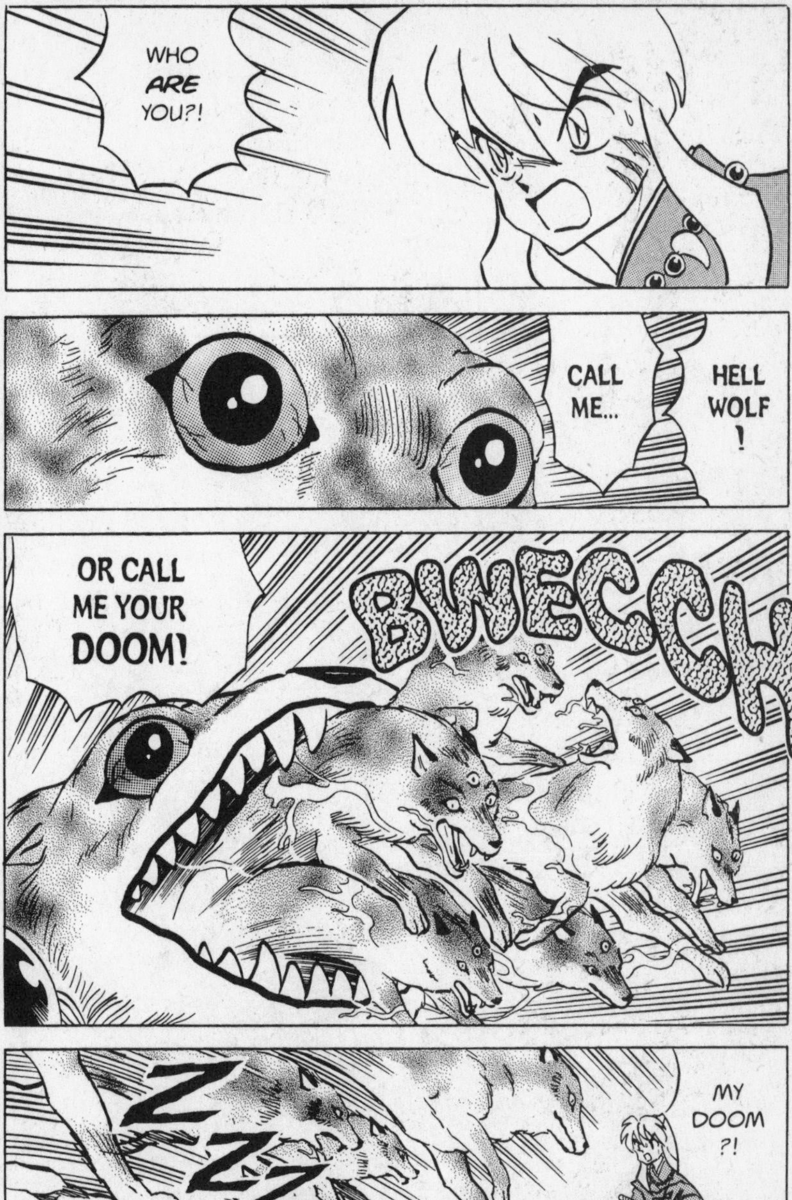
WHO ARE YOU?!
CALL ME...
HELL WOLF!
OR CALL ME YOUR DOOM!
BWECCH
ZZZZZZ
MY DOOM ?!

152

153

154

SCROLL NINE

WHEN WE ARE TWO

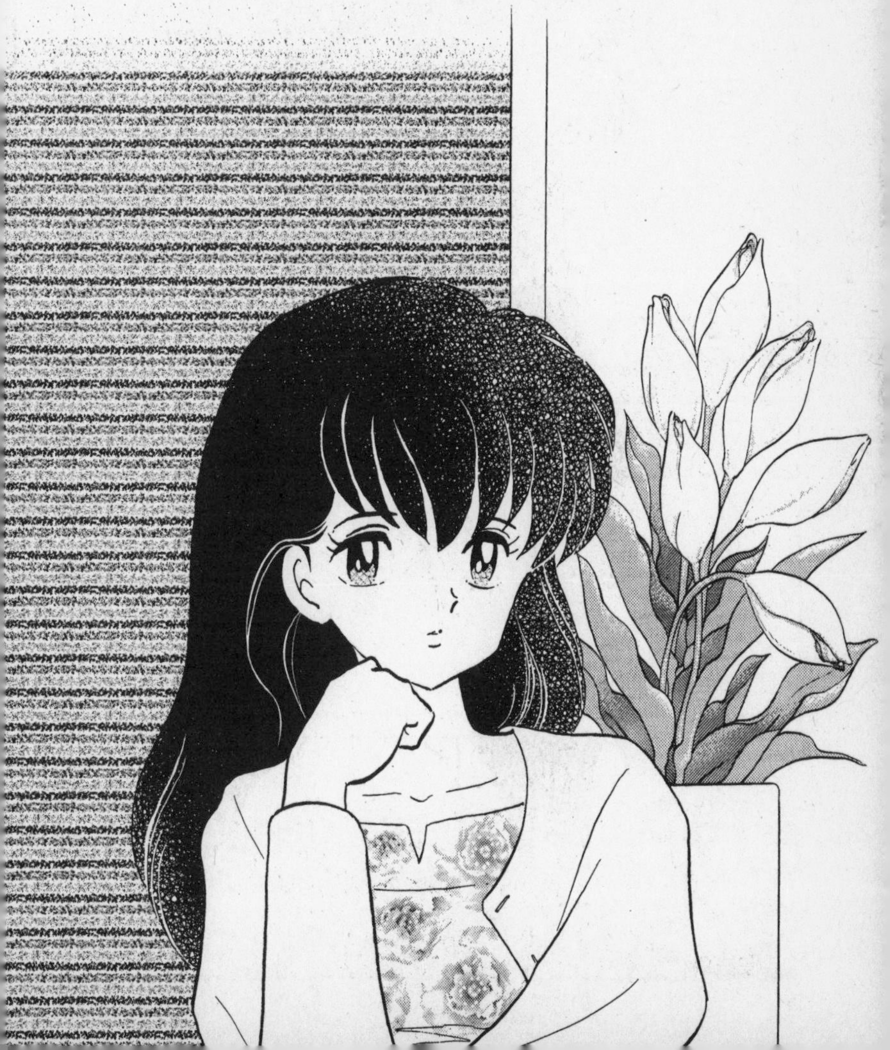

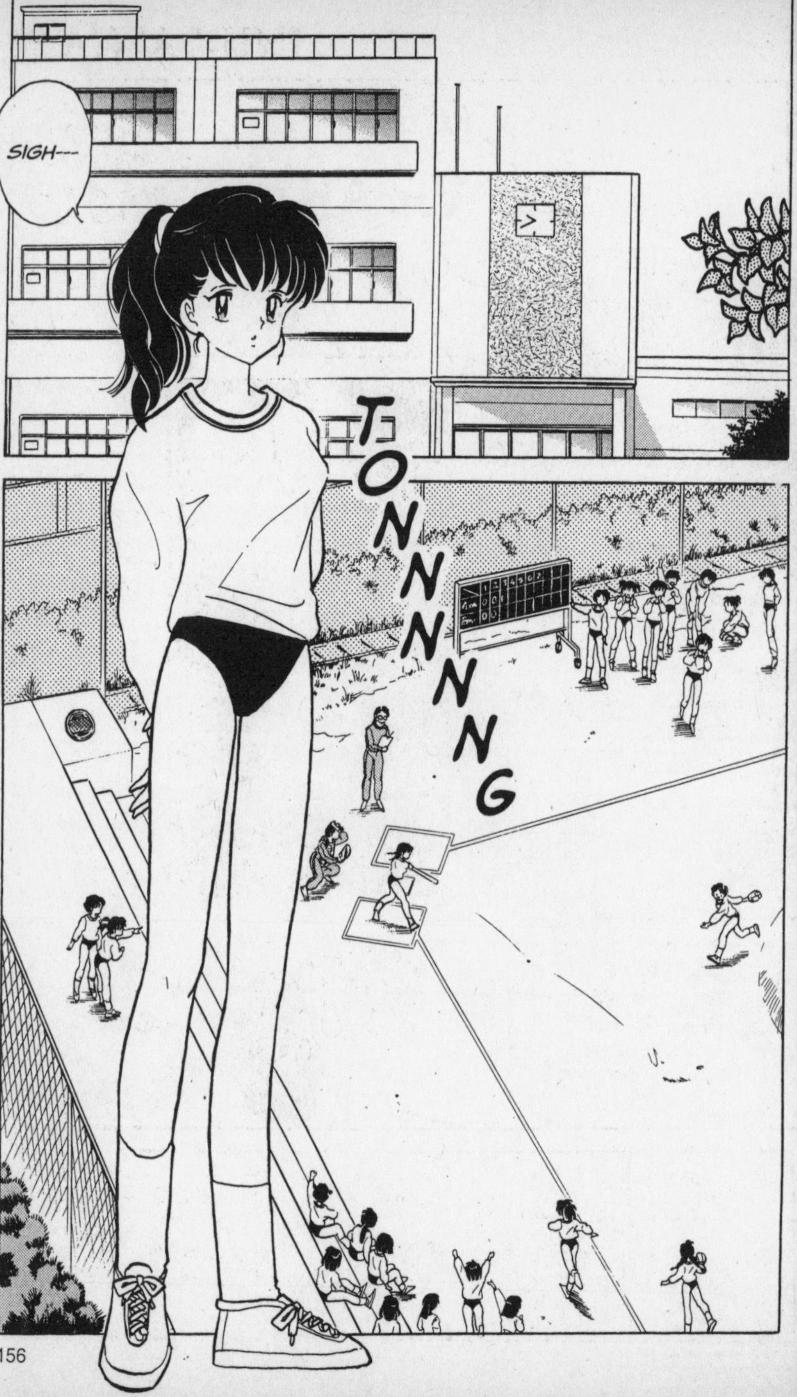
SIGH---
TONNNNNG

AND DON'T YOU *EVER* COME BACK HERE!

INU-YASHA!

IT'S BEEN THREE DAYS SINCE THEN...

DOES HE REALLY NEVER WANT TO SEE ME AGAIN?

INU....

KAGOME!

HM?

HOJO FROM CLASS B!

HE SAYS HE WANTS TO TALK TO YOU!

157

158

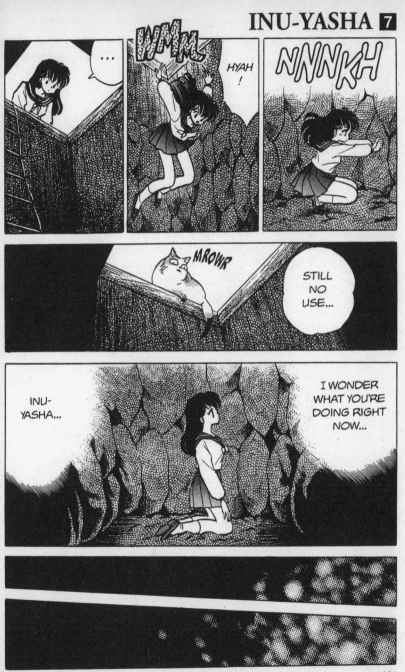

164

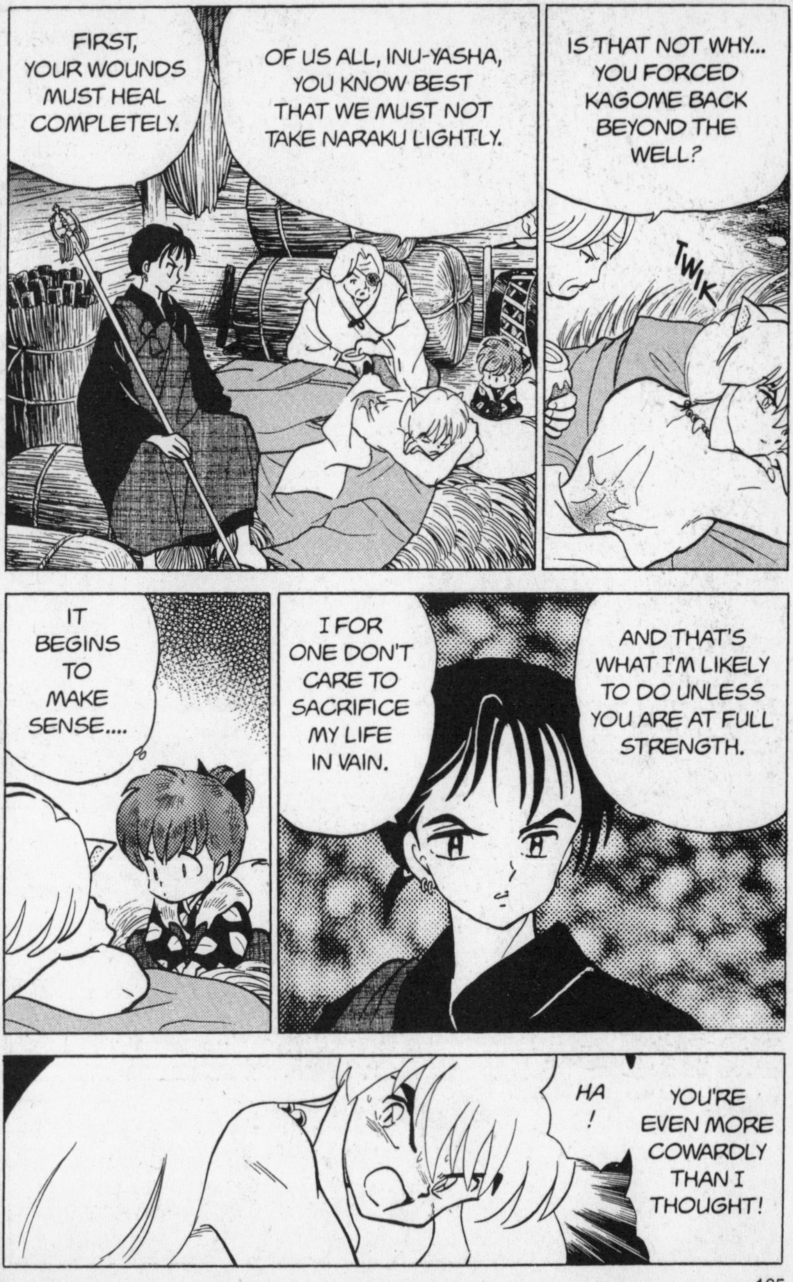
FIRST, YOUR WOUNDS MUST HEAL COMPLETELY.
OF US ALL, INU-YASHA, YOU KNOW BEST THAT WE MUST NOT TAKE NARAKU LIGHTLY.
IS THAT NOT WHY... YOU FORCED KAGOME BACK BEYOND THE WELL?
TWIK
IT BEGINS TO MAKE SENSE....
I FOR ONE DON'T CARE TO SACRIFICE MY LIFE IN VAIN.
AND THAT'S WHAT I'M LIKELY TO DO UNLESS YOU ARE AT FULL STRENGTH.
HA!
YOU'RE EVEN MORE COWARDLY THAN I THOUGHT!

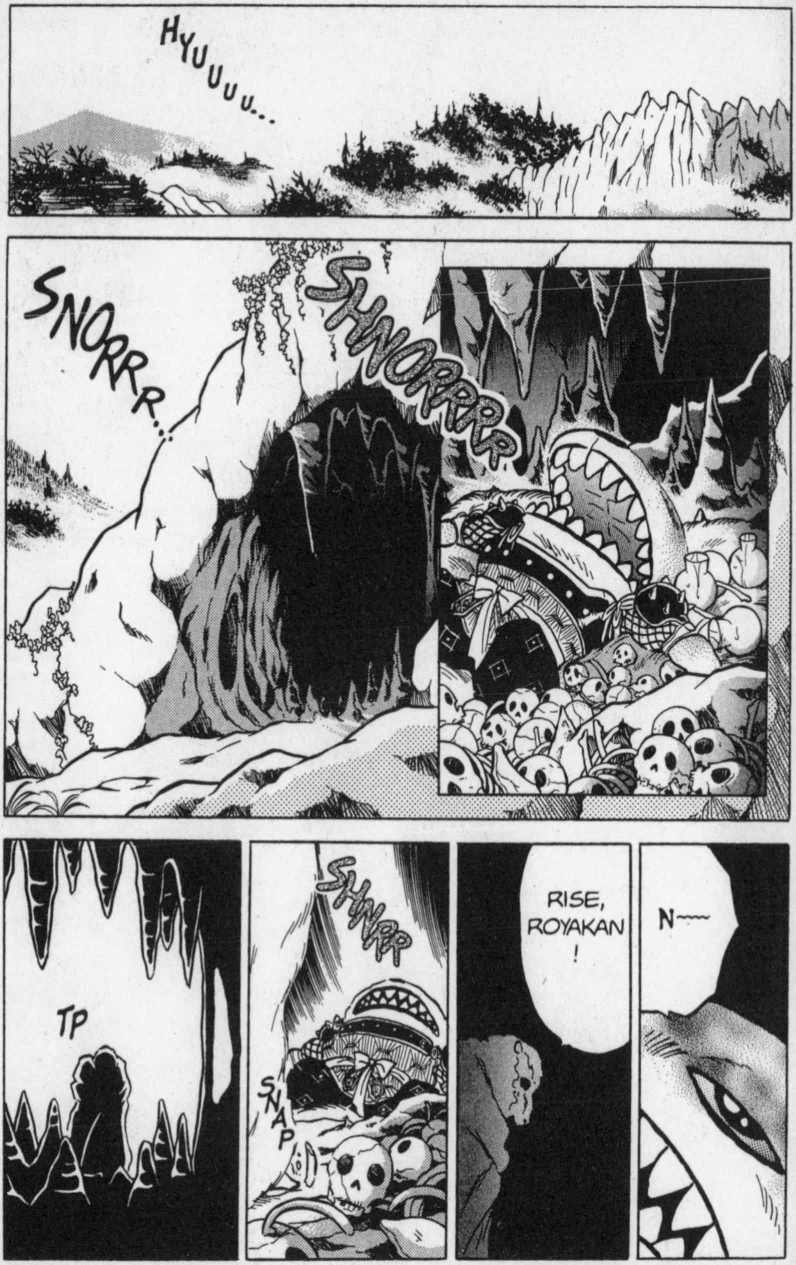
HYUUUUU...
SNORRRR...
SHNORRRR
TP
SHNRR
SNAP
RISE, ROYAKAN!
N~~~

169

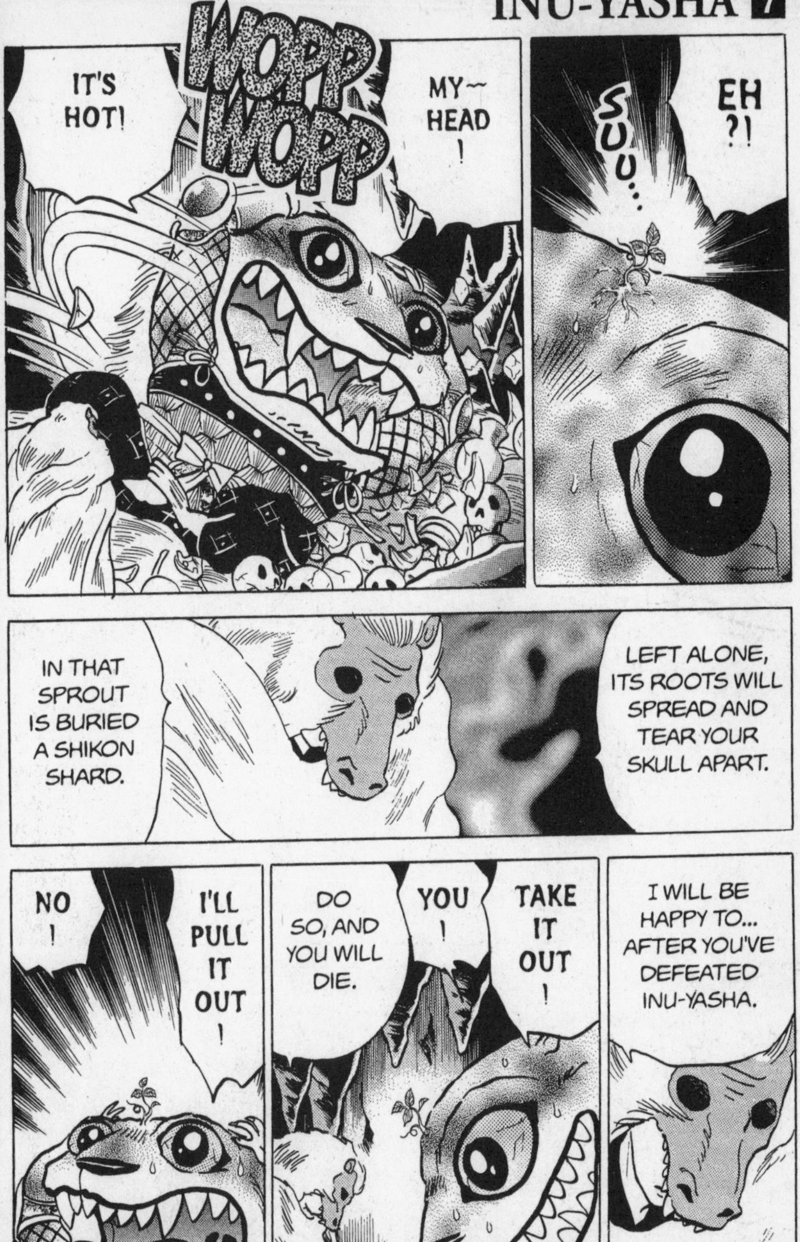
IT'S HOT!
WOPP WOPP
MY~ HEAD !
SUU...
EH ?!
IN THAT SPROUT IS BURIED A SHIKON SHARD.
LEFT ALONE, ITS ROOTS WILL SPREAD AND TEAR YOUR SKULL APART.
NO !
I'LL PULL IT OUT !
DO SO, AND YOU WILL DIE.
YOU !
TAKE IT OUT !
I WILL BE HAPPY TO... AFTER YOU'VE DEFEATED INU-YASHA.

SCROLL TEN

THE PIERCED WALL

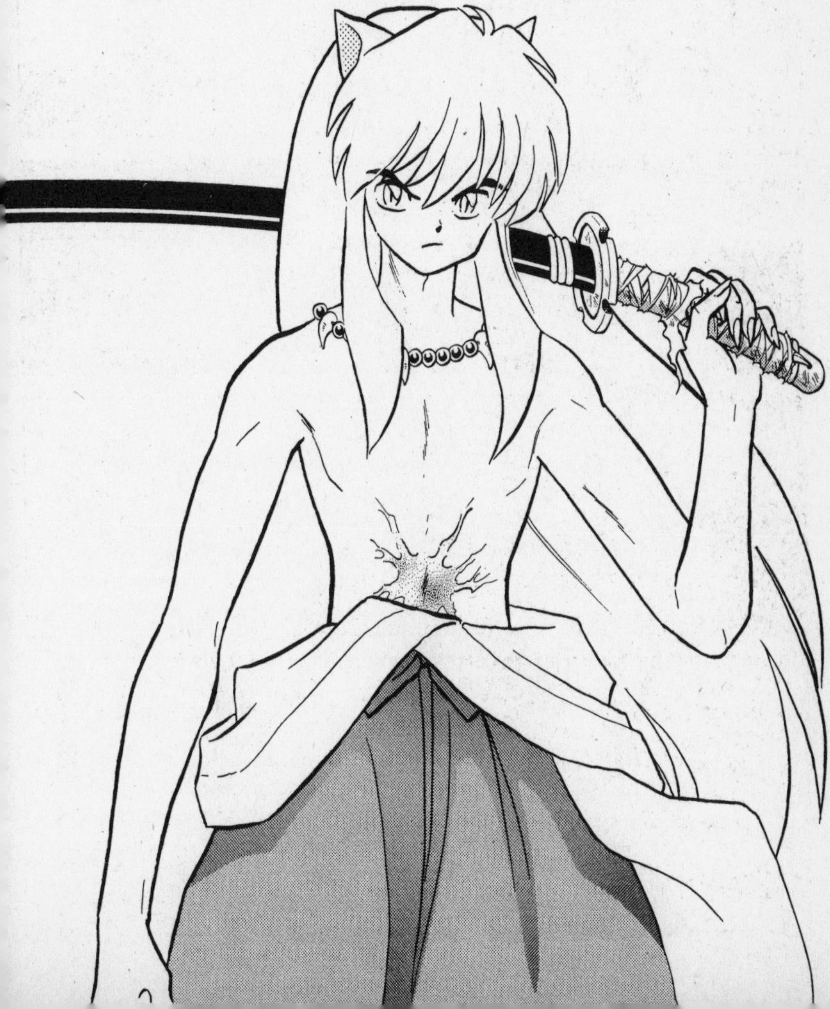

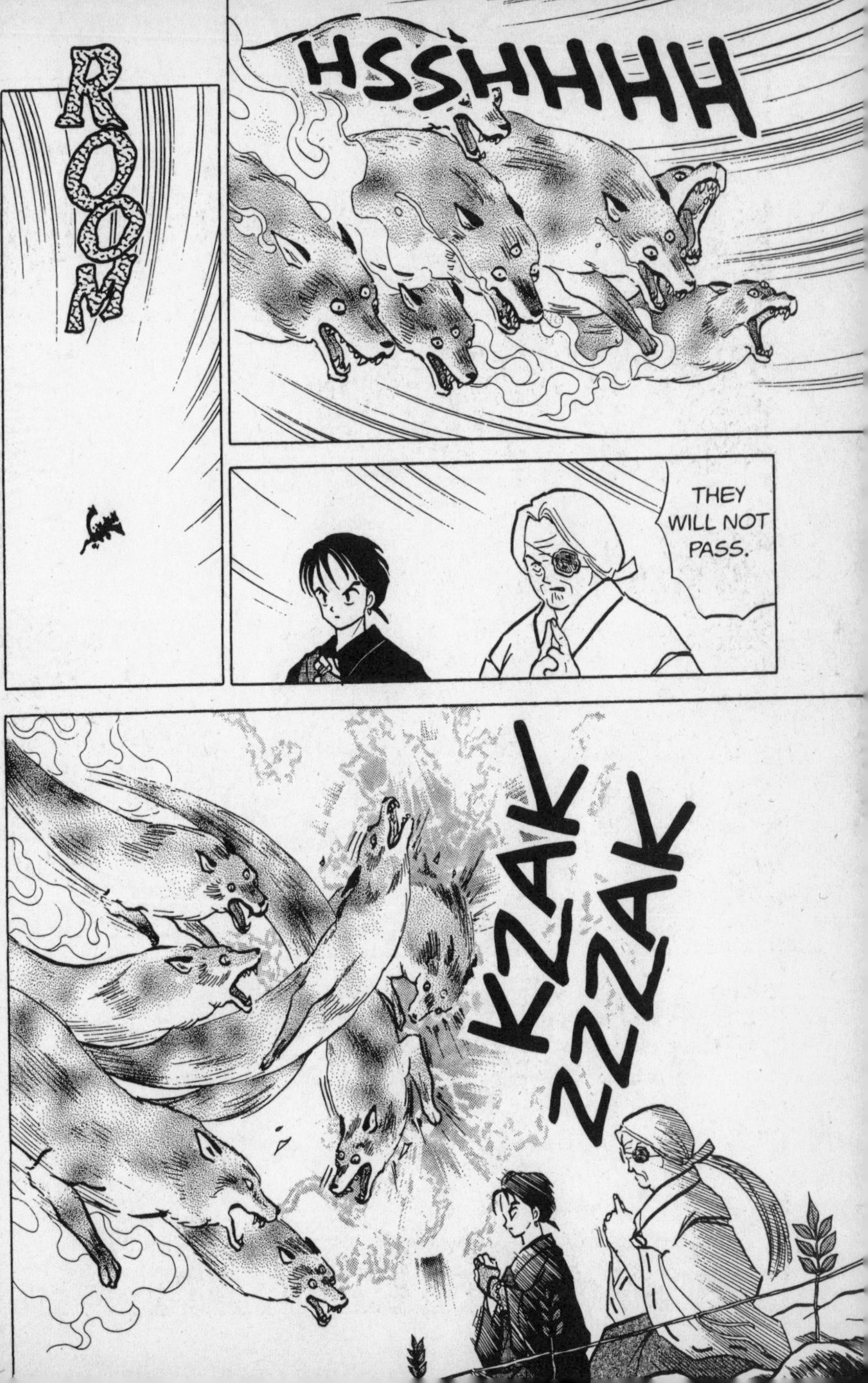
ROOM
HSSHHHH
THEY WILL NOT PASS.
KZAK
ZZZAK

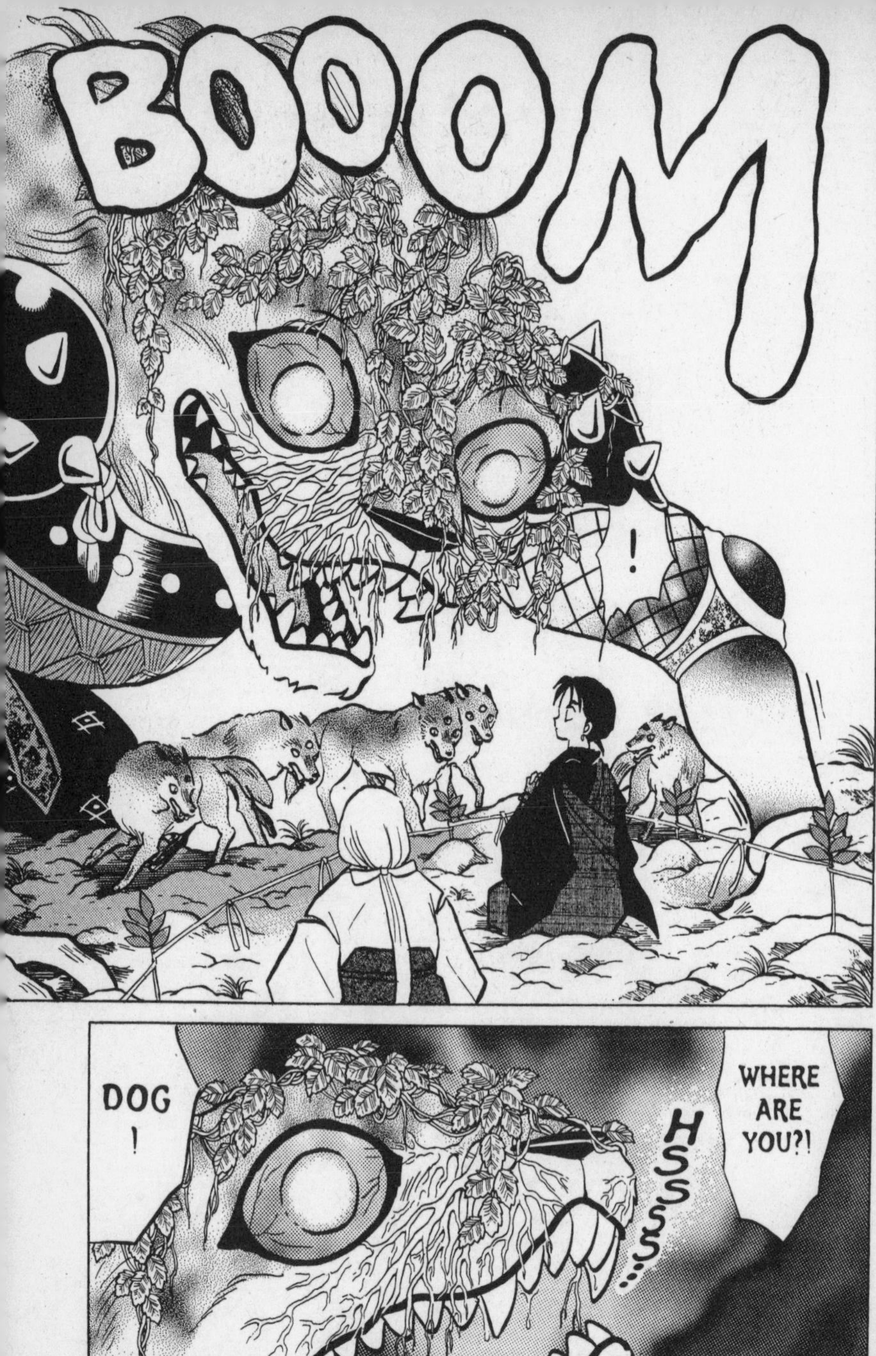
BOOOM
!
DOG
!
HSSSS...
WHERE
ARE
YOU?!

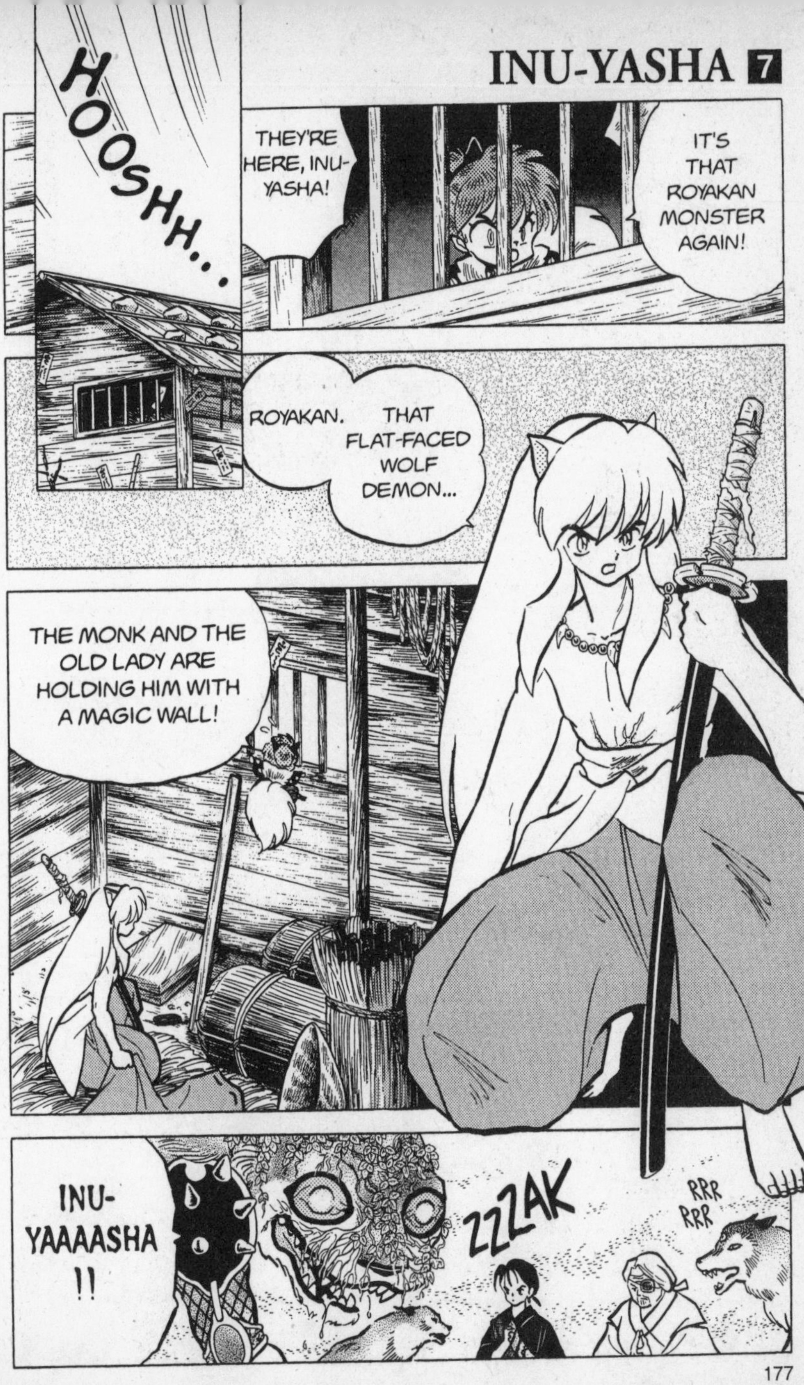
HOOSHH...
THEY'RE HERE, INU-YASHA!
IT'S THAT ROYAKAN MONSTER AGAIN!
ROYAKAN. THAT FLAT-FACED WOLF DEMON...
THE MONK AND THE OLD LADY ARE HOLDING HIM WITH A MAGIC WALL!
INU-YAAAASHA!!
ZZZAK
RRR RRR

179

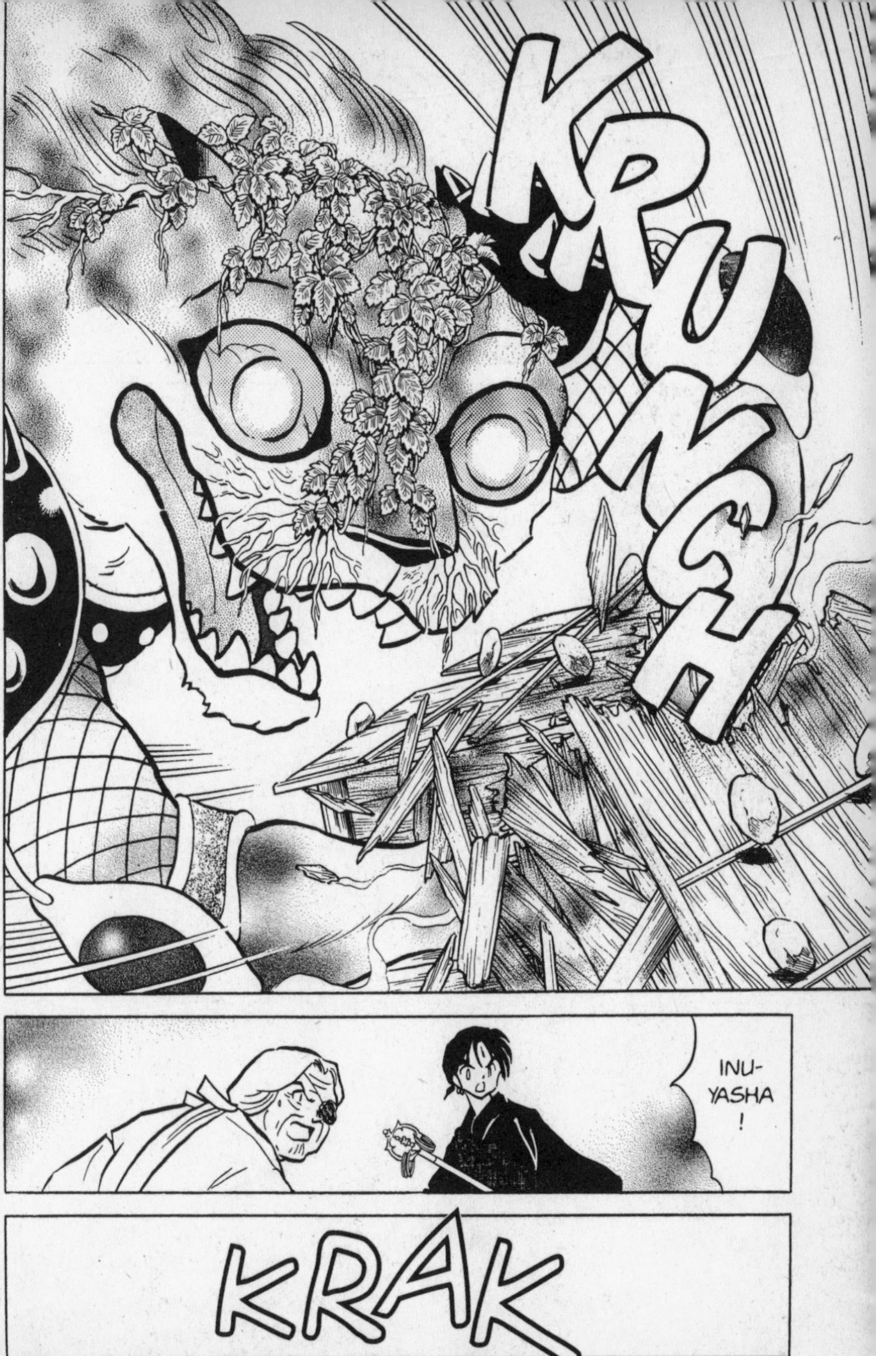
KRUNCH
INU-
YASHA
!
KRAK

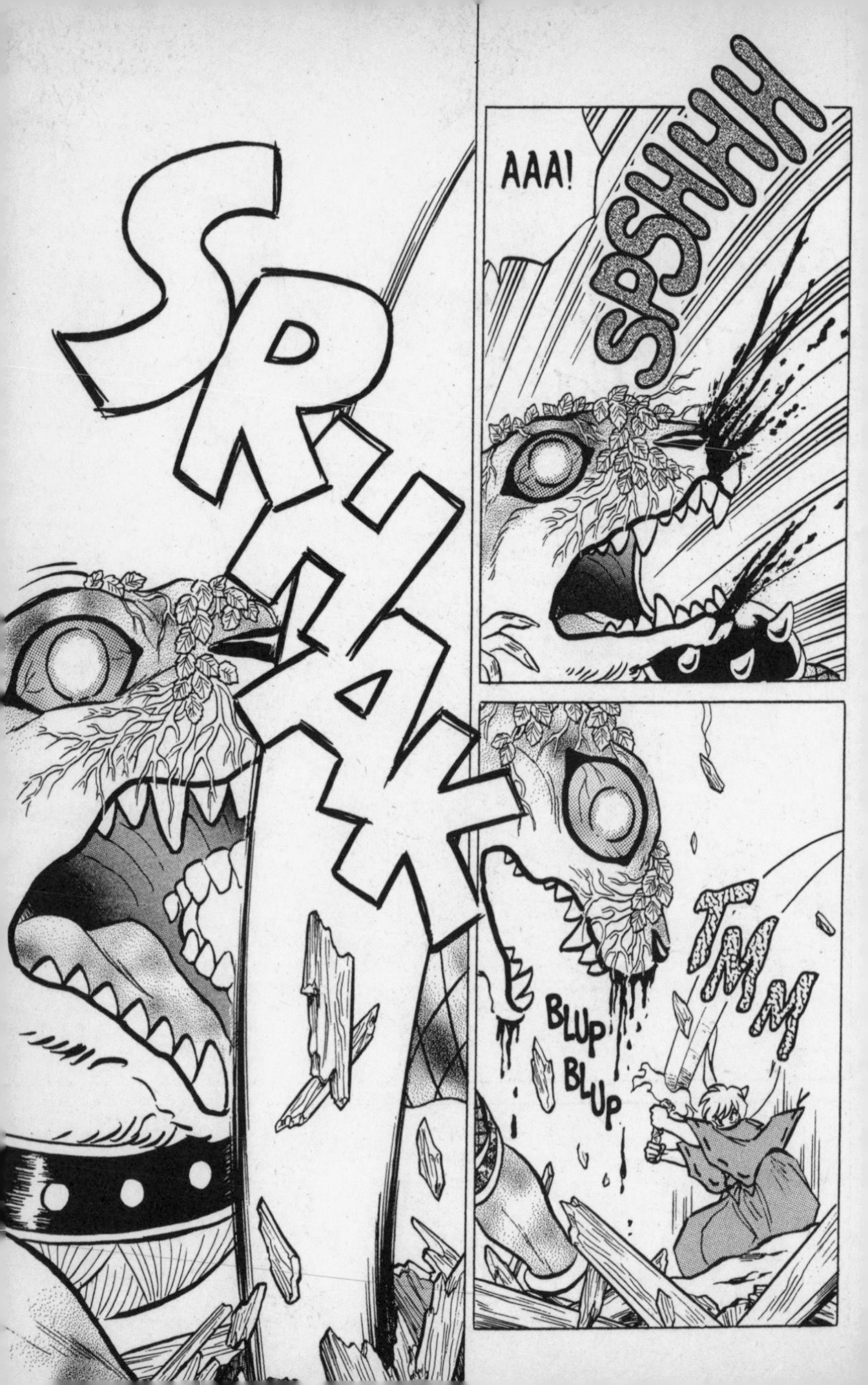
SPLAK
AAA!
SPSHHH
BLUP
BLUP
TMM

THANKS FOR LETTING ME OUT, ROYAKAN.

S-SHA!

THOSE *FOOLS* HAD ME TRAPPED, YOU KNOW!

HE NEVER WAS VERY GRATEFUL.

I'M NOT SURPRISED.

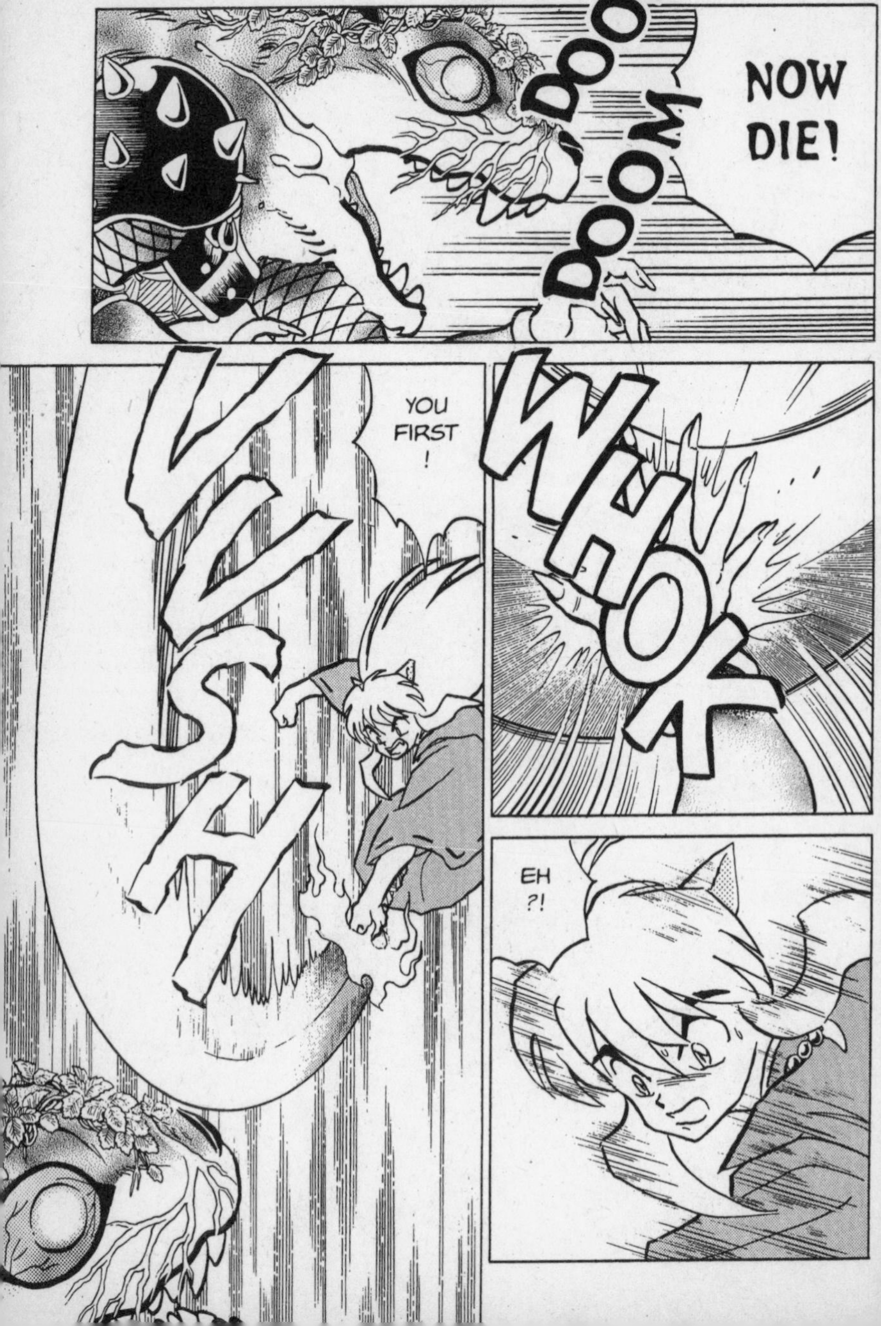
DOOM DOOM
NOW DIE!
VUSH
YOU FIRST!
WHOK
EH?!

187

BZZZZZZ

!

THOSE ARE... NARAKU'S WASPS!

I CAN'T LET THEM STING ME!

RRGH.

KLAK

INU-YASHA-- WE'RE IN TROUBLE!

BZZ

DOOM

I SEE WHY THEY MADE YOU A MONK!

TO BE CONTINUED...

COMPLETE OUR SURVEY AND LET US KNOW WHAT YOU THINK!

☐ Please do NOT send me information about VIZ products, news and events, special offers, or other information.

☐ Please do NOT send me information from VIZ's trusted business partners.

Name: _____

Address: _____

City: _____ **State:** _____ **Zip:** _____

E-mail: _____

☐ **Male** ☐ **Female**   **Date of Birth** (mm/dd/yyyy): ___ / ___ / ___   (Under 13? Parental consent required)

What race/ethnicity do you consider yourself? (please check one)

☐ Asian/Pacific Islander ☐ Black/African American ☐ Hispanic/Latino

☐ Native American/Alaskan Native ☐ White/Caucasian ☐ Other: _____

What VIZ product did you purchase? (check all that apply and indicate title purchased)

☐ DVD/VHS _____

☐ Graphic Novel _____

☐ Magazines _____

☐ Merchandise _____

Reason for purchase: (check all that apply)

☐ Special offer ☐ Favorite title ☐ Gift

☐ Recommendation ☐ Other _____

Where did you make your purchase? (please check one)

☐ Comic store ☐ Bookstore ☐ Mass/Grocery Store

☐ Newsstand ☐ Video/Video Game Store ☐ Other: _____

☐ Online (site: _____)

What other VIZ properties have you purchased/own? _____

_____

How many anime and/or manga titles have you purchased in the last year? How many were VIZ titles? **(please check one from each column)**

ANIME	MANGA	VIZ
☐ None	☐ None	☐ None
☐ 1-4	☐ 1-4	☐ 1-4
☐ 5-10	☐ 5-10	☐ 5-10
☐ 11+	☐ 11+	☐ 11+

I find the pricing of VIZ products to be: **(please check one)**

☐ Cheap ☐ Reasonable ☐ Expensive

What genre of manga and anime would you like to see from VIZ? **(please check two)**

☐ Adventure ☐ Comic Strip ☐ Science Fiction ☐ Fighting

☐ Horror ☐ Romance ☐ Fantasy ☐ Sports

What do you think of VIZ's new look?

☐ Love It ☐ It's OK ☐ Hate It ☐ Didn't Notice ☐ No Opinion

Which do you prefer? **(please check one)**

☐ Reading right-to-left

☐ Reading left-to-right

Which do you prefer? **(please check one)**

☐ Sound effects in English

☐ Sound effects in Japanese with English captions

☐ Sound effects in Japanese only with a glossary at the back

THANK YOU! Please send the completed form to:

NJW Research
42 Catharine St.
Poughkeepsie, NY 12601

All information provided will be used for internal purposes only. We promise not to sell or otherwise divulge your information.